THE INCA PRINCESSES

THE INCA PRINCESSES

TALES OF THE INDIES

STUART STIRLING

SUTTON PUBLISHING

First published in the United Kingdom in 2003 by
Sutton Publishing Limited · Phoenix Mill
Thrupp · Stroud · Gloucestershire · GL5 2BU

British Library Cataloguing in Publication Data
A catalogue record for this book is available from the British
Library.

ISBN 0-7509-3079-9

Typeset in 11/14.5 pt Sabon.
Typesetting and origination by
Sutton Publishing Limited.
Printed and bound in England by
J.H. Haynes & Co. Ltd, Sparkford.

Contents

Contents

For my parents,
and to the memory of my uncle Alfredo Peláez Díez
de Medina and Fernando Díez de Medina

Acknowledgements

I would like to thank Peter Clifford of Sutton for encouraging me to write this book, and Christopher Feeney, my commissioning editor, for his steadfast support. I am grateful to Doña Magdalena Canellas Anoz, Director of the Archivo General de Indias at Seville, for her constant assistance, and the directors of the Archivo General de la Nación at Lima, and the Archivo Regional at Cusco. I would also wish to thank the following museums and collections: the Archivo General de Indias, Seville; the Museo Inka, the Museo de Arte Religioso, the Church of La Compañía, Cusco; the Museo Pedro de Osma, Lima; the Museo Casa de la Moneda, the Church of San Francisco, Potosí; the Museo Nacional de Arte, La Paz; and the librarians at the British Library, the Institute of Historical Research and Canning House.

Preface

On the morning of 22 October 1822 an elderly Augustinian friar was seen accompanying an Andean Indian, not much older than himself, along the gangway of the British barque *Retrieve*, and stepping onto the landing quay at Buenos Aires. The two men soon lost themselves in the crowd of passengers who had made the seventy-day sailing journey from the Spanish port of Cádiz to the Argentine capital. No one, not even the ship's captain, an Englishman called Hague, knew who they were, nor what fate had befallen the old Indian, now dressed in the peasant clothes of a Spanish labourer, his frail figure wrapped in a black threadbare cloak. Some of his fellow passengers had thought him an oddity, while others imagined him to be a freed slave or possibly the servant of his companion.

Five years later, on 5 September 1827, an obituary notice appeared in the Argentine newspaper *Crónica Política y Literatura de Buenos Aires*, stating: 'Don Juan Bautista Túpac Amaru, fifth lineal grandson of the Incas of Peru, died in this city of Buenos Aires on the second of this month, at the age of eighty, having suffered forty years of imprisonment in Spain.'[1] The old Indian was the last Inca of Peru, but the empire of his ancestors was by then little more than a distant memory.

From the Inca princesses of Cusco, who were the mistresses of the conquistadores, to their eighteenth-century descendants, some of whom played a part in the winning of South America's independence, are to be found the seeds of this book and its depiction of the Andes in colonial times. Its writing owes a debt both to the Peruvian scholar Ella Dunbar Temple, who carried out research into the Inca dynasty in the 1940s and to Josefa García Tovar, who transcribed for me innumerable manuscripts of eyewitness accounts of the Conquest and of the Inca royal family from the Archives of the Indies at Seville, some of which are published herein for the first time.

ix

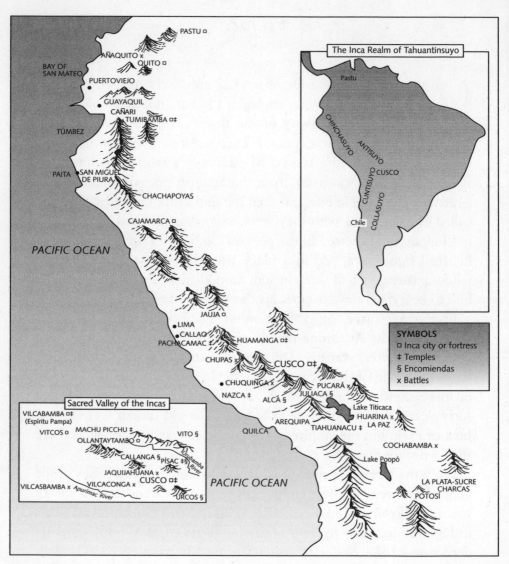

PASTU ▫

AÑAQUITO x
QUITO ▫

BAY OF
SAN MATEO
PUERTOVIEJO

GUAYAQUIL
CAÑARI
TUMIBAMBA ▫‡

TÚMBEZ

PAITA • SAN MIGUEL
DE PIURA

CHACHAPOYAS

CAJAMARCA ▫

PACIFIC OCEAN

JAUJA

• LIMA
• CALLAO
PACHACAMAC ‡   HUAMANGA ▫‡

CHUPAS x   **CUSCO** ▫‡

• CHUQUINGA x   PUCARÁ x
NAZCA ‡   ALCÁ §   JULIACA §
                                 Lake Titicaca
AREQUIPA   HUARINA x
QUILCA   TIAHUANACU   LA PAZ

COCHABAMBA x
Lake Poopó

LA PLATA-SUCRE
CHARCAS
POTOSÍ

The Inca Realm of Tahuantinsuyo

Pastu

CHINCHASUYO

ANTISUYO

CUNTISUYO   CUSCO

COLLASUYO

Chile

SYMBOLS
▫ Inca city or fortress
‡ Temples
§ Encomiendas
x Battles

Sacred Valley of the Incas

VILCABAMBA ▫‡
(Espíritu Pampa)
VITCOS ▫   MACHU PICCHU ‡   VITO §
OLLANTAYTAMBO ▫
CALLANGA §   PÍSAC ‡§
JAQUIJAHUANA x   CUSCO ▫‡
VILCASBAMBA x   VILCACONGA x
Apurímac River   URCOS §

Vilcanota River

PACIFIC OCEAN

Map of Peru.

ONE

The Galleons of Seville

5 December 1553

At first they thought it a trick of the light, flickering on the distant horizon, until at last they could see the great galleon, its small shadow cast across the open sea, its sails stretched and its worn wooden frame blackened and scarred by a voyage of over a thousand miles. Soon after, a second vessel appeared on the horizon, its bows beating into the wind and its fluttering pennant also bearing the scarlet and gold arms of Castile and León, and within the hour both ships had entered the sound of San Lúcar de Barrameda. All along the estuary of the River Guadalquivir the news of the arrival of the vessels spread, and in the nearby villages and hamlets men stared in wonder or ran to catch a closer glimpse of the returning conquistadores, laden with the treasures and booty they had brought back with them from the New World.

It took almost eight hours for the ships to reach Seville, its cathedral and crenellated walls silhouetted against the fading winter light, its whitewashed convents and mudéjar palaces almost hidden by shadows. All that day its citizens, young and old alike, had awaited the arrival of the galleons, eagerly following their entry into the port as they were rowed upriver, their decks illuminated by lanterns and crowded with the jubilant figures of their passengers. Among them was the thirty-year-old conquistador Cristóbal de Mena, a native of Ciudad Real and the first of the veterans of Francisco Pizarro's conquest of the Inca empire to return to Spain, bringing with him his share of the Indies treasure of Cajamarca.

It had been over a quarter of a century since Columbus's discovery of the New World – which he had at first thought to be part of

1

India, for which reason its indigenous people to this day are known as Indians – and three years since Hernán Cortés, the conqueror of Mexico, had sailed from that very same quay in Seville to return to his newly founded colony in the continent only recently named by a German mapmaker in honour of Seville's pilot-general, the Florentine Amerigo Vespucci. Each of these men, like the returning conquistador, had knelt in the semi-darkness of Seville's cathedral to thank its Madonna for his safe return, on the site where once the great mosque of the Calif Abu Yusuf had stood.

The city to which Cristóbal de Mena had returned after almost twenty years in the new colony of Nicaragua, in the conquest and exploration of which he had also served, had altered little in appearance: its old square of San Francisco, where on feast days the young hidalgos, astride their Arab mares, fought the finest bulls in Andalusia, and its numerous taverns and brothels, where many a returning veteran of the Indies would take his bars of gold and silver, and listen to the troubadours and gypsies singing the legends of their lost Moorish homeland.

One of the few contemporary accounts of the city was left by the Venetian ambassador Andrea Navagero, a historian and Renaissance poet whose portrait Raphael had painted. He wrote in a letter to his cousin the geographer Gian Battista Ramusio:

You find me in Seville, a city set in a plain on the left bank of the Guadalquivir river; its circumference is some four or five miles, and resembles more an Italian city than a Spanish one; its streets are wide and elegant, though the greater part of its houses are not so fine; even though there are some palaces whose beauty can not be rivalled in all of Spain, and in which there are numerous gardens.

There are also some fine churches, especially the cathedral, which is beautiful and far larger than the cathedral at Toledo, though not so richly decorated; alongside the cathedral is a cloister or patio, joined to it by a wall and which appears to be one single structure; along side of which are various porticoes and chapels, among them the chapel where the body of the saint king lies, and which is said to exude a scent when the coffin is opened for veneration.* The patio is planted with orange trees of great beauty, at the centre of which is a fountain; around the entire building there is a market place, enclosed by chains, whose steps descend into the street; here all day hidalgos, merchants and passers-by assemble, for it is the most lively place in all the city, and known as the 'Steps'. In the street and adjoining square a great number of people can be found, and where many thefts take place and rogues abound, and which is also a type of market place; the square is both wide and large. Beside the cathedral is a bell tower of much beauty, with fine large bells; to reach its top one climbs up a ramp, and not stairs as at the tower of St Mark's in Venice, though the climb is comfortable and steady.†

Not very far from the cathedral is the Alcázar, which is the palace that once belonged to the Moorish kings and very beautiful, its masonry richly decorated in the style of the Moors, and with magnificent marble and fountains, the waters of which pass through various chambers and bath houses. It has a patio filled with orange and lemon trees, and gardens of the greatest beauty, among which there is a wood of only orange trees, where not even the sun can penetrate, and which is possibly the most beautiful sight in all Spain.[1]

The city was the seat of some of Spain's wealthiest families, many of them Jewish converts who had invested in Columbus's expeditions and who held most of the trading concessions to the New World. Among the city's nobility, which had also involved itself in the Indies' trade, was Seville's leading grandee, the Duke of Medina Sidonia. The duke was a recluse, whose every movement was subject to his wife's control, and Ambassador Navagero recorded of him somewhat ungenerously, 'It was necessary to teach him what to say

---

* King Ferdinand III of Castile, who reconquered Seville in 1248.
† The Giralda tower. Its weathervane – the Giraldrillo – was added in 1568.

when ever he met someone; once when a bishop visited him, he asked after his wife and children.'[2] His son and heir would one day be the commander of the ill-fated Spanish Armada.

Though the official purpose of Navagero's visit to Seville in 1526 had been to attend the marriage of the young Emperor Charles V and the Portuguese Infanta, he had been instructed by the Venetian Senate to report on Spain's commerce with its newly established colonial empire, principally with regard to the Sevillian trade. In the two years of his embassy he collected every available manuscript and chronicle connected with the exploration and conquest of the New World, copies of which he also sent to his cousin Ramusio, himself a former ambassador to the French court and at that time secretary to the Venetian Senate. Many of these manuscripts he obtained from the Italian priest Pietro Martire d'Anghera, a keen historian who lived in Toledo and who had at one time served as Queen Isabella of Castile's envoy to the Sultan of Egypt. They would eventually form part of his cousin Ramusio's monumental publication *Navigationi e Viaggi*, an account of the discovery of the New World which to this day serves as a primary source for the history of the Americas.

In his letter to his cousin Navagero also noted the increasing migration of Seville's men to the Americas and Caribbean islands:

So many men abandon the city to seek their fortune in the New World that it is virtually in the possession of its women . . . all the wine and wheat that is grown here is sent to the Indies, as is soap, shirts, stockings and other such items, and which as yet are not manufactured there, and for which a great profit is made. The Casa de la Contratación de las Indias is also situated in the city, and to which are brought all the goods and produce of those lands, for no shipping is allowed to unload in any other port; on the arrival of each fleet a great quantity of gold is brought to the Contratación each year; a fifth of which is marked for the king. Some merchants say that for some time less gold is brought, but the expeditions continue and all year ships come and go there. I saw many items from the Indies in Seville and was given and eat some roots called batatas, potatoes, which have a taste of chestnuts. . . .[3]

Founded in 1503 as the legal and administrative authority for all trade and shipping to the Spanish colonies, the Casa de la Contratación was also the city's school for mariners and pilots, among them cartographers and astronomers, ship builders and sea captains, some of whom had already received some training at the Portuguese naval academy at Lisbon, established by King Henry the Navigator. Mapmakers, adventurers and travellers of every persuasion had over the years made their way into the tiled and mosaic-floored chambers and gardens, created by the eleventh-century Almoravid Muslim dynasty behind the palace of the Alcázar, each bringing their proposals and diagrams for expeditions they had spent years in planning. One such proposal had been sent by the Nicaraguan conquistador Vasco Núñez de Balboa, who in 1513 discovered the Pacific Ocean. Even the preparations and maps produced for Ferdinand Magellan, who circumnavigated the world in the years 1519–22, had been submitted to its authority.

It was probably while he was waiting for the officials of the Contratación to release his share of the booty he had brought back with him from Peru that the conquistador Cristóbal de Mena, one of Francisco Pizarro's captains of horse, finished writing his chronicle of the conquest of the Inca Empire. Just four months after his return the printing house of Bartolomé Pérez published the work in Seville.

In simple prose Mena recalled the early days of his adventures. He had first joined the expedition at the Pacific port of Panama, from where he sailed in Pizarro's small armada of caravels, comprising 150 Spaniards, a number of African and isthmian slaves and 50 horses. At some length he described the landing on the Ecuadorian coast of South America and the year they had spent waiting for reinforcements. The foot-soldier Diego de Trujillo, who had served under Mena, recorded in his own memoir the stifling heat and the lack of food and fresh water, remarking that they had been forced to kill and eat the island's wild dogs in order to survive and that before the winter rains 'the sun had turned the soil into broken and withered dust'.[4] His words reflect the sorry state of the Spanish encampment: many of the men were confined to their tents and hammocks because of an outbreak of skin sores which caused them excruciating pain and bleeding, made worse by the incessant number of mosquitoes, lice and other vermin that plagued them day and night. Some forty years later Pizarro's sixteen-year-old kinsman from Toledo, Pedro Pizarro, wrote that when the slaver Hernando de Soto's reinforcements finally joined them from Nicaragua, the new arrivals had shown 'little joy, for they found [us] in an anguished state . . . and most of the men sickly, and no gold for them to see . . .'.[5]

Dressed in the extravagant and exotic manner of the Nicaraguan slaver, Soto, then aged thirty-four, cut a dashing figure amid the mainly barefooted and bedraggled men who had waded out to greet him: his ear-lobes were adorned with pearls, his coat armour decorated with gold and Indian amulets and his helmet embellished with the plumage of tropical birds. 'He was', recorded the chronicler Garcilaso de la Vega, 'one of the finest lances in the Indies.'[6] Soto was to command the expedition's cavalry.

The disembarkation of Soto's reinforcements took several hours to complete, the horses and their African handlers swimming alongside the Indian rafts laden with provisions, while a long line of men and isthmian camp women waded to the shore. Among the latter was Soto's Moorish slave Juana Hernández, reputedly the first Spanish woman to set foot on the continent of South America.[7] It rained for most of the day, the rain beating across the animal-hide tents, whose exhausted occupants slumbered peacefully, already oblivious to the endless sound of the rain and the stifling heat. As night approached, a group of Soto's African slaves, fettered by leg irons, huddled around the perimeter of the stockade and watched in silence the smouldering camp fires. A human barrier of sweating bodies, their task was to guard their master's prized Andalusian mares, moving restlessly from side to side of their enclosure, trying to escape the approaching storm.

Few of the 228 conquistadores on the equatorial island of Puna had any experience of soldiering, let alone of Indian fighting. Armed with home-made pikes and shields fashioned from the wooden staves of discarded isthmian wine casks, the majority of them comprised a motley collection of diehard adventurers, more accustomed to labouring in the farmlands of their homeland or eking out a living in the crowded slave markets of Panama. Most of them, as their testimonials and wills prove, were Andalusians or Castilians. Of the 168 men who would march to Cajamarca only 36 were from Estremadura and only 58 of them could read and write.[8]

For a further four months, until the end of the winter rains, Pizarro's small army was forced to remain on the island, encountering sporadic hostility from the native Indians. In the first week of April the entire contingent of men finally crossed to the mainland aboard Soto's two caravels and Pizarro's remaining ship, accompanied by a small flotilla of canoes and rafts. Three men were killed by the Indians during the initial stages of the crossing; their naked bodies, skewered and hacked to pieces, were left on the shore for their companions to see, as their scalps fell prey to the small colony of sea crabs. They arrived at the coastal township of Túmbez, where Pizarro in his last voyage had left two of his men, Morillo and Bocanegra, but the town was deserted and bore no evidence of their presence. The ruins of the mud-and-thatch buildings sheltered hundreds of unburied corpses, riddled with flies, and everywhere they encountered the smell of death and human misery. It was a pitiful sight – and the first evidence they would find of the civil war then being waged by the Inca lords of the empire they had come to conquer.

Nothing, it seemed, could raise the men's spirits, not even the arrival of a provision ship from Nicaragua bringing a further twenty volunteers. The Greek Pedro de Candia, who had accompanied Pizarro in his last voyage and had so openly boasted of the settlement's great riches, now became the butt of ridicule. Not even Pizarro's purported discovery of a note written by the unfortunate Gines, claiming that more gold and silver could be found in the land than all the iron of Vizcaya,* lessened the hostility and ill-feeling among the conquistadores, many of whom, principally the Nicaraguan contingent, felt justifiably deceived by the lack of any evidence of gold and by the desolation that surrounded them.

Shortly before leaving the settlement Pizarro ordered the executions of thirteen caciques who had been captured in the vicinity of Túmbez and who had refused to assist him in transporting his men on to the mainland. They were to be garrotted and then burnt before the entire encampment in reprisal for the deaths of two of his conquistadores. It was as much a demonstration to his own men as to the Indians.

Few doubted Pizarro's resolve. Fear soon diminished the rumours of rebellion, and once more the small contingent of men struck out into the endless swamp and equatorial forest, their leather and steel-coated armour soaked with their sweat, their bearded faces burnt by the sun, as they marched alongside the columns of African and isthmian slaves – men and women alike – carrying on their heads the provisions and tents, their chains beating against the mud and undergrowth as they struggled forward under their heavy burdens. A number of men and horses fell prey in the mangroves to the caymans, their bodies dragged down into the depths of the waterpools, their passing marked only by traces of blood in the water. Each day the conquistadores' difficulties mounted as they searched desperately for food and fresh water, and the fevers and dysentery from which most of the men suffered gripped ever harder.

It took them almost two months to reach the southern coastal lands of Tangarara, a distance of almost 100 miles. On 15 July 1532 Pizarro founded there the settlement of San Miguel. Abandoning the original encampment because of its oppressive climate, he soon moved his settlement further inland, to the banks of the River Piura. Among the fifty Spaniards who were to remain there were Soto's

---

* The northern Spanish province of Biscay – Vizcaya – reputedly possessed the greatest iron ore reserves in Europe.

Moorish slave Juana, whose freedom he had granted, and the future chronicler Pedro Pizarro.

Two months later Pizarro led a column of men out of the settlement, among them Mena, who commanded a squadron of cavalry. In total, the force numbered 62 horse and 106 foot-soldiers, together with a number of African and isthmian slaves. Their march took them across some 70 miles of treeless desert until they reached the village of Serrán. Here Pizarro again heard reports from the local tribesmen that much of the northern coastal region had surrendered to the army of one of the warring Inca princes, Atahualpa, who had declared himself sovereign of the empire. In order to clarify the situation Pizarro ordered Soto and a squadron of horse to ride inland to the township of Cajas. After riding for two days and a night, stopping only for food and to rest their horses, de Soto's forty horsemen finally reached the township, where they made contact with its cacique and one of the Inca warrior chiefs, who had some two thousand men under his command.

Mena and Diego de Trujillo, who both accompanied Soto's squadron, recorded the events that followed:

[The township] was greatly destroyed because of the war . . . and many Indians could be seen hung [from the buildings] . . . the Captain [Soto] sent for the cacique of the township and soon he came, complaining bitterly about Atahualpa, and how his warriors had killed so many of his people, some ten or twelve thousand, and that no more than three thousand were left . . . and he said he had no gold, for Atahualpa's warriors had taken it all . . . even though he gave four or five bars of mined gold. It was then one of Atahualpa's lords came: and the cacique was greatly frightened, and he stood up in his presence, but the Captain made him sit beside him. This lord had brought us a present from Atahualpa of stuffed ducks: and which made us imagine a similar fate; he also brought us two small fortresses made of clay, saying that there were many such as them in his land. There were three houses of women, called mamacunas, virgins of the sun. And as we entered their houses and took the women into the square, some five hundred of them, the Captain gave many of them to us Spaniards, something which greatly infuriated the Inca lord, who said: 'How dare you do this? With Atahualpa only twenty leagues from here? Not one of you will be left alive. . . .'[9]

No single eyewitness describes the mass rape of the mamacuna by Soto's men, recording only that Soto ordered his harquebusiers to fire into the air, causing the trembling women to fall to their knees from fear of being killed.

Cajas offered the Spaniards the first real indication of the grandeur of the empire they had come to conquer: its streets and buildings, though gutted and burnt, were built of stone and laid out in an orderly and geometric manner, with the large square and temple forming a central point. The rich dress and evident authority of the Inca lord were a far cry from the primitive clothing of the caciques of the coastal region, whose villages were constructed in wood and mud.

Having inspected the neighbouring village of Huancabamba, which also possessed some fine stone buildings, Soto led his men back to Serrán, taking with him the Inca lord and the women. The booty from Cajas and the rich clothing they had also found, woven with gold thread and plumes, prompted Soto's horseman Gavilán to note that 'great merriment was had by all, for the Adelantado [Soto] declared he had discovered a land as rich as Castile!'[10] After meeting Pizarro, who presented him with a lace shirt and some Venetian glass, the Inca lord left the camp, taking Pizarro's message of friendship to his master Atahualpa. He left behind a number of guides to lead the Spanish to Atahualpa's encampment in the valley of Cajamarca.

In early October the conquistadores broke camp and began their march into the Andes, the foothills of which they reached in the first week of November. Mena recorded their journey:

We were only to find the roads destroyed, also their villages, whose caciques had fled . . . and as we approached the mountains Hernando Pizarro and Hernando de Soto went on ahead with some men, swimming across a great river [the Saña], for we had been told that in a village beyond we would find much treasure . . . before we reached the village we captured two Indians in order to get information about Atahualpa: the Captain [Soto] ordered them tied to two poles, for they were scared and would not speak; one of them said he knew nothing of Atahualpa, and the other said he had only left his encampment a few days before, and that he was waiting with many of his people for us in the valley of Cajamarca. He also told us that many warriors were guarding two passes in the mountains ahead, and that for their banner they now used the shirt the Governor [Pizarro] had sent Atahualpa: but neither by the torch nor any other inducement did they tell us more.[11]

In small groups, and at times reduced to single file, they began their ascent of the great cordillera, climbing to an altitude of some 13,000 feet above sea level, almost to the very tops of the mountains. Here, for the first time they gazed in wonder at the huge condors that hovered above them, drifting in the changing air currents above the snow-capped peaks. Exhausted by the thinness of the air, some of the men doubtless resorted to chewing the coca leaves their guides carried with them to counter their dizziness and lack of oxygen.* Mile after mile they hauled their frightened horses and mules along the stone trails of the Inca highway; chiselled out of the bare mountainside, at times these trails were no wider than a few feet. Climbing even higher, they crossed the cordillera's great canyons on the few reed bridges that had survived the Indian fighting. These flimsy structures seemed barely able to take a man's weight, let alone a horse. They inched forward, some of the men crawling on hands and knees, as the bridges swayed thousands of feet above the rivers and ravines far below, and only the occasional scream of a man falling to his death pierced the silence. The seemingly endless march exacerbated their sense of abandonment, but they tried to lift their

---

* Coca – a narcotic plant, indigenous to the Andes, from which cocaine is derived.

spirits by praying, led by the black-and-white-robed Dominican friar Valverde, their voices resounding across the giant snow-clad mountains that seemed to engulf them at every turn. Even the most hardened of the isthmian veterans had never witnessed such human misery, their frostbitten hands and feet numbed by the bitter cold of the Andean nights, but after almost a week they finally reached the great valley of Cajamarca, its green and lush pastures enclosed by the cordillera. Here the Inca Emperor Atahualpa awaited them, his tents spread across a distance of almost 2 miles.

For several hours Atahualpa had awaited their arrival, staring across the valley towards the northern hills and the blackened winter sky. The first indication of their coming was a noise that sounded like the recurring beat of rain, but his scouts told him this was the sound of horses; soon he could see their plume-helmeted riders moving along in a cloud of dust, their lances sloped across their shoulders. Marching behind them at some distance was the tall black-bearded figure of Pizarro at the head of his foot-soldiers; he was accompanied by the friar Valverde, the large wooden cross he had brought with him from Panama strapped to his mule.

The following is an account of the events that took place that day, recorded by Mena and by the foot-soldier Diego de Trujillo:

It was six o'clock in the evening and it began to rain, and huge hailstones were falling, forcing the men to shelter in the buildings . . . then the Governor [Pizarro] entered with the infantry, all of whom were much frightened . . . for we could now count on no other rescue other than from God . . . the Captain Hernando de Soto asked the Governor for permission to go with five or six horsemen and an Indian to speak with Atahualpa . . . and against his better judgement the Governor agreed to his going. All the area near the encampment was guarded by squadrons of warriors with lances and archers . . . the Spaniards rode through their ranks without any hindrance until they reached the Cacique: seated as he was in front of the door of his lodging, and with many of his women . . . and then Hernando de Soto rode right up to him, and so close to him that his horse's nose touched his headdress: and not once did the Cacique make a movement. The Captain de Soto then took off a ring from his finger and gave it to him, as a sign of peace and friendship, and which he took with little mark of esteem. . . .

And as he did not return and suspecting that he may have been killed, the Governor ordered [his brother] Hernando Pizarro to take with him horsemen and foot-soldiers, and I [Trujillo] among them, to discover what had taken place. When we reached his camp we found the Captain de Soto with the men he had taken, and Hernando Pizarro said to him, 'My lord, what is happening?' And he replied: 'As you can see, we are still waiting', and then said: 'Soon Atahualpa will come out' – who was still in his lodging – 'but until now he has not.' Hernando Pizarro shouted at the interpreter: 'Tell him to come out!' The man returned and said: 'Wait, he will see you shortly.' And Hernando Pizarro said to him: 'Tell the dog to come out immediately!' . . . and then Atahualpa came out of his lodging, holding two small gold cups in his hands that were filled with chicha [maize wine], and gave one to Hernando Pizarro and the other he drank.

And Hernando Pizarro said to the interpreter: 'Tell Atahualpa that there is no difference in rank between myself and the Captain Soto, for we are both captains of the King, and in his service we have left our homelands to come and instruct him in the Faith.' And then it was agreed Atahualpa would come the following day, which was a Saturday, to Cajamarca. Guarding his camp were more than forty thousand Indian warriors in their squadrons, and many principal lords of the land. And on departing Hernando de Soto reared the legs of his horse, near to where were positioned the first of these squadrons, and the Indians of the squadrons fled, falling over each other. And when we returned to Cajamarca Atahualpa ordered three hundred of them killed because they had shown fear and fled, and this we discovered another day when we found their bodies. . . .

The following day Atahualpa came with all his people in procession to Cajamarca, and the league they travelled took them until almost an hour before sunset . . . it was as if the entire valley was in movement . . . six hundred Indians in white and black livery, as if pieces of a chessboard, came ahead of him, sweeping the road of stones and branches . . . wearing headdresses of gold and silver . . . and the Governor, seeing they were taking such a great time, sent Hernando de Aldana, who spoke their language, to ask him to come before it was too dark. And Aldana spoke to him, and only then did they begin to move at a walking pace . . . in Cajamarca there are ten streets that lead from the square, and in each of these the Governor placed eight men, and in some, fewer number, because of the few men we had, and the horsemen he positioned in three companies: one with Hernando Pizarro, one with Hernando de Soto with his own men, and one with Sebastián de Belalcázar with his, and all with bells attached to their bridles, and the Governor positioned himself in the fortress with twenty-four of his guards; for in all we were a hundred and sixty: sixty horsemen and a hundred on foot.

As Atahualpa entered the square of Cajamarca, and as he saw no Christians he asked the Inca lord who had been with us: 'What has become of these bearded ones?' And the Inca lord replied: 'They are hidden.' And he asked him to climb down from his throne litter on which he sat, but he refused. And then the Friar Vicente de Valverde made himself seen and attempted to inform him of the reason why we had come on the orders of the Pope and one of his sons, a Christian leader who was the Emperor, our lord. And speaking of his words of the Holy Gospel Atahualpa said to him: 'Whose words are these?' And he replied: 'The words of God.' And Atahualpa said to him: 'How is this possible?' And the friar Vicente told him: 'See, here it is written.' And he showed him a breviary which he opened, and Atahualpa demanded to be given it and took it, and after looking at it he threw it on the ground and ordered: 'Let none of them escape!' And the Indians gave a great cry, shouting: 'Inca, let it be so!' And the shouting made us very frightened. And the friar Vicente returned and climbed to the wall where the Governor was and said to him: 'Your Excellency, what will you do? Atahualpa is like Lucifer!'

And then the Governor climbed down and armed himself with a shield and sword and put on his helmet, and with the twenty-four men who were with him, and I [Trujillo] among them, we went directly to Atahualpa's litter, pushing our way through the crowd of Indians, and as we tried to pull him off his litter the horsemen charged to the great sound that was made from their bridle bells, and there in the square fell so many people, one on top of the other, that many were suffocated, and of the eight thousand Indians who died, over half died in this manner. The killing of those who fled continued for half a league and into the night. . . .[12]

In less than an hour, and without the loss of a single man, Pizarro's conquistadores changed for ever the course of world history and laid the foundations of South America's Hispanic heritage. Native accounts recorded by missionaries and Crown officials almost half a century later offered a more damning insight into the massacre. The Indian Sebastián Yacobilca recalled that twenty thousand warriors were killed and claimed that he personally witnessed Pizarro and his brother Hernando 'and his other brothers, and various Spaniards, who were with them, take from Atahualpa's encampment to their lodgings in the township all his treasures of gold, silver and jewels, which he kept for his use and for the use of his women and children'.[13] The smell of death hung over the township for days, and all that could be heard was the wailing of the Indian women, many of whom had witnessed the dramatic end of the Inca lords. To the last man the escort had held aloft the litter of their emperor; some of them had lost their arms, and used instead the bleeding and mutilated stumps of their shoulders to support him. Others had stood by in silent disbelief, mesmerised by the sight of their living god, naked and chained like an animal, pleading with his captors for his life and promising to fill two chambers with gold and silver in exchange for his freedom. 'With a white line,' recalled Trujillo, 'he marked the height of two men,' in each chamber.[14]

Several conquistadores left descriptions of Atahualpa. Pizarro's notary, the Sevillian Francisco López de Jerez, recorded that he was 'some thirty years of age . . . somewhat stocky, his face imposing, beautiful and ferocious, his eyes bloodshot'.[15] The conquistador Miguel de Estete recalled that during his captivity Atahualpa 'let it be known what he had planned to do with us, for it had been his intention to take our horses and mares, which was what had impressed him most, for breeding, and to castrate some of us for his service to guard his women, as was their custom, the rest of us he would have sacrificed to the sun'.[16]

Pedro Pizarro, who later served as one of Atahualpa's guards, wrote that during his captivity the Inca emperor

was served by his women, who were his sisters; each spending eight or ten days with him, and who were also served by a great number of the other women, daughters of his lords . . . he also had a number of caciques with him, who remained outside in the courtyard: and if any one of them were called by him he entered barefoot and in homage carrying a burden on his back. . . .

On his head he wore a llautu, which are braids of coloured wool, half a finger thick and a finger in width, in the manner of a crown . . . on his forehead he wore a fringe attached to the llautu, made of fine scarlet wool, evenly cut and adorned with small gold strings. His hair, like that of his lords, he wore cut short . . . the clothes he wore were very thin and fine . . . over his head he wore a mantle which partly covered his neck: so as to hide the wound to his ear he had suffered.

One day when he was eating the food his women had brought him, and which they placed on fine green leaves on the floor, seated on a wooden stool, a foot in height, and made of reddish and very pretty wood, he pointed as was his custom at whatever food he wished and it was brought to him by his women, and from whose hand he ate. On one occasion, as he was being fed by his sisters and when he raised some food to his mouth, a particle fell on his clothing, and giving his hand to one of the women to lick clean, he stood up and went into his chamber to put on new clothing, and when he came back he wore a shirt and dark brown mantle. I felt the mantle which was smoother than silk, and I said to him: 'Inca, of what is this cloth made?' And he said to me: 'It is made of birds who fly at night in Puerto Viejo and Túmbez and who bite my people.' And on my asking him what he kept in his chests, he showed me they contained the clothing he had worn and all the garments that had touched his skin. And I asked him: 'For what purpose do you have these garments here?' He answered that it was in order to burn them, for what had been touched by the sons of the Sun must be burnt to ashes, which none was allowed to handle, and scattered to the wind.[17]

Cajamarca also marks the first recorded mention of the Inca princesses, the sister-wives and royal concubines of the Emperor Atahualpa, numbering possibly several hundred women, who had formed part of his harem at his encampment. Their faces hidden behind masks of beaten gold and their gowns adorned with precious stones, they would have presented a fabulous sight that few of Pizarro's men could ever have envisaged in the poverty and squalor of their homeland. Pedro Pizarro recorded:

They were carried in litters or in hammocks, which were blankets tied at each end to thick poles, the thickness of one's arm, and finely designed, and in these the princesses lay, their bodies shaded and hidden by canopies attached to their litters or hammocks. They were attended by a multitude of servants, who treated them with great reverence, and they were of a very fine appearance . . . their robes of a very delicate and soft cloth . . . their hair, which was black, they wore long, over their shoulders . . . almost all of them were very beautiful.[18]

Several princesses were allowed to remain with Atahualpa during the eight months of his captivity until his execution in the township, among them his half-sister Quispe Sisa, then aged possibly no more than twelve, whom he gave to Pizarro. Another of the princesses was his niece Cuxirimay, formerly his favourite wife; she was later raped by the Indian interpreter Felipillo. Only recently has the identity of several of the other princesses at Cajamarca been made known, principally from the evidence they gave in their petitions to the Spanish Crown; most had become the mistresses of Pizarro's principal captains and bore them numerous mestizo children.

Four weeks after the conquistador Cristóbal de Mena's arrival at Seville – and almost a year after the Emperor Atahualpa's capture at Cajamarca – another of the Indies ships, the small galleon *Santa María del Campo*, piloted by Pedro Bernal, docked at its quay amid even greater fanfare than that which had greeted the two previous Indies ships; it was carrying the Crown's initial share of the Cajamarca treasure, which Pizarro's brother Hernando had brought with him from Peru. It took almost an entire day for the labourers of the Contratación to unload the wooden crates of gold and silver, amounting to some 100,000 gold pesos, and pile them onto the oxen carts waiting to make the short journey to the depository at the back of the palace of the Alcázar.*

Records show that Pizarro had ordered the smelting of the Cajamarca treasure in nine separate forges. Over seven days and seven nights 11 tons of gold and silver artefacts had been fed into the furnaces, yielding some 13,420 lb of 22.5 carat gold in ingots and 26,000 lb in silver. The distribution of the treasure – which included 700 sheets of gold removed from the Inca temple of Coricancha at Cusco – had taken a whole month to complete. A document bearing Pizarro's mark recorded the full amount of treasure smelted at Cajamarca as 1,326,539 pesos of gold and 51,610 marks of silver.[19] Neither of these figures included the gold and silver artefacts and jewels that the conquistadores seized as personal booty, nor Atahualpa's gold throne which Pizarro appropriated for himself. Years later the conquistador Diego Maldonado, known as el rico, the rich, married a Spanish nobleman's daughter and gifted her an Inca necklace of emeralds, together with a gold statue of a puma, which he probably looted either at Cajamarca or at the sacking of Cusco four months later.

---

* Peso – coinage, the name originally meaning weight. Estimated present-day value of gold and silver: Gold Peso – £25. Silver Peso or Mark – £17. The value in Spain in the early colonial period would have been possibly threefold.

Each of Pizarro's horsemen was awarded approximately 8,800 pesos of gold and 362 marks of silver, each of his foot-soldiers 4,440 pesos of gold and 181 marks of silver. His own share of the booty was 57,740 pesos of gold and his principal captains also received a far greater share of the treasure than the other men. Hernando de Soto was awarded 17,740 pesos of gold – the fact that some years later he would bring with him to Seville a personal fortune of 100,000 pesos of gold demonstrates the enormous discrepancy between the official records and the actual amount of booty seized by the conquistadores at Cajamarca and later at Cusco – booty that was never declared to the Crown.

The notary Francisco López de Jerez recorded that a reckless spending spree followed the distribution of the few available goods to be found in their encampment, all paid for with bars of gold and silver: a jug of wine cost 60 pesos of gold; a pair of boots or breeches from 30 to 40 pesos; a cape 125 pesos; a clove of garlic ½ peso; a sword 50 pesos; and a sheet of vellum paper 10 pesos.[20] The foot-soldier Melchor Verdugo purchased a horse, two isthmian slaves (one male, one female) and twenty chickens for 2,000 pesos. A horse in poor condition was valued at 94 pesos and one in good condition at 3,000 pesos. Juan Pantiel de Salinas, one of the farriers, is recorded to have spent several days shoeing horses with silver.

For a number of weeks the treasure was left on public display at Seville in the courtyard of the Contratación. Many of the ornaments had been looted from the Inca coastal city of Pachacamac, and the Indian Sebastián Yacobilca recalled: 'A great quantity of gold and silver vessels, jugs, pitchers, images of the puma and of foxes, of men and women, of maize, frogs and snakes was taken to a great chamber and given to Hernando Pizarro, and which he took to Cajamarca with him, and it was carried by more than ten thousand Indians.'[21] Among the items listed was a life-size gold statue of a young man and a huge silver eagle.

People flocked to see the spectacle, among them the future historian Pedro de Cieza de León, who as a young boy had queued up to see the treasure, all of which formed part of the royal fifth of the Emperor Charles V's share of the booty. Sadly, the officials of the Contratación ordered the treasure to be smelted in February 1534, just a month after Hernando Pizarro's arrival at Seville.

The conquistador Cristóbal de Mena never signed his chronicle. Its authorship remained unknown until 1935, when the Peruvian scholar Raúl Porras Barrenechea identified him as its author. The date and place of his death is unrecorded. The foot-soldier Diego de Trujillo's memoir was only discovered a year earlier, in 1934, in the library of the Royal Palace in Madrid. The Venetian ambassador Andrea Navagero died in France three years after leaving Seville. Among his papers was discovered his translation into Italian of the chronicler Gonzalo Fernández de Oviedo's summary to his history of the Indies, *Historia Natural y General de las Indias*, which his cousin Gian Battista Ramusio published at Venice, together with Mena's anonymous chronicle, entitled *Relatione d'un capitano spagnuolo della conquista del Peru*.

Ramusio died at Padua at the age of seventy-two and was buried in a quiet and unassuming square in Venice, in a tomb he had originally built for his mother at the church of the Madonna dell'Orto, where the painter Tintoretto is also buried.

TWO

The Kingdom of the Snow Mountains

On a winter's morning in the year 1572 a procession was seen winding its way through the narrow cobbled streets of Cusco headed by thirty-seven Inca princes and nobles, dressed in their finest regalia and holding aloft the standards of their respective families, emblazoned with the coats-of-arms awarded them by the Spanish Emperor Charles V. Next came four veteran conquistadores on horseback, dressed in velvet and taffeta, and wearing the black capes of hidalgos, the bridles and stirrups of their horses embossed with gold. The Plaza de Armas, the city's great central square, was lined by hundreds of spectators, many of them newly arrived settlers from the isthmus of Panama, curious to catch a glimpse of the surviving veterans of Pizarro's army of conquest, and to see the few remaining members of the city's Inca nobility.

The procession finally reached the newly built council chamber, where a platoon of Spanish halberdiers and Cañari Indians stood guard. One by one the men entered the building, where they were received by the 57-year-old Viceroy Don Francisco de Toledo, the breast of his cape embroidered with the green cross of the Order of Alcántara; fourteen years previously he had been present at the death of the Hapsburg Emperor Charles V at the desolate Estremaduran monastery of Yuste.[1] His portrait shows him to have been a pale and thin-faced man, but he had important family connections: fourteen years later El Greco himself would depict the burial of one of Toledo's ancestors in one of his greatest masterpieces, *The Burial of Gonzalo Ruiz de Toledo, Count of Orgaz*, which still hangs in Toledo's church of Santo Tomé.

No portrait, however, has survived of the men he had assembled that morning in the city's council chamber, among them the lawyers

21

Juan de Matienzo and Juan Polo de Ondegardo, the priest Cristóbal de Molina and the explorer Pedro Sarmiento de Gamboa, who had recently returned to the colony from an expedition to the western Pacific. (This expedition had discovered the Solomon Islands, and but for the cowardice of its naval commander would have reached the eastern coast of Australia some 200 years before Captain Cook.) Each of these men was an authority on Indian matters, and at his request had compiled separate accounts of Inca history, based on a series of similar enquiries held across the Andean region.

The Viceroy Toledo had also commissioned Pizarro's kinsman Pedro Pizarro and the elderly conquistador Diego de Trujillo to write their reminiscences of the march into the Andes almost half a century previously. His intention, as the small group of Spaniards assembled that morning in the council chamber was aware, was to establish a historical account of Inca history which would prove that the Inca rulers had had little right to the empire they had conquered from their subject tribes. Such evidence as could be found, he had earlier informed the commissioners of his enquiry, headed by the lawyer Gabriel de Loarte, would be regarded in Spain as a refutation of the charges levelled against the Crown by its critics, principally the renowned social reformer the Dominican Bartolomé de las Casas. He had questioned his country's right of conquest, and his literary legacy had helped to fuel further anti-Spanish sentiment among the country's European neighbours, who over the years had viewed Spain's ever-increasing colonial trade with growing envy and suspicion.

The four elderly men he had called as the main witnesses to his enquiry were encomenderos of the city and held its highest offices; through their children, whose mothers had been Inca princesses, they maintained close ties with the remnants of the Inca royal family.* Alonso de Mesa, the wealthiest of the four, had joined Pizarro's expedition of conquest in his native Toledo at the age of fifteen, and had been the youngest conquistador present at

---

* Encomienda – encomendero: land grant of Indian vassals awarded by the Crown in lieu of feudal service and conditional upon their evangelization.

Cajamarca. A semi-invalid, his crippled arms the legacy of the torture he had endured at the hands of Pizarro's brother Gonzalo for opposing his rebellion against the Crown, he had only recently succumbed to the pressure exerted on him by the city's clergy to marry one of the six Indian mothers of his numerous mestizo children. Two of his daughters he had sent to Spain and placed in a convent at Toledo under the care of his brother, a priest of its cathedral. His eldest son he had also sent to Spain, where he had purchased for him the lordship of a Castilian township.

Pedro Alonso Carrasco, an Estremaduran and native of Zorita, had also enlisted in Pizarro's expedition but had not been present at the capture of the Emperor Atahualpa, having been forced to remain in the coastal settlement of San Miguel before joining the expedition's final march to Cusco.

Not much is known of the third man, Juan de Pancorbo Celiorigo, other than that he owned the mansion in which Toledo stayed during the earlier part of his lengthy sojourn in the city.

Of the fourth witness, the mestizo chronicler Garcilaso de la Vega recorded:

At the time the Spaniards first entered the city of Cusco the gold Inca image of the sun from its temple was taken in booty by a nobleman and conquistador by the name of Mansio Serra de Leguizamón, who I knew and who was still alive when I came to Spain, which he lost in a night of gambling, and where, according to Father Acosta,* was born the refrain: 'He gambled the sun before the dawn.' Many years later the council of that city, seeing how destitute and lost this son of theirs had become due to his gambling, in order to save him from his vice elected him one of its mayors on condition that for the year's term of his office he would refrain from gaming; an office he served with all diligence and care, for there was much of a gentleman about him, and for that

---

* The Jesuit José de Acosta, author of *Historia Natural y Moral de las Indias*, who later met the Viceroy Toledo at the city of La Plata during his tour of inspection.

year he never once touched a card or a pair of dice. Seeing this, the city honoured him for many more years with public office.[2]

Though in fact he never lost his passion for gambling, as the gaming debts listed in one of his wills demonstrates, the Biscayan Mansio Serra de Leguizamón, whose name appears in a number of testimonials over the years on behalf of the Inca princesses of Cusco, had taken a prominent part in the capture of the Inca capital under the command of Hernando de Soto. He had also served in the defence of the city against the native uprising some three years later, when on one celebrated occasion he had been mistaken for the apostle St James, as the chronicler Friar Martín de Murúa recorded:

For I wish to refer to what I have heard told by Spaniards and Indians alike, who swear to the truth of what they say, and who recall that in the most difficult time of the fighting a Spaniard appeared mounted on a white horse and killing many Indians, and many of the Spaniards believed him to have been Mansio Serra de Leguizamón, one of the leading conquistadores of Cusco; yet later, when they enquired about this they discovered that he had not been fighting there, but in another part of the city, even though there was no other among the Spaniards who possessed a white horse other than he. It was understood by many that it had been the Apostle Santiago, patron and defender of Spain, who had appeared there.[3]

Each of the elderly veterans knew that the native nobility who had accompanied them into the chamber had three days previously accepted what had been read to them of the history the Viceroy had commissioned from Pedro Sarmiento de Gamboa concerning the origin and government of their ancestors. All that day the lawyer Loarte read the manuscript to the four conquistadores, one of whom, Pancorbo, may have been illiterate, pausing from time to time to ask them for their opinion of certain passages. They were also asked to verify various painted cloths depicting the portraits of

Inca rulers in the form of medallions, together with a genealogy of their lineages. The conquistadores recorded that:

> They had always been told by the older Indians, and by others, that from the first until Huáscar, who was the last, there were twelve in number . . . and that they had heard it said that Túpac Inca Yupanqui, father of Huayna Cápac, had been the first who by force of arms had made himself lord of the whole of Peru, from Chile to Pastu, reclaiming various provinces in the vicinity of Cusco which his father Pachacuti had conquered, and which had rebelled . . . and that Huayna Cápac, his son, inherited his sovereignty and conquered further lands, and that at his death Huáscar, his legitimate son, succeeded him; and while the realm was at war between Huáscar and Atahualpa, his bastard brother, Don Francisco Pizarro by order of His Majesty came to these kingdoms, and with him the said Alonso de Mesa, Mansio Serra de Leguizamón, Pedro Alonso Carrasco and Juan de Pancorbo.[4]

Serra de Leguizamón also informed the enquiry that 'he had heard it said that Huayna Cápac had died some six or seven years before the Marquis Don Francisco Pizarro entered these realms, for that is what I have always been told by their elders, and even by the Incas themselves, who were his brothers and cousins'.[5]

The enquiry was to record that the Inca empire – numbering possibly seven million subject people – had been established by military conquest in less than a hundred years, its society ruled by a hereditary nobility of the Quéchua tribe of the Cusco region, known as Inca, which had dominated the central Andes, instilling in their conquered tribes the cult of sun worship, since they claimed their divine origin from the sun. Serra de Leguizamón was also to testify many years later:

> They were a people of great importance, great lords and sons of kings, who governed this realm, and as such they ruled at the time I entered in the discovery and conquest of this kingdom, and witnessed the Incas command and govern this land . . . for the

term Inca is what we would call in Spain lords of vassals, dukes and counts, and others of that caste. For they were sovereigns of these kingdoms they had conquered, from Chile to Quito, and beyond . . . for they were persons of great knowledge, and by the government they held, though possessing no written word, they ruled like the Romans in ancient times.[6]

Much of the Inca oral tradition recorded by the priest Cristóbal de Molina, possibly the best informed of the enquiry's historians with regard to Inca religion, ascribes their origin to their sacred lake at Titicaca, lying 12,000 feet above sea level and bordering the present-day republics of Peru and Bolivia. Covering some 3,200 square miles, the lake was revered by the Incas as the site of the divine birth of their first ancestors, Manco Cápac and Mama Ocllo, 'children of the sun and of the moon'. In his reminiscences the conquistador Pedro Pizarro recorded that 'these Indians claim that the first of their lords came from an island of Titicaca . . . and where they kept an idol of a woman, life-size and of medium height, and which from the waist upwards was of solid gold, and from the waist down, of pure silver, and which I saw when it was brought [to Cusco]'.[7]

The Andean lake had also been the site of an ancient pre-Colombian civilization – the Tiahuanacu – a military religious community that by the year AD 700 had been the nucleus for some seventy thousand people. Though its temple city on the southern shores of the lake had for centuries been no more than a barren ruin, some of its traditions and religious iconography had survived among its Aymára tribal descendants, and had been assimilated by the Quéchua in their years of expansion.

Tiahuanacu's deities included Viracocha, the Quéchua and Aymára meaning of which denotes 'the Creator', whose image can still be seen carved on the frieze of its Gate of the Sun. The soldier-chronicler Pedro de Cieza de León, who visited Tiahuanacu sixteen years after the Conquest, recorded that its ruins 'are of the oldest antiquity in all Peru . . . for I heard it said by many Indians that the Incas constructed their buildings in Cusco in their form and manner, and it is where they first held their court, here at Tiahuanacu'.[8] In a similar way the Spanish missionaries were themselves later to transform another of the region's deities, Thunupa, a Christ-like figure, into either the apostle St Thomas, the Apostle of India, or St Bartholomew, both of whose religious symbols can be found in the paintings and carvings of the area's colonial churches.

The Spaniards discovered three principal temple shrines of the cult of the sun, where the human sacrifice of virgin women and children was practised. These were at Copacabana, on the south-eastern shore of Lake Titicaca, later the site of the seventeenth-century colonial sanctuary dedicated to the Virgin of Copacabana; at Pachacamac, a coastal shrine south of Lima, from which Hernando Pizarro took much of the treasure he took back with him to Seville; and at the temple of Coricancha at Cusco, the gold wall sheets of which had also formed part of the Spanish booty. The conquistadores also recalled how the Incas instructed their subject tribes 'in the veneration of their idols of the sun and of the stars, teaching them how to make sacrifices in the mountains and holy sites of each province . . . forcing them to kill their sons and daughters to this effect . . . and to sacrifice their women, so that they could serve them in the afterlife'.[9]

Inca society was integrally linked to the spiritual life of its people and their belief in the supernatural: a world with which they communicated in their worship of nature, and which brought them into communion with an invisible world. Even in death it was a society governed by order and contained by an earthly structure, binding the supernatural to the living world.

As the lawyers Polo de Ondegardo and de Loarte recorded, almost every aspect of Inca government, from the detailed instructions given to each province concerning the need to supply artisans and agricultural workers for its sustenance, to the distribution of land, to the punishments (usually death) inflicted on adulterers, rapists and thieves, was registered by the quipucamayoc, the Inca historians, on their quipu or coloured string cords, which were also used for numeration and for astronomical and magical formulae. Their usage had been handed down from father to son for some three hundred years, and they also chronicled the Inca genealogies and historical events, the quantity of crops and every article that was transported or stored in the empire's warehouses, and even the measurements of the construction of buildings, 'something that merits great admiration and is difficult to believe for those who have not examined them, or witnessed their usage'.[10]

A manuscript compiled by an unknown conquistador, who had lived in the Collasuyo region of the Bolivian highlands and whose testimony would have been known to the enquiry, recorded:

> In each of their provinces the Incas had governors, ruling with great account and order . . . there were others of lesser rank who were known as sayapaya: inspectors who gathered the ordinances of the Inca and of the realm, visiting the storehouses and herds of llamas that belonged to the sun and to the Inca. And they would also inspect the mamacuna, virgins of the sun, and the veneration and sacrifices they would offer to the sun and to the huacas, which were the idols they worshipped. In each village were located the storehouses of every item and produce; for laziness and vagabondage were severely punished, and all laboured in the produce of these goods; and in the lands where maize was unable to grow, storehouses of chuño [dehydrated potatoes] were kept, as were other products of each region, none of which were consumed unless in times of war or necessity: then they would be distributed in great order.
>
> The Inca lords who would visit the governors of the provinces would be received with great honour, as if they were the emperor himself, and they would be informed of all the labour commanded of the people . . . and those caciques who had served the Incas well would be rewarded with women and servants, livestock and fine clothing, and be granted the privilege of being carried in litters or hammocks, and be given yanacona, servants, for that purpose; they would also be given the right to use parasols and be served with bowls and plates of gold or silver: something no one would make use of without the authority of the Inca; these privileges would also be granted them when they came to Cusco each year with their tribute from as far as Chile or Las Charcas.

In the month of May all the principal caciques from the different suyos would assemble before the emperor in the great square of Cusco with their tribute of gold, silver, clothing, livestock, and also their tribute of women, after which they would hold their feasting and perform their ceremonies and sacrifices.[11]

Trains of llamas transported the empire's produce on the four principal stone-paved roads that led to Cusco from its four suyos or provinces: the northern Chinchasuyo, the westerly Cuntisuyo, the Antisuyo to the east, and the Collasuyo to the south, covering a distance of some 14,000 miles. Pizarro's brother Hernando, in a letter sent from the island of Hispaniola while on his way to Seville, described the Inca roads as 'something to be believed, for in all truth, in a land so arid, there is nowhere in all Christendom to match their beauty . . . all the rivers have their own bridges, of either stone or reed. At one great river, which was very turbulent and wide, over which we twice crossed, there was a bridge made of reeds, which was a marvel to see, and which the horses also crossed.'[12]

At the time of the conquest some two hundred thousand people in an area of 40 square miles helped sustain the life flow to the capital Cusco, which the Incas referred to as the 'navel of the world'. The mystical pre-eminence of the Inca capital, lying in a mountain valley 10,500 feet above sea level, was reflected in the person of their emperor, and maintained in the afterlife by the panaca, houses of the dead, one for each of the emperors' respective families, which were living shrines to their immortality.

Each emperor in his lifetime established his own panaca in one of the city's palaces, staffed by about a thousand of his relatives and attendants to oversee his personal wealth and estates after his death. When the Spaniards first entered Cusco eleven panacas were venerated in the city, to which all the princes and higher nobility belonged, through their maternal or paternal descent, entitling them to unparalleled privileges and prestige among the Quéchua and their subject tribes. The aristocracy was divided into two distinctive groups: Hanan Cusco, the dominant military and secular grouping, and Hurin Cusco, its spiritual and mystical equivalent. Even some twenty years after the conquest, at a tribunal held in the city of Potosí, the Indian witnesses referred to the Spanish Emperor Charles V as the 'Hatun [apu, lord], of Castile', the dominant Hanan panaca.[13]

The several thousand Inca lords and their family dependants made up almost the entire population of the city. Along the Huatanay River and its lower valley were housed the yanacona, a servant caste, responsible for the cleaning of the city's streets and the maintenance of its buildings. Also populating the lower valley were the mitimae, communities of subject tribes, who lived under the rule of their caciques; in their thousands they had been brought to Cusco from their tribal lands for their own annual service of labour. In a rotary system known as mita, which the Spaniards themselves would later adopt, the subject tribesmen served as bondaged workers for a specific purpose and period of time in the four regions of the empire, in either agriculture or mining or as warriors of the imperial armies. Pedro Alonso Carrasco in his evidence stated that in order to keep the tribes in servitude and to prevent rebellion 'the Incas took their people from one region to another, those from Quito to Cusco, and those of Cusco to even more remote lands'.[14]

It is also thanks to the Venetian geographer Gian Battista Ramusio that the finest account of Cusco has survived, originally written by Pizarro's secretary Pedro Sancho de la Hoz and published in 1550 in his third volume of *Navigationi e Viaggi*, the original Spanish manuscript of which was subsequently lost:

The city, being the principal seat of these lords, is so grand and beautiful it would be worthy of being seen even in Spain, filled as it is with the palaces of its lords; for no poor people live there, and each lord possesses his own house, as do the caciques, even though they do not live there permanently. The majority of these houses are made of stone, and the others are part stone; many are of brick, and are constructed with great symmetry, as are their streets, in the form of a cross, all of them straight and paved, and through which run drains, also of stone. Their only detriment is that they are narrow, allowing only a single horseman to ride on one side of the drainage. This city is situated at the height of a mountain, and there are many buildings on its side and embankments, and in the plain below.

Its square is a quadrangle and in the most part flat and paved with pebbles; alongside the square there are four mansions of their lords, which are the principal palaces of the city, painted and constructed in stone; the finest of which is the palace of the Emperor, the old cacique, the gate of which is of white marble and decorated with various other colours, and which has also other buildings, with flat roofs, that are also worthy of note. There are in the city many other buildings of much grandeur: two rivers run on either side, the source of which is a league above Cusco, and which flows for a further two leagues below to the valley; the waters of which are both clear and clean running, and each has a bridge crossing into the city.

Above, on the mountain, which on the side facing the city is circular and very arid, there is a great stone fortress of great beauty, which has large watchtowers that overlook the city, and which gives its appearance even greater splendour. Inside this there are many buildings and a main tower, of cylindrical shape, with four or five smaller towers, one above the other: the chambers and halls within are small, though their walls are of fine workmanship, and very well assembled, their stone joinery in perfect order, like that which can be seen in Spain, one against the other, though without any evidence of sand, and so smooth they appear polished. It possesses so many adjacent towers and courtyards that a person would be unable to inspect them all in a day: and many Spaniards who have travelled in Lombardy and other foreign realms say that they have never seen the like of such a fortress or castle. It could garrison five thousand Spaniards: neither can it be besieged by battering ram, nor can it be mined from underground, because of its mountainous position. . . .[15]

In death, as in life, the Incas celebrated their divine origin before the mummies of their dead emperors, paraded in Cusco's central square in throne litters in front of thousands of their people. Preserved with ointments and aromatic herbs, and bound with white linen in an oval shape, their faces masked in gold, the mummies were symbolically 'fed' by their attendants with chicha, maize wine and coca leaves (a plant sacred to the panaca), and then entertained through the speech of mediums. In a ritual that acclaimed their divinity, the Inca princesses, the concubines and sister-wives of the emperor, would act out a theatre of the dead, miming the yuyaycucuy, the timeless frozen past of their people.

Little remains of Coricancha, Cusco's great Temple of the Sun, where many of these ceremonies took place, other than its foundation walling and some of its chambers; most of its vast structure was robbed for use in the construction of the monastery of Santo Domingo. The soldier-chronicler Pedro de Cieza de León, who as a young boy had seen the Cajamarca treasure displayed in the Casa de la Contratación in Seville, and who interviewed several of the Inca princes and conquistadores during his stay at Cusco, described the temple as four hundred paces in circumference, surrounded by a high wall of the finest masonry and precision. He wrote:

In all Spain I have not seen anything to compare to these walls, nor the placement of their stones . . . the stone is somewhat black in colour, rough, yet excellently cut. There are many doors and their arches are of a fine construction; at mid height of the walls runs a band of gold, of some seventeen inches in width and two in depth. The doors and arches are also embossed with sheets of this metal. Within the enclosure are four houses, not very large but of similar construction, the interior and exterior walls of which are adorned with sheets of gold, and their ceilings are of thatch. Built into the inner walls of these houses are two stone benches, illuminated by shafts of sunlight and decorated with precious stones and emeralds. On these benches sat the emperors, and if any person would have done the same he would have been condemned to death . . . at each of the entrances were porters who guarded the virgins, of whom there were many, being the daughters of the principal lords and chosen for their beauty; they would remain in the temple until old age; and if any would have had dealings with men they would have been killed or buried alive, as would also be the man's punishment. These women were called mamacuna, who knew no other role than to paint the woollen garments for service in the temple, and in the making of chicha, of which containers were filled in ample quantity.

In one of these houses, the grandest of them all, was the figure of the sun, of great size and made of gold, and encased with precious stones. There also were placed the mummies of the Incas who reigned in Cusco, each surrounded by a great quantity of treasure . . . around the temple house were a number of smaller buildings, which were the dwellings of the Indians who served in the temple, and an enclosure where they kept the white llamas and the children and men they would sacrifice. There was also a garden, the earth and grass of which was of fine gold and where artificial maize grew, also of gold, as were their stems and ears, and so well planted that even in a strong wind they would stand. As well, there were twenty llamas of gold with their lambs, and shepherds with their stone slings and staffs, all of gold. . . .[16]

Most of the witnesses to the enquiry recorded that the succession to the Emperor Huayna Cápac's throne had remained unresolved. Though neither primogeniture nor legitimacy in the European sense of the word were established requisites among the Quéchua, the purity of his bloodline favoured the succession of the son of a sister-queen. It was a succession that depended also on the allegiance of the panacas of Cusco and the sanction of the High Priest of the Sun, known as the Villaoma.* The conquistador Mansio Serra de Leguizamón, who had taken the Villaoma prisoner, had been awarded his image on his family coat-of-arms by the Emperor Charles V.

After the death of his sister-queen the Coya Cusi Rimay, who was probably the mother of his son Ninancuyochi, the emperor married

---

* Villaoma – as spelt in the testimonies of various conquistadores.

their younger sister the Coya Rahua Ocllo, who for many years had been his concubine.* Renowned for her exceptional beauty and the magnificence of the court over which she presided, she was said to have been accompanied during her travels across the empire by a thousand musicians. The eldest of their sons was Topa Cusi Huallpa, known as Huáscar, whom Huayna Cápac appointed Governor of Cusco and of his southern empire. The youngest of their daughters were the Coyas Marca Chimbo and Quispiquipi – these girls were the only imperial children to survive the massacres ordered by Atahualpa, and after the Conquest they were known as Doña Juana and Doña Beatriz.[17]

Atahualpa was one of the hundreds of other sons born to the emperor, but he became Huayna Cápac's favourite son, despite the fact that his mother was only a cousin of the emperor, not a closer relation. Two other sons, the Incas Manco and Paullu, both from different mothers, were to feature in the history of the conquest. Pedro Sarmiento de Gamboa recorded in his history that in the last years of Huayna Cápac's reign his empire was devastated by a plague, probably smallpox, which had spread from the northern borders of his realms as far south as Cusco. Years later the Jesuit Bernabé Cobo wrote that in an act of penitence the emperor had gone into seclusion and fasted in order to bring an end to the suffering of his people, and that during his fast he saw the ghosts of three dwarfs enter his chamber, which he interpreted as a sign of his impending death. Sarmiento de Gamboa also describes in some detail how the emperor then summoned his diviners to guide him in his choice of successor. The carcass of a young llama was brought to his presence and its entrails were read by the High Priest Villaoma, who informed him that the auspices for the succession of his son Ninancuyochi were unfavourable. The carcass of a second llama was brought in, but the same auspices were predicted for the succession of his son Huáscar. It was a divination that would never be repeated. It was the year 1527.

---

* Coya – title of the sister-wife of the Inca emperor and of their daughters.

A thousand of his servants were killed in sacrifice to serve him in the afterlife, and for ten days the tribes of Quito mourned his passing with traditional weeping before his body was taken to Tumibamba to be mummified. In less than five years the Inca realm of Tahuantinsuyo had virtually disintegrated, and circumstances had laid it open to its final and inevitable destruction by the small army of Pizarro's conquistadores who had disembarked on its northern shore.

The thirteen reports assembled by the Viceroy Toledo were made into a folio of 213 leaves which he sent to the Council of the Indies. He also informed King Philip II that the Indian population of Peru had been greatly reduced. Recurrent outbreaks of smallpox, and the huge fatalities suffered by the Inca warriors in their own civil wars and later in the rebellions of the conquistadores, where they had served in the various private armies, had reduced by almost a third the male population of the former Inca empire.

Some twenty years previously the Crown official Antonio de Ribera, in a letter to the Council of the Indies, recorded that:

> It has been some fifteen years since the Marquis Don Francisco Pizarro ordered the counting of Indians of the encomiendas of the conquistadores, and which numbered 1,550,000 Indians. And when Pedro de la Gasca was to make a similar enquiry [in 1548] . . . it was discovered that in all the land there were no more than 243,000 tributary Indians, as recorded by the testimonies that were made to the inspectors, I being one of them.[18]

Pedro Sarmiento de Gamboa's history of the Incas, *Historia Indica*, commissioned by the Viceroy Toledo, was discovered in a library in Denmark in 1906.

THREE

The Marquis of Las Charcas

26 July 1541

It had taken Francisco Pizarro a great deal of time to decide on the name for the marquisate bestowed on him by the Emperor Charles V. The matter was still unsettled that morning, when he discussed the subject with his secretary Picado, who was in charge of all his correspondence, signing his name with a customary flourish beside the mark he would make. The southern region of Las Charcas, where he held one of his largest grants – the twenty thousand Indian vassals the Crown had awarded him – was in Picado's opinion the more suitable title.[1]

His enemies nevertheless still referred to him simply as the 'bastard' or the 'swineherd', a calumny frequently bandied about by the dispossessed supporters of his fellow-slaver the Adelantado* Diego de Almagro, whose execution he had condoned, and who claimed that as an infant he had been suckled by pigs. He had been called worse names, even by his brother Hernando, the only legitimate son of their impoverished hidalgo father, who had refused to acknowledge their kinship until he had returned to their native Estremaduran township, a hardened man of the Indies with the royal warrant of conquest in his possession. Nor, when he met his other half-brothers for the first time, did he know whether they would accept him, or whether they would follow him halfway across the world in search of the empire they would eventually conquer together – and over which he now ruled like a god with

---

* Adelantado – military title denoting a governor of a frontier region.

36

power of life and death over every living soul from his newly built palace at Lima, the coastal settlement he had founded on the Feast of the Epiphany seven years previously, which he had named the City of the Kings.

No one really knew his age or much about him, except that he was an old man who had spent most of his life in the isthmus of Panama, where he had acquired a small encomienda, earning his living as a slaver, and that he had also been among the men with Balboa who had first seen the Pacific.[2] A tall, dark-featured man, although by now his hair and beard were grey, he was by nature silent and remote, and had always maintained the simple peasant habits of his childhood. His only extravagance was the gilded coat armour he commissioned from the armourer Ximenez in Seville, which he wore on special occasions. His only recreation, other than working in the small garden at the far end of his compound, was playing bowls, a passion he shared with his secretary Picado.

Sunday 26 July 1541 marked the eighth anniversary of the killing of the Inca Emperor Atahualpa at Cajamarca; it was a day Pizarro regarded as ominous, even though it was also the day on which he had been granted by the Empress Isabela at Toledo the Capitulación, the Crown's official permission for his expedition of conquest. At ten o'clock that morning he had received in the patio of his lodging his lieutenants Velázquez and Chávez, who had accompanied Picado. Mass was said in the small chapel at the back of the building by a Biscayan priest, a man Pizarro neither cared for nor trusted, but whose habit it was to make himself available to perform that simple duty. It is reported that after the Mass the priest warned him to take care of himself, but it is more likely that he said nothing to him at all, simply taking the silver peso always left for him and departing.

Shortly after eleven the wife of the conquistador Chávez, María de Escobar, heard shouting coming from the square. Though her lodging was situated in front of the newly erected convent of Santo Domingo, a little distance from the square, the noise was sufficient to arouse her suspicions, partly because her husband had earlier commented on having seen more people there than usual, many of whom were not known to him. Even the young Indian woman

Cuxirimay, the mother of Pizarro's two youngest children Francisco and Juan, noticed the noise but thought it had nothing to do with her people; she attributed it to the Spaniards, for she too had seen many of them assembled near the wood and stone church that served as a cathedral.

By the time María de Escobar herself reached the square, some three hundred armed men, many of them mounted on horses and mules, had sealed off each of its narrow streets. It was then she saw the small procession of Negro slaves, led by Pizarro's Spanish servant Juan de Barbarán. It took her a few seconds to understand what she was staring at, amid the shouting and curses of the armed men surrounding the Negroes. But on they walked, like men in a trance, their huge shoulders almost dwarfing the object they carried – and which María could now identify because of the calf-booted leg and silver spurs, trailing through the dusty earth.

She never saw his face but she was told by the Negroes who carried his body to the church and buried him that night that it was clean though greatly disfigured; before taking him out into the square they had washed his body and dressed him in his finest clothes, covering him with his white cloak of the Order of Santiago. That night the woman Escobar buried her husband, in silence and alone, also the victim of Almagro's mestizo son.

On 18 June 1977 four workmen restoring the crypt of Lima's cathedral discovered in one of its walls a metal casket and box containing a man's skull and bones, together with fragments of a sword and a pair of silver spurs. The casket bore the emblem of a six-pointed star within four concentric circles, and the words:

Here is the head of the Lord Marquis Don Francisco Pizarro, who discovered and conquered these realms of Peru, and who placed them in the Royal Crown of Castile.[3]

FOUR

The Nephews of Doña Inés

On 26 February 1547 a large crowd gathered in the main square of the City of the Kings at Lima to witness the execution of an Indian sorceress known as the witch Yanque. Among the officials standing on the square's podium, waiting to witness the execution, was the city's alderman Francisco de Ampuero, the victim of the witch's enchantments. Standing beside him, dressed in her native costume, was his Indian wife, an Inca princess; it was she who had instigated the acts of witchcraft, but she had been pardoned by the city's magistrate at the behest of her husband.[1] Most of the colonists assembled in the square had also attended the lengthy court hearing, in which the sorceress and her accomplice, the princess's Negro slave Simón, had been interrogated by the public prosecutor and admitted their guilt after being tortured.

The descriptions they gave both startled and infuriated the spectators, as they related how they had magically summoned Alderman Ampuero's shadow and cast a spell restraining him from beating and maltreating his wife. But the alderman's wife had again complained to the sorceress that her husband had continued in his maltreatment of her, and this was the reason, the witch Yanque claimed, why she had been forced to conjure the devil himself, in the form of a four-legged animal. Both of the prisoners had received the severest sentences, while their client was left to the mercy of her husband.

At precisely six o'clock that evening a small wooden cart drawn by four Indians entered the main square. Seated with her head bowed and wearing a yellow coned hat, on which was written the word 'Blasphemer', was the witch Yanque. Not once did the princess take her eyes off the unfortunate witch, not even when they tied her to the stake, surrounded by kindling wood, and set it ablaze.

Nothing more is recorded of the Inca princess until eight years later, when she attended the same courtroom as a witness on behalf of the orphaned children of her brother, the former Emperor Atahualpa.[2] In faltering Castilian she gave her name as Doña Inés and declared that her Indian name had been Quispe Sisa, and that she was Atahualpa's sister and the wife of the Spaniard Francisco de Ampuero, alderman and encomendero of the city. Though most of the colonists assembled in the courtroom knew that she had once been Pizarro's mistress and had borne him two children, Doña Francisca and Don Gonzalo, few were aware that her husband had once been Pizarro's servant and that she had been forced to marry him, once her lover had discarded her. It was something that still shamed her.

Asked by the royal notary whether the plaintiffs were known to her, she answered that they were the sons of her brother, the Emperor Atahualpa, and that their names were Don Diego and Don Francisco. She was then questioned about the identity of their mothers. She stated that she had known both of them at Cajamarca, and that they had been her brother's concubines: 'and as they were Atahualpa's women, and publicly revered, they were obeyed and respected; and as was the custom among the native lords, men as well as women, no single person could speak to them, nor have any contact with them; and if anyone would have looked upon their faces, they would have been killed'.

Once more referring to her nephews, she told the tribunal that neither of them had ever received any gratuity from the Spanish Crown, despite their former high status as her brother's sons, and that they now lived in great poverty, sustained only by the charity of the friars of the monastery of Santo Domingo at Cusco. She then made her mark on the document of her evidence, stating that she could neither read nor write.

The testimony of two conquistadores was then read to her. Both of them were known to her. The older of the two, Pedro de Alconchel, who was also illiterate, had been Pizarro's trumpeter at Cajamarca and had for several years kept a small boarding-house in the city for veterans of the Conquest. Asked whether he had seen any of Atahualpa's wives at Cajamarca, he replied:

Atahualpa had had several women with him, some of whom served him, and others with whom he had carnal relations; and these were much respected and lived apart from the other women, and were held in great esteem by the many Indians, men and women, who were their servants; and if any Indian lord or cacique had touched them, or had had carnal relations with them, he would have been killed; for neither would he have dared to do so, let alone to look upon their faces. . . .

Alconchel's testimony was followed by the evidence of the conquistador Mansio Serra de Leguizamón. He stated that 'he had also known Atahualpa at Cajamarca when the Marquis Don Francisco Pizarro made him his prisoner, for he had come to this land with the Marquis, and that the two petitioners, Don Diego and Don Francisco, the sons of Atahualpa, were known to him since they were young boys, when they had been brought to Cusco from Quito'. When questioned about the Cajamarca treasure, he recalled that 'Atahualpa had promised to give the marquis a hut filled with gold, but, because the hut had been destroyed in a fire, he gave him an even greater quantity of gold, which was partitioned among all the men, and he gave more than he had promised him'.

To the fourth question of the interrogation, he replied

he saw Atahualpa die, and that at the moment he was about to be killed he addressed the interpreter, and, weeping, he said to the Marquis that he charged him with the care of his sons and his daughter, for in Quito he had left two small sons and a daughter, and this he must do; and the Marquis, with tears in his eyes promised him he would care for them; and some time later, he witnessed the Commander Don Diego de Almagro go to the province of Quito, from where he brought back with him Don Francisco and Don Diego and their sister, and they were brought to this city of Cusco, where they had lived in the monastery of Santo Domingo, where they had been instructed and looked after by the friars, and always throughout these realms they had been recognized as the sons of Atahualpa.

In answer to the fifth question, he said that 'after they had been brought to Cusco, which was some twenty years ago, it was known to him that they lived in great poverty, and not how the sons of Atahualpa should live, for they own neither encomienda lands, nor any such possessions, not one single thing; for they have only what the friars give them for food, and this is publicly known'. Finally, in reply to the seventh question, he said that 'it would be a just and a saintly thing if His Majesty the Emperor were to favour Don Francisco and Don Diego with an encomienda of Indians with which they could sustain themselves and their wives and children, being whose sons they are; for their father Atahualpa was lord of all this kingdom and these realms obeyed him and served him, and this he witnessed before they killed him'.

At this point the princess left the courthouse, her memory haunted by the events of those days, seeing in her mind's eye the image of her brother in the square at Cajamarca, tied naked to a wooden pole; his body had remained there all that night, his eyes open wide, and his face and hands smeared with his blood. She remembered how she and her cousin Cuxirimay had gone to the chamber where they had shared his imprisonment, searching for his spirit and calling out to him, but there was only silence and her distraught cousin had tried to kill herself. Then it was that Pizarro took Cuxirimay for his other woman, and later gave her the name Doña Angelina.

The Princess Doña Inés was to remain married to Ampuero until her death in May 1575; she was buried in the church of the convent of La Merced at Lima. Her nephews Don Diego and Don Francisco Atahualpa, who for several years had been cared for in Cusco by the elderly conquistador Diego de Trujillo, were awarded an annual pension of 600 pesos of silver by the Crown. The chronicler Garcilaso de la Vega, who was a school companion of Don Francisco, recorded that he was 'a handsome young man, in body and face . . . and who died young'.[3]

The fate of Doña Angelina, who was Pizarro's mistress for several years and was the mother of his two sons Don Francisco and Don Juan, was less fortunate. Soon after being discarded by Pizarro she left Lima and returned to her native Cusco. There is some evidence that at the time of the Adelantado Diego de Almagro's seizure of the city at the outbreak of his rebellion against the Pizarros she was made his prisoner and suffered the rape of many of their women. Several years later she married the Spanish immigrant Juan Díez de Betanzos, who made a living as a translator of quéchua; he helped obtain for her a small encomienda near Cusco, which after her death he appropriated for himself and his new Spanish wife.

Nothing is known for certain of Betanzos's background, other than his birth at Valladolid, but he played a minor role in the rebellion of Pizarro's brother Gonzalo. His *Suma y Narración de los Incas* is one of the earliest accounts of the Inca people and their culture, most of the background information for which he obtained from his wife's relatives and through his work as an interpreter during the enquiry held at Cusco by Governor Vaca de Castro. The first part of his manuscript was discovered in the library of the Escorial and was published in 1880. A second section, which had found its way into the library of the Dukes of Medinaceli, was discovered in Mallorca and first published in 1987. A dictionary of quéchua which he compiled as an addendum to his history has never been found.

FIVE

The Child Empress

She was a lonely figure, mounted on a mule overlooking the plain of Chupas, on the outskirts of the township of Huamanga, where four centuries later the Independence of the Andean republics of South America would be decided by the defeat of Spain's army at the Battle of Ayacucho. For most of that day she had watched the mustering of the rebel forces of the Panamanian mestizo Diego de Almagro, the Adelantado's son, who had avenged his father's killing by murdering Pizarro.

Along the great plain Spaniards wearing armour and their Indian vassal warriors were positioning themselves into squadrons in front of the loyalist army of Governor Vaca de Castro. She could clearly make out the white mare of the mestizo's general, the Spaniard Juan Balsa, whose woman she had been for almost two years, as he crossed the ridge of mountains and entered the plain at the head of his horsemen. An escort of her Indian servants surrounded her and the ten mules he had told her to keep saddled, their packs laden with the gold and silver bars he had looted from Pizarro's lodging. Their young son she cradled in her arms.

She had no love for the mestizo, nor for the memory of his elderly father, to whom she had been given by her bastard half-brother the Inca Manco, Pizarro's puppet ruler, when she was just thirteen years old. She had seen his corpse taken to the gallows in Cusco, his head spiked on the end of Hernando Pizarro's lance, his one eye staring blankly at the crowd of his fellow countrymen who had defeated him in battle.

The friar-chronicler Cristóbal de Molina, who had accompanied the Adelantado Almagro on his ill-fated expedition to Chile, and had also watched his execution at the hands of Pizarro's brother, recorded that the Inca Manco:

gave Almagro a great quantity of gold and also one of his sisters, Marca Chimbo, a daughter of the Emperor Huayna Cápac, who was the most important of all the women in the kingdom, and who – had she been a man – would have inherited the Inca realm; and she gave Almagro a pit filled with gold and silver, which in bars weighed 27,000 pesos alone; and to another captain she gave from the same pit the equivalent of 12,000 pesos of silver; and not even by these acts was she honoured by the Spaniards, being raped various times, for she was of a mild and gentle disposition and very beautiful, though later marked by syphilis.[1]

As she surveyed the field of battle, she knew that once more her fate would be decided by men who had abused her, and who would doubtless abuse her again. But nothing seemed to trouble her any more, her only concern being the survival of her child.

The conquistador Lucas Martínez Vegazo, who fought at Chupas that September's day in the year 1542, recalled the battle:

The rebels began their advance across a mountain ridge to almost a league in distance of our troops as their cavalry scouts rode out to inspect our positions . . . placing their artillery in line and their squadrons, of some 230 horse, accompanied by some 50 foot-soldiers; their infantry consisted of 200 arquebusiers and 100 pikemen, all so well armed that not even troops from Milan could match them in their armour and weapons . . . the governor then ordered the advance, and we marched to within reach of their arquebusiers' shot, advancing further still, until we engaged them with our lances, pikes and swords in a battle that lasted for almost an entire hour; and never was witnessed such cruel and brutal fighting, in which neither brother, relative nor friend spared each other's lives. . . .[2]

As night fell the dead and wounded could be counted in their hundreds, among them Juan Balsa, the father of her son, who had been cut down by his own Indian escort as he tried to flee the battlefield. That evening, together with the other Indian women prisoners, she was taken before the Governor Vaca de Castro, who awarded her in marriage to the conquistador Francisco de Villacastín, an elderly man who for years had made a living as an Indian interpreter. He was widely ridiculed by his own countrymen for having lost his front teeth to a stone thrown by a monkey.[3] At her baptism in Cusco she was given the name Doña Juana.

Villacastín was to die six years later, executed for his part in the rebellion of Pizarro's brother Gonzalo, whom he had served as Governor of Cusco. Reduced to penury, the young princess, who would have inherited the Inca throne had she been born a boy, lived out her days in Cusco in absolute poverty in the company of her only son Juan Balsa, who made a scant living as an interpreter and Indian guide. The year of her death is unknown.

SIX

The River of the Holy Ghost

It was almost dawn and the chorus of wildfowl could be heard across the banks of the great river the Apalachee people called the Mississippi, its shoreline of mud flats hidden by woodland and pine trees. The contingent of some forty Spanish and Portuguese men, dressed in buckskins and buffalo hides, watched in silence as the two dugouts slipped into the swirling current, their oars cutting into the water. Behind them they towed a large oak log containing the body of their leader. At Luis de Moscoso's orders the men had covered the makeshift coffin with animal skins and filled it with sand so that it could be 'buried' in the great waters of the river they had named the River of the Holy Ghost. His property was then sold: 'two male and two women slaves, three horses, and seven hundred pigs'.[1]

Hernando de Soto's amulets were buried beside him, together with the magic mirrors he had always carried on his person. These, he said, would foretell his death, and he told the Indians that they also enabled him to converse with his god. He was, recorded the chronicler Garcilaso de la Vega, a man of above medium height and a dark complexion.[2]

The fate of the largest armada of conquest ever to sail from Seville to the New World, and the suffering and losses endured by Soto's men, would remain virtually unknown to the Spanish public until fifteen years later when one of the survivors, calling himself simply 'an hidalgo from the township of Elvas',* published an account of their expedition during the years 1539 to 1543.[3]

---

* A Portuguese township on the Spanish border of Badajoz.

Few of the veterans of the conquest of La Florida or the 'land of
the flowers', the name given to the territory by the early Spanish
explorer Juan Ponce de León, would recall the events that had
brought their leader to such an ignominious end that summer's
morning, his body racked by fever. Only a handful of his men had
known him in the early years of the conquest of Nicaragua, or later,
when he had worked for the colony's governor, Pedrarias,* as his
slaver. One or two of them remembered some of the stories they had
heard: how Balboa,† his elderly friend and patron from the
Estremaduran township of Jerez de los Caballeros, had been hanged
like a common criminal by Pedrarias, and how the elderly governor
had then spent hours contemplating his victim's fly-ridden head,
which he had ordered to be placed on a lance in the small square of
his settlement at León, and how for weeks afterwards he had spoken
to no one, not even to Pedrarias's crippled daughter, who would one
day be his wife. Only the chronicler Fernández de Oviedo, who had
hated Pedrarias possibly more than any other man, would record
that their governor had spent the rest of the day of Balboa's murder
beside the coffin he kept in his wooden stockade house.

One of Soto's men remarked that at the height of his fever he had
called out Balboa's name, for it was said that an astrologer had once
told him he would not live to be older than Balboa, who had died at
the age of forty-two. The chronicler Hidalgo de Elvas left a vivid
account of the days before their leader's death, and recalled the
orders he had issued from his sickbed:

> All that night the horses were left bridled, and from each of their
> companies the men rode in groups of two to check on the
> sentinels, who kept guard on the road outside the camp, and the
> crossbowmen, guarding the canoes on the river . . . and he sent
> Tovar with fifteen horse, and Guzmán with his footmen upstream
> in canoes . . . and at night they crossed the river. At daybreak

---

* Don Pedro Arias Dávila, known as Pedrarias.
† Vasco Núñez de Balboa, who discovered the Pacific Ocean in September 1513.

Tovar and his horsemen fell upon the Indian village, of some five or six thousand souls. He ordered that not one Indian should be spared. The cries of the women and children were so loud that they deafened the ears of those who pursued them. A hundred or so Indians were killed there, and many more were badly wounded by our lances. There were men there that day, so cruel and such butchers, they killed old and young alike. . . .[4]

The chronicler recorded that after Soto's death it would take almost a year for the men now under Moscoso's command to attempt a crossing into Mexico through the hills and desert plains of Texas, but the conditions were so harsh that they were eventually forced to turn back to spend the winter on the banks of the Mississippi, after a march of some 4,000 miles. Desperate to escape, they built brigantines from the snowbound forest trees, and these they sailed down the great river and into the open sea; after fifty-two days they finally reached the small Spanish settlement at Pánuco in the Gulf of Mexico on 10 September 1543. Of the 600 conquistadores only 311 had survived.

In his will, written in Cuba before the departure of his armada, the Adelantado Hernando de Soto, Knight of Santiago, had ordered that 'five hundred ducats be left to a boy, who they say is my son, called Andrés', and that one thousand ducats be given to his daughter María whom he had left in Nicaragua.[5] He made no mention of any other children. The fortune he had acquired in the conquest of Peru had financed his new expedition, and what little remained he left to his wife Doña Isabel de Bobadilla, Pedrarias's daughter, whom he had appointed Governor of Cuba during his absence. For years to come her ghostly image was said to haunt the Giralda tower of Havana's harbour, her eyes searching the skyline endlessly for his return.

In the Archives of the Indies at Seville there exists a curious manuscript in the form of several petitions, dated between 1562 and 1586, presented to the Royal Chancery Court at Lima by an Inca princess who claimed to be the daughter of the Adelantado

Hernando de Soto, and calling on the Spanish Crown to redress the poverty in which both she and her children had been forced to live.[6] Among the conquistadores who gave evidence on her behalf at Lima were three women who had taken part in the Conquest: Beatriz de Salcedo, a freed Moorish slave who had accompanied the conquistadores to Cajamarca; María de Escobar, an elderly Spanish woman who as a young girl had been a maid to the wife of Pedrarias, the Governor of Panama; and the Inca Princess Doña Inés, Pizarro's former mistress.

The following extracts from the petition give an indication of the fate of many of the Inca princesses after they were abandoned by their conquistador lovers, most of whom were obliged by the Crown to marry low-born Spanish immigrants, prepared to accept their illegitimate children in return for an award of Indian vassals.

NOTARY: In the City of the Kings in these realms of Peru, on June 20, 1562, before the President and judges of this Royal Chancery Court, García Carrillo, on behalf of his wife Doña Leonor de Soto, a granddaughter of the Emperor Huayna Cápac, once lord of these kingdoms, declares she is the natural daughter of the Adelantado Hernando de Soto, His Majesty's Governor of Florida, and of the Coya Doña Leonor, who are diseased. And he begs Your Highness that he may present the following witnesses to verify the truth of his words, and that they be asked the following: If the Adelantado and Doña Leonor Coya was known to them, and whether their daughter, Doña Leonor de Soto, is also known to them. And that the Coya Doña Leonor, whose Indian name was Tocto Chimbo, was the daughter of Huayna Cápac and of Chumbe Yllaya, lady of the valley of Yca, and that she was held as such in these realms of Peru, and that she gave birth to her daughter, when both she and the Adelantado were unmarried and at a young age.

And if it be known to them that the Adelantado was one of the foremost discoverers and conquistadores of these realms of Peru, and that he was the captain-general of the Marquis Don Francisco Pizarro, His Majesty's governor, and that he served Your Majesty with great valour and loyalty, because of which the Marquis charged him with the most important commissions in the conquest of these realms. And that once these realms of Peru had been conquered and secured, the Adelantado returned to the kingdoms of Spain to offer his services to His Majesty, leaving behind two distributions of Indian vassals he had been awarded as an encomienda. And that His Majesty, holding him in such high regard, sent him as his governor of Florida, in which conquest he served His Majesty well, and that he spent from his own purse some hundred thousand pesos of gold in the discovery and conquests of Peru and of Florida. And that after he left for Spain, Vaca de Castro, His Majesty's governor of these realms of Peru, obliged Doña Leonor Coya to marry Bautista, el Galán, the handsome, the son of the Emperor Don Carlos's armourer, to whom he awarded the encomienda of Guaro Canas and of Layo Supa, in recognition of his wife being the daughter of Huayna Cápac. And if it also be known to them that Bautista, the handsome, was a loyal servant of His Majesty, and that during the rebellion of Gonzalo Pizarro, Alonso de Toro, his rebel governor of Cusco, hanged him, and that shortly afterwards, Doña Leonor, robbed of all her goods and bereft of a husband, died of sorrow. And that Doña Leonor de Soto, her daughter, married García Carrillo by the rites of the Holy Mother Church of Rome, and that they have two sons and a daughter, and that they live in extreme poverty.

LUCAS MARTÍNEZ VEGAZO: Once these realms and the Indians of their provinces had been pacified, Hernando de Soto, who was an encomendero of Cusco, possessing there a fine mansion and a large distribution of Indian vassals, which now is possessed by some three or four Spaniards, left these lands for Spain; and this I know, for on his departure from the city I accompanied him for almost a league.

GONZALO DE MONZÓN: I witnessed the Adelantado, on his return to Spain, marry by order of Our Holy Mother Church Doña

Isabel de Bobadilla, the legitimate daughter of Pedro Arias Dávila, and being present, I also saw His Majesty the Emperor entrust him with the conquest and pacification of Florida, naming him also governor of the island of Cuba. And it is known to me that at the time Don Hernando de Soto left these realms of Peru for Spain, he took with him some eighty thousand castellanos,* all of which he spent in the service of His Majesty in supplying his armada for the conquest of Florida. This I witnessed at Havana, when the accounts of the expedition were discussed by him with his partner Hernán Ponce de León. And all this is known and witnessed by me, for I took part in the said expedition and conquest.

BERNABÉ PICÓN: I knew both the Adelantado and the Coya Doña Leonor, and I was present at the Adelantado's house in Cusco when their daughter was born at the time he was Don Francisco Pizarro's governor of the city; and I later saw their daughter living in the household of the Captain Hernán Ponce de León, his companion in arms. This is known to me, for the Adelantado was a close friend of mine, and I shared his house in Cusco and I witnessed the Coya serve him as his woman, and where she gave birth to their daughter, whom I also saw baptised. And I know that he had no other child in this realm of Peru, for it would have been known to me, and because he confided in me. Neither of them were married. And at the time of Cajamarca, when Atahualpa, whose woman she had been, gifted her to the Adelantado, she was some twenty-two years of age.

DOÑA INÉS: It is true that Doña Leonor Coya, whose Indian name was Tocto Chimbo, was a daughter of Huayna Cápac, King and lord of these realms of Peru, though I do not remember the name of her mother, nor whether she was lady of the valley of Yca. For I knew her well, and had much friendship with her, being as she was my sister. It is also true that Doña Leonor de Soto,

---

* Castellano – a gold coin of 24 carats.

who is the wife of García Carrillo, is her natural daughter and of the Adelantado.

BEATRIZ DE SALCEDO: I knew Doña Leonor Coya intimately. At Cajamarca she was called by the Indians Tocto Chimbo, and she was held as the daughter of Huayna Cápac. And I witnessed that Manco Inca, his son, treated her as his sister, and this I know, for I was the first Spanish woman to enter Cajamarca. And I spent much time there in the company of Atahualpa's women, and speaking to them. And I saw that the Adelantado Hernando de Soto took possession of her, and that neither of them had any other children in these realms. I heard it said that Bautista, the handsome, who married her daughter, was a loyal servant of His Majesty, because of which they hanged him in Cusco, and that a few days afterwards Doña Leonor Coya, seeing herself abandoned and without a husband, died from sheer anger.

MARÍA DE ESCOBAR: Doña Leonor de Soto is well known to me, for she was placed in my care. Her mother was also known to me, and also placed in my care by the Marquis Don Francisco Pizarro so that she could be instructed in our customs and discipline, and taught our Holy Catholic Faith. And being the daughter of Huayna Cápac at various times caciques would come to my house to see her, and render her homage. Her daughter greatly resembles the Adelantado in her features, and I raised her and had her living in my house until the day she married García Carrillo. It is also known to me that the Governor Vaca de Castro arranged for the marriage of Doña Leonor Coya with Bautista, the handsome, the son of the Emperor's armourer, and that on their marriage he gave him a distribution of Indian vassals; and that during the rebellion of Gonzalo Pizarro he was killed, and that Doña Leonor Coya died shortly afterwards, and that her daughter was still a very young child, and I had no choice but to take her with me. And she and her husband and children now live in great poverty. . . .

SEVEN

The Old Soldier

Shortly before the Feast of the Epiphany marking the twenty-seventh anniversary of the founding of the viceregal capital, one of the few surviving veterans of Cajamarca, his bearded features scarred by war and marked by the years he had spent in the Indies, rode into Lima's main square, accompanied by a retinue of his Negro slaves and Indians. His weary horse was covered in dust and mud after a journey that had brought the veteran across the cordillera of the Andes from Cusco to the Pacific coast. With no outward sign of sentiment he had ridden past the iron cages at the far end of the square that contained the skulls of Pizarro's brother Gonzalo, his lieutenant Carbajal and the encomendero Francisco Girón, men who had once been the veteran's companions in arms – and whose executions he had witnessed some fourteen years previously. Driven by debt, he had come to the capital to present his testimonial of his past service to the Crown and his petition to King Philip II for an award of Indian vassals.[1]

For three months the veteran conquistador Mansio Serra de Leguizamón and his witnesses duly appeared before the viceregal court, recalling their role both in the Conquest and in the later rebellions of their countrymen, and reliving the legends of their past deeds. They were old men now, very different from the callow, untried youths brought to the Indies by their dreams of riches. We may not see their faces but their words still carry across the centuries.

The Witnesses

LUCAS MARTÍNEZ VEGAZO
Testimony: 16 February. Age: 49. Born in Trujillo, Estremadura. Literate. He had enlisted in the expedition of Conquest when Pizarro

had returned to his native township of Trujillo in 1529. Appointed by Pizarro as a founding encomendero and the first mayor of the city of Arequipa, he was one of the wealthiest conquistadores, building his fortune from the revenues of his mines and trade as a merchant. In 1543 he had sent the first ship with supplies to the newly founded settlement of Chile. A leading partisan of Gonzalo Pizarro's rebellion, he had served as his rebel Governor of Arequipa. Stripped of his lands, he had spent years litigating in the civil courts of Lima for the restitution of his encomienda. Though he fathered an illegitimate daughter by his Moorish slave and a son by his mistress Doña Isabel Yupanqui, an Inca princess, he was to leave most of his fortune to his young Creole bride, the daughter of the witness Nicolás de Ribera, whom he married just a few weeks before his death, five years after his testimony.

LUIS SÁNCHEZ

Testimony: 16 February. Age: over 50. Origin unknown. Illiterate. Though he was awarded an allotment of land in Cusco, nothing is recorded of his later years. In a decree signed by the Cardinal of Seville and dated 24 November 1541, he was awarded a coat-of-arms, the crest of which was the fortress of Cusco enveloped in Indian plumes, in commemoration of the part he had played during the Inca siege of the city in 1536.

PEDRO SUÁREZ DE ILLANES

Testimony: 26 February. Age: 35. Origin unknown. Illiterate.

BERNABÉ PICÓN

Testimony: 27 February. Age: 55. Born at Cáceres, Estremadura. Able to sign his name. One of the first explorers of northern Argentina, he had served in Diego de Rojas's expedition of 1542. A partisan of Gonzalo Pizarro's rebellion, he was taken prisoner at the Battle of Jaquijahuana and exiled from Cusco.

HERNÁN GÓMEZ

Testimony: 28 February. Age: 35. Origin unknown. Literate.

NICOLÁS DE RIBERA

Testimony: 3 March. Age: 70. Andalusian. Literate. Known as el viejo, the old man, to differentiate him from another conquistador of the same name. He was a veteran of Pizarro's second voyage of discovery in 1527, and one of the famous thirteen men who had remained behind with him at the Island of Gallo, for which he was awarded by the Crown the rank of hidalgo. An encomendero of Lima, he was also its first mayor and was one of the most influential grandees of Peru's founding colonial nobility. A principal source for the chronicler Agustín de Zárate, who stayed with him in his mansion in Lima, he died a year after giving his testimony.

JUAN DE RIVAMARTÍN

Testimony: 4 March. Age: 44. Andalusian. Literate. Army commander.

FRANCISCO DE ILLESCAS

Testimony: 4 March. Age: 50. Born in Torrejón de Velasco, Toledo. Illiterate. An encomendero of Guayaquil, he was a veteran of Gonzalo Pizarro's ill-fated expedition to the northern Amazon in search of the legendary kingdom of El Dorado in 1540. He also took part in Gonzalo Pizarro's rebellion. Five months after he gave his testimony, the Viceroy the Count of Nieva awarded him an annual pension of 800 pesos – a benevolence that aroused considerable protest among the settlers of Guayaquil, one of whom described him as 'the most fallen of men we have in these parts, whole sole distraction is to gamble day and night'.[2]

PEDRO DE ALCONCHEL

Testimony: 10 March. Age: 70. Born in Estremadura. Illiterate. An encomendero of Lima, he was one of the oldest veterans of the Conquest, and in his latter years opened a boarding-house in Lima for his fellow veterans. It was his custom to have his name signed for him with the words 'Alconchel, trumpeter', to commemorate his role as Pizarro's trumpeter.[3]

DIEGO CAMACHO
Testimony: 10 March. Age: 43. Origin unknown. Literate.

HERNANDO DE CESPEDES
Testimony: 10 March. Age: 45. Origin unknown. Able to sign his name.

RODRIGO LÓPEZ BERNAL
Testimony: 10 March. Age: 55. Origin unknown. Illiterate.

The Royal Notary

The royal notary Francisco López added the following words to the testimonial:

> . . . inscribing my signature Francisco López, who had been among the men who had gone immediately afterwards [from Cajamarca] to place Cusco under the royal jurisdiction, in the company of the reserves of the Captain Hernando de Soto and Mansio Serra and Martínez Vegazo, as they marched southward from Vilcasbamba to Cusco, all of which he witnessed. . . .

These words positively identify him as Francisco López de Jerez, Pizarro's secretary and notary during the Conquest, and the author of the chronicle *Verdadera Relación de la Conquista del Perú*, published at Seville in 1534, shortly after the conquistador Cristóbal de Mena's chronicle. Historians had previously assumed that a leg wound he had suffered at Cajamarca had forced him to return to Spain directly from the township. His testimony, now published for the first time, proves that he was in fact present at the capture of Cusco in November 1533; leaving shortly afterwards for the isthmus of Panama, he arrived at the port of Seville, as he affirms in his chronicle, in June 1534.

The few surviving records show that in 1554, signing himself simply Francisco López, he was granted permission to return to Peru as notary to the Viceroyalty. Historians have always assumed that he never filled this post, since they were unable to prove that he was the same man as the notary accredited to the Chancery Court of Lima between the years 1559 and 1565.

The Testimony

CONQUISTADOR: Most Powerful Lord, I, Mansio Serra de Leguizamón, encomendero of Cusco, declare that I have been in these realms of Peru thirty-one years, in which time I have served Your Majesty in all that has been commanded of me at my own expense and purpose; of which I wish to inform Your Royal Highness so that my past services be known to him, and which I ask and beg be sent him, in conformity with these documents and royal seal: and in so doing petition Your Royal Highness to grant me in this realm the favour of an encomienda, of an annual income of ten thousand pesos in gold, and that my heirs may also be shown Your Majesty's favour; and such evidence I commend to the testimony of my witnesses, and for which they be questioned regarding the following: That in the conquest of Veragua, in the province of Nicaragua, I served in the company of the captains Juan de Pánes and Juan Téllez, and which province we placed under His Majesty the late Emperor's dominion, and where I experienced great risk to my life and the loss of many pesos of gold.

NICOLÁS DE RIBERA: I first met Mansio Serra in the province of Veragua when he had gone there in its conquest with the captains he mentions. And then a second time, when I went there in the company of the Adelantado Don Diego de Almagro, who had been provisioned to go there by the Licentiate Gaspar de Espinosa, Governor of Panama, in order to recruit men from its province; and he was among those he brought with him to this realm, and this is known to me for I accompanied Don Diego de Almagro; and as for what he says of the province of Veragua, so devastated by rain and with such bad prospect, it would have been impossible for him, and for those who were with him in its conquest, not to have suffered great danger and hardship.

CONQUISTADOR: I came to these realms of Peru in the company of the Adelantado Don Diego de Almagro, bringing with me my arms, horses and servants, in search of Don Francisco Pizarro, who had departed previously. And so as not to show disservice to His Majesty, the ship in which I came, belonging to Juan Díaz, a citizen of Panama, sailed ahead of the armada. And I took part in the imprisonment of Atahualpa among the company of Don Francisco Pizarro, His Majesty's Governor, and did all that was ordered of me, and I helped place this land at peace; and by so doing rendered His Majesty singular service, because of which Atahualpa gave us a great sum of gold which was sent to His Majesty.

LUIS SÁNCHEZ: What I know is that Mansio Serra was among the men who sailed with the Adelantado Don Diego de Almagro, and who landed in this realm at the bay of San Mateo . . . and that all those who marched with them experienced great hardship in the fighting, hunger and deprivations, for the land was at war,* and in the crossing of the mountains and many rivers, clearing the roads along which we marched; and the Governor Don Francisco Pizarro was greatly pleased with the arrival of so important a reinforcement, and at such good time: for he was much stretched in men and hindered by having Atahualpa as his prisoner and surrounded by so many of his warriors; and this is known to me because I served with Don Diego de Almagro and took part in what I record, and in which Mansio Serra also served, doing all that was commanded of him as the fine soldier he was. It is also well known that before our arrival the Governor had been on the point of losing all: for those who were with him were few, and the Indian warriors in great numbers; and it is true that Atahualpa gave for his ransom great treasure in gold and silver which was sent to His Majesty with Hernando Pizarro, and much more remained behind for it was not possible then to take it all.

---

* The war between Atahualpa and his brother Huáscar was still being waged at this time.

CONQUISTADOR: I accompanied the governors Don Francisco Pizarro and Don Diego de Almagro on their march to Cusco, on the way to which we met with many difficulties and risks because of the state of the roads; until we reached the valley of Jauja where we encountered a great number of warriors who had burnt its bridges, and against whom we fought in several engagements, making use of our arms and horses to disperse them.*

LUCAS MARTÍNEZ VEGAZO: In the valley of Jauja Mayta Yupanqui, Atahualpa's general, who was in command of a great multitude of warriors, attacked us Spaniards; against them we fought until we broke and dispersed their squadrons, pursuing them and killing them for some 12 leagues, and among our men was Mansio Serra, who greatly served Your Majesty, and this I know, for it is what I witnessed.

CONQUISTADOR: In the advance on Cusco the Captain Hernando de Soto went ahead with seventy hand-picked soldiers, I among them, for a great deal of the land was still at war, and we reached the province of Vilcastambo, where again we were met by a multitude of their warriors, and I took prisoner many of their scouts after a great deal of fighting and risk to my life.

LUIS SÁNCHEZ: It is true that a few days after we had defeated the natives in the valley of Jauja Don Francisco Pizarro sent up to 120 men, footmen and horse, to accompany him for the seizure of Cusco, and ordered that the rest of our comrades remain in the valley with the treasurer Riquelme, guarding the treasure of His Majesty, which was some million pesos of gold, and also guarding the treasure of those who were to leave with us. And on the way he ordered the Captain Hernando de Soto to go ahead, taking

---

* Pizarro's army which advanced on Cusco consisted of some 120 men and about 1,000 Indian auxiliaries. The armies of Atahualpa's generals defending Cusco numbered possibly some 10,000 warriors.

with him sixty or seventy footmen and horsemen, and they went forward in advance to secure the road: for the Indians we had defeated in the valley had retreated to Cusco, and had destroyed bridges and recruited more men; and the Captain went ahead with the men, among them Mansio Serra, till we came to the province and township of Vilcas where we fought a long and bloody battle with the native warriors, which was very hard, and at great peril we defeated them; and then we went in pursuit of them until we reached the mountain crest of Vilcaconga, fording and swimming across a river with much difficulty, for they had burnt its bridges, and it was winter and the rivers were in flood.

CONQUISTADOR: At Vilcaconga, 8 leagues distance from Cusco, we once more did battle with the native warriors, and with much difficulty; and in the fighting many of our men were killed and wounded, as were many horses, and those that remained were wounded. And among all the men the Captain de Soto took with him, I alone was chosen to return and show the governors where to ford the river, and bring them and the rest of our men to where we were; and in great danger I returned through the lines of the Indians who surrounded us, and I was able to inform Don Diego de Almagro of what had taken place, and to show him and those who were with him the way to where the Captain Soto was besieged, and urge them to go there at once. And having informed Don Diego, within hours they relieved the Captain and his men after marching a full day. And at the behest of Don Diego, I remained by the river in guard of it and to show the Governor Don Francisco Pizarro and the reinforcements where to ford and the way to take; and this I showed him, and with all speed we marched to relieve our men, where I helped bury our dead and cure our wounded, and also bury the horses so the Indians would not discover our losses.

PEDRO DE ALCONCHEL: I was at the River Apurímac, in the company of the Governor Don Francisco Pizarro and the Adelantado Don Diego de Almagro, when we were told by our

Indian scouts of the number of warriors Quisquis, one of Atahualpa's generals, had with him at Vilcaconga. And the Governor ordered Don Diego to take with him some thirty horsemen and foot-soldiers in search of Captain Soto, including myself. And walking as fast as we could along the road we heard the news from Mansio Serra, of how the Captain Soto was surrounded on the mountain crest, and that five Spaniards had been killed and seventeen or eighteen were wounded. Don Diego reached them that same day of the battle when it was already dark, and then in groups, the rest of the men arrived who had walked the whole of that night. Don Diego then chose Mansio Serra, for being not only young but conscientious and a strong runner, to return and inform the Governor of what had taken place, and to show him the way across the river, the bridge of which had been burnt; and I saw him leave on that mission, which was one of great risk and danger, and he then returned with the Governor to the crest where we were all gathered; and it was a great service he performed that day, and of so much importance. And if that same night the Adelantado Don Diego de Almagro and this witness and other horsemen had not come to their aid, some thirty men, more or less, not one of the Captain Soto's company would have escaped because of the number of warriors that surrounded them.

LUCAS MARTÍNEZ VEGAZO: With less than a shot left of our crossbows, and being positioned high up the crest and encircled by the natives, the rescue arrived in the middle of the night, in groups of ten and twenty, each one making their way to the crest till dawn; and I know of this because it is what I witnessed with my own eyes, and in which I took part, and with great difficulty and danger to our lives.

CONQUISTADOR: The governors and those who went with them, I among them, marched in good order towards the city of Cusco. Close to the city, some half a league in distance, thousands of Indian warriors came out to confront us in three squadrons, and we fought them until we dispersed them. A number of Spaniards were wounded and horses killed, and we had to delay our march for another day. In the morning in battle order we entered the city of Cusco and its square and took possession of its strongholds.

BERNABÉ PICÓN: In the morning the Governor and all the men entered the city of Cusco and took possession of it . . . for in all we were no more than one hundred and twenty men.

CONQUISTADOR: Once the city had been captured, the Governor Don Francisco Pizarro ordered the Captain Soto to go to the province of Cuntisuyo with fifty horsemen and some footmen in pursuit of Atahualpa's warrior chiefs, and I was one of those who served there for more than two months, fighting and following them into the most rugged of country and suffering great hunger, until we finally found their chiefs and their warriors, some of whom we captured. The Governor then ordered us to return to Cusco, fearing an attack; and we returned to where he and the rest of the men were guarding the city, which the Indians had surrounded, putting our lives in much danger because of their numbers and the hunger and deprivations from which we suffered.

LUCAS MARTÍNEZ VEGAZO: It is true that the Captain Soto left the city of Cusco after we Spaniards had won it, taking with him horsemen and footmen in pursuit and in search of the chiefs and warriors of the Inca, and we had many encounters with them, crossing the mountain passes and rivers, which were of great danger; and I do not recall the time the expedition lasted, only that great risk and difficulty were experienced, which Mansio Serra could not have failed to also have experienced, for I was there and saw this with my own eyes.

LUIS SÁNCHEZ: A few days after our return the Governor Don Francisco Pizarro distributed to the Spaniards who had come there with him, and those who had remained at Jauja, the gold and silver which had been collected, and later he founded the city of Cusco and distributed the land among eighty encomenderos, and one of those he named was Mansio Serra, to whom he awarded Indians and lands, which he retains to this day.

CONQUISTADOR: In recognition of the service I rendered Your Majesty and the great expenditure I had incurred, I was among those when the land was divided to be awarded two encomiendas as a person of rank,* and for my service, and for which I was given seals.

PEDRO DE ALCONCHEL: I saw that the Governor was always conscious of those who served him well in the war, and because he also was greatly fond of Mansio Serra for being so diligent and so deserving he made him an encomendero of Cusco and gave him a distribution of Indians.

CONQUISTADOR: I was one of the forty soldiers chosen to remain in the city of Cusco in its defence, in the company of the Captain Beltrán de Castro, which was when the governors had gone to meet with Don Pedro de Alvarado who had come from Guatemala with his soldiers. While on guard of this city, it was learnt that the Incas planned to kill us all and recapture Cusco, bringing with them as their chief Villaoma.† In order to forestall them, I and a number of my comrades disguised ourselves as Indians, and taking with us our arms we went on foot to where Villaoma was encamped with a great number of warriors. And I was the first to seize him, and we brought him as our prisoner to Cusco and handed him over to the Captain Beltrán de Castro, and this was a great service we rendered Your Majesty. And as Villaoma was our prisoner the Incas wished to pay us a ransom

* Alluding to his hidalgo rank.
† Villaoma: the Inca High Priest of the Sun.

for his freedom, and they gave us a great sum of gold worth more than 200,000 pesos, which we gave to the Captain Beltrán de Castro, and we soldiers, who had been responsible for his capture, refused any share of the ransom which was sent to His Majesty and his royal officials.

PEDRO DE ALCONCHEL: I know that Mansio Serra was one of the forty Spaniards left in guard of Cusco under Beltrán de Castro, and this is publicly recorded; for I was present with the Governor Don Francisco Pizarro at Jauja when the news of this was brought, for he received a letter concerning the event in question; and I believe Mansio Serra did what he says, for he was brave and diligent in warfare. And though I was not in the city of Cusco when these events took place, I know them to be true and publicly held, and those who had remained in guard of the city gave that amount of gold to the Governor who received it on behalf of His Majesty, and which was spent by him.

DIEGO CAMACHO: I know Mansio Serra remained in guard of the city of Cusco, for I went there for the first time before its later siege, and met there Mansio Serra, who was one of its encomenderos, possessing there a house, horses and Indians. And being in the city of Cusco news reached us of how Villaoma was with many warriors in the province of Cuntisuyo; and it was agreed that one night he be captured and brought back prisoner: an act Mansio Serra carried out, together with another encomendero called Francisco de Villafuerte, and nine or ten other soldiers. And I saw him brought back to the city and placed in the custody of the Captain Beltrán de Castro. It was an action of great boldness and one which could not have been carried out without much danger and courage, especially as Villaoma was camped in such barren terrain and among so many of his warriors, and it was of great service to His Majesty.

CONQUISTADOR: On their return from Quito and the City of the Kings, captains and soldiers were commissioned to go to the province of Callao,* I among them, together with the Governor's brothers;† and we went to the said province with our arms and horses and served there, pacifying and conquering the land after many engagements with the natives who were in considerable numbers, and we Spaniards, few, ill-fed and with a great many tasks to perform. After which I accompanied Juan Pizarro and Gonzalo Pizarro, His Majesty's captains, to the province of Cuntisuyo where the native warriors had killed their Spanish masters, and we subdued them after much fighting and effort.

DIEGO CAMACHO: Because of the killings by the Indians in the province of Cuntisuyo of an encomendero by the name of Pedro Martín de Moguer and another encomendero called Simón Suárez, I saw the Captain Juan Pizarro and Gonzalo Pizarro, and Mansio Serra among them, leave the city with other soldiers to exert reprisal on that province; and being as I was in the city of Cusco I heard it said that the reprisal had been carried out at the capture of the mountain fortress of Ancocagua, where more than eight thousand Indian warriors had taken refuge, and that a great deal of fighting took place; I saw them leave for the reprisal and also return from there, for Pedro Martín, whom the Indians killed, was my brother.

CONQUISTADOR: I was in Cusco at the time of the Inca uprising, and I served much in its defence and did all that was commanded of me; experiencing both lack of food and basic necessities; for the natives took possession of the city's fortress of Sacsahuaman, and were some two hundred thousand in number,‡ and the Spaniards were few in number, many of whom had been

---

* Callao – the highland region of Bolivia.
† Pizarro's half-brothers, Hernando, Juan and Gonzalo.
‡ Though Indian witnesses record the same figure, the likely number of warriors was some one hundred thousand, accompanied by their porters and yanaconas. There were no more than two hundred Spaniards in Cusco, together with several thousand of their native auxiliaries.

killed and wounded; and the siege and fighting continued for some three to four months until in battle order we went to the fortress which was defended by some thirty thousand of their finest warriors; but by day it could not be captured and we were to wait for a further year before I and other soldiers dared enter the fortress: in which action I fought and was wounded in the stomach; and even though badly wounded and on the point of death, and though seeing the Captain Juan Pizarro and others killed, I was the first to cry victory.

DIEGO CAMACHO: I saw and know that when the natives' uprising broke out, and when they laid siege to Cusco, Mansio Serra fought in defence of the city, serving there all the time, which was some fourteen months, with his arms and horses, in the day and at night, taking part in the engagements and battles with the natives, in which we all ran great risk and fought with much hardship: for we were surrounded by more than three hundred thousand Indian warriors, and they had put us under such duress that they burnt the greater part of the city; and seeing this, and realising the danger, the Captain Juan Pizarro decided that we had to capture the fortress, where a great number of warriors had fortified themselves; and so it was decided, and among those who went up there was this witness and Mansio Serra, and some seventy soldiers in all; and for some days we had the fortress besieged and one night Mansio Serra and a few others volunteered to gain entry through a small opening they had seen, and thus they entered, and all the others after them, and we captured the surrounding area to the fortress at great peril and with much fighting, and that night Juan Pizarro was killed. Hernando Pizarro, who had remained in the city, then came up and we held to the siege until the fortress was captured: scaling its walls with ladders, and in all this, as in the earlier siege of the city, Mansio Serra's service was of principal importance.

LUCAS MARTÍNEZ VEGAZO: Manco Inca Yupanqui, Atahualpa's brother, whom the Indians of this land had begged the Marquis Don Francisco Pizarro to recognise as lord of these realms, saying he was descended from God, as was his sovereignty, and after rewarding him, and seeing himself obeyed by the natives of the land, he attempted to rise up against the Spaniards and kill them: and this he put into effect by his siege of the city of Cusco with some two hundred thousand Indian warriors, a number recorded by both Indians and Spaniards; and they put the Spaniards who were in the city under great pressure, for they burnt the houses they captured and put barricades across the streets and fought us from the roof tops, and took control of the city in great order, killing some Spaniards and horses, and wounding others; and as the city was on the verge of being lost, and with it the whole of the realm, some men were selected to capture the fortress, and it was won at night: for in the day on a number of occasions it was found impossible to enter because of the multitude of warriors in its defence; and through a gap in its walls, in a remote part of the fortress and away from where the Spaniards were laying siege, some twelve or fifteen Spaniards entered, killing and wounding the natives and shouting 'Spain! Spain!' and 'Victory!' And from the other sides of the fortress the rest of the Spaniards made their entry and also took part in the killing, during which the Captain Juan Pizarro was killed from a deep wound in his head from a stone, and also a certain Gallego was killed, and other Spaniards were wounded; and in all this Mansio Serra took part, and it is evident he fought well, being a good soldier and fine young man; though I took part in this I do not remember whether or not he was the first to enter the fortress and cry victory.

CONQUISTADOR: I was among those who later accompanied Hernando Pizarro to Ollantaytambo, where Manco Inca had retreated with many of his men to a fortress* beside a river, and here we engaged his warriors who killed six Spaniards and

---

* The valley and fortress ruins of Ollantaytambo are 45 miles north-west of Cusco, in the Sacred Valley of the Incas.

wounded many others, and because of this we were forced to return to Cusco in great danger of our lives.

DIEGO CAMACHO: In the company of Mansio Serra this witness and seventy horsemen went to the said province and fortress, which we attacked on the day of our arrival. The Indian warriors having ventured out of the fortress, a great battle took place until nightfall, in which many Spaniards were killed and wounded; and abandoning our encampment and tents we were forced to flee to Cusco that very same night, losing everything we had taken with us; for had we remained until morning not one of us would have returned alive because of the great number of warriors and the ruggedness of the land.

CONQUISTADOR: I was also among the men who accompanied the Captain Heredia* to the Cuntisuyo for its pacification, in which expedition I served some seven or eight months as caudillo with forty of my soldiers, who by their labour and in great danger destroyed the fortress encampments of the Indians, placing them under the royal dominion.

RODRIGO LÓPEZ BERNAL: What I know is that some Spaniards had been killed in the province of the Cuntisuyo, which had risen against His Majesty, and I accompanied the Captain Nicolás de Heredia, together with Mansio Serra, to that province, and he served there as captain and caudillo with his horses and arms, both day and night, in all that was expected of him; and much was risked, for there were few of us Spaniards in comparison to the great number of Indians who attacked us and surrounded us in very barren terrain, making it impossible for us to reach a river for the water we needed to drink; and that night in the native fortress of Alca, Mansio Serra and the Indians in his service left our encampment in order to break the siege, entering

* Captain Nicolás de Heredia, one of the early explorers of northern Argentina.

the fortress from the high ground of a slope, passing their sentries and putting them to the sword so that they could not warn their warriors; and in this manner, in the middle of the night, they climbed to the upper villages where the great multitude of warriors were camped, and catching them asleep they killed many of them, and then gave the Spaniards who had remained below the signal to climb up and follow them. In these and other acts I wish to inform Your Majesty that Mansio Serra was one of those who served with the greatest diligence and valour, and with the lustre of a soldier and hidalgo, at his own cost and mission; which expedition I recall lasted eight or ten months.

FRANCISCO DE ILLESCAS: Many of my friends went on the expedition, and when they returned they told me on a number of occasions that Mansio Serra had been one of the most hard-working among them, as was always the case with him, being as he was such an agile man and so fine a soldier; and in which conquest, of great risk and hardship, I heard he lost a horse.

CONQUISTADOR: Together with the Captain Gonzalo Pizarro I went in pursuit of Manco Inca into the Andes, where he was encamped; and I was one of the first of the squadron in the subsequent battle in helping to capture the Inca's wife and his warrior chief, who was called Cusi Rimache; and I assisted in the pacification of the province where I served for eight months, suffering hardship and hunger and the expenditure of a large sum of pesos of gold: for I went there well armed, with my horses and servants, and served there as a caudillo until all the land was at peace. And in the campaign I captured a bridge that is close to Vilcabamba,* which is the first fortress the Inca possessed there, and I captured many of their scouts, and served Your Majesty greatly.

---

* Vilcabamba is known today as the Lost City of the Incas. It was the fortress refuge of the Inca Manco in the subtropical Andean valleys north-west of Cusco.

FRANCISCO DE ILLESCAS: I know that Mansio Serra went with the Captain Gonzalo Pizarro in pursuit of Manco Inca, who had retreated to the province of the Andes, for I served on that expedition with the Captain, though because of illness I had to return to Cusco. And Mansio Serra, who went on ahead, I know served throughout the expedition; and it is commonly known that a great deal of work was carried out, and at great risk, as the land was rugged and of dense forest, where the natives ambushed them along the mountain passes of its roads; and in that journey they captured Cusi Rimache, brother of the Inca, and the Inca's wife and a great number of warriors; and I know for certain that Mansio Serra did all that he records, and I saw him well armed and on horseback, in the service of Your Majesty.

CONQUISTADOR: At the time of the rebellion of Don Diego de Almagro the younger,* and the death of the Marquis Don Francisco Pizarro, I left Cusco for the coast in order to take a caravel in search of the Licentiate Vaca de Castro, accompanied by eight friends, all well armed, mounted and provisioned; and because Almagro had been informed that I had gone in search of the Licentiate, he took from me my house in Cusco and my Indians; and I and my friends were captured by García de Alvarado, his captain, who dispossessed us of our arms, horses and Negro slaves, all of which were worth some eight thousand pesos of gold; and having robbed us and hanged one of our companions he brought us to Cusco as his prisoners.

LUIS SÁNCHEZ: What I know of this is that after the death of the Marquis Don Francisco Pizarro, Don Diego de Almagro the younger was informed by his captain Gregorio de Soto, who had gone to Cusco, that Mansio Serra was in the province of Cuntisuyo in his encomienda together with some friends of his,

---

* Don Diego de Almagro the younger was the Panamanian mestizo son of the Adelantado; his supporters had been responsible for Pizarro's murder.

and he ordered they be taken prisoner; and hearing of this they fled towards the coast where they were captured by Don Diego's captain García de Alvarado, who brought them prisoner to Cusco. And I later saw Don Diego award Mansio Serra's encomienda to Martín de Bilbao,* another captain of his, and he also took from him his house.

FRANCISCO DE ILLESCAS: Being as I was in the city of Cusco at the same time as Don Diego, I heard it said that Mansio Serra and Mazuelas and Montenegro† and others had gone to the coast in search of the Governor Vaca de Castro; after which I saw García de Alvarado, Don Diego's captain, enter the city with prisoners, among them Mansio Serra and other soldiers; and I heard it also said that García de Alvarado had hanged one of them, Montenegro, and robbed them of all their goods and arms. And as Mansio Serra was his prisoner, Don Diego de Almagro took from him his Indians and awarded them to Martín de Bilbao, his captain, who acquired their tribute, and who I saw bring him tribute; and during the time Mansio Serra was a prisoner he suffered ill treatment and torture because he had stood against them.

CONQUISTADOR: Because of my later refusal to follow Gonzalo Pizarro, when he came to Cusco and was declared Procurator General, accompanied as he was by many armed men, he ordered I be tortured and caused me much injury, and he seized from me my Indians and my house, which he gave to his ally and vassal Guerrero; and he kept me prisoner and threatened to have my head cut off, which he would have done had it not been for his fear of people's reaction.‡

---

* Martín de Bilbao was one of Pizarro's assassins.

† The conquistadores Gómez de Mazuelas, Mansio Serra's future father-in-law, and Francisco de Montenegro. Diego de Almagro's rebellion ended with his defeat at the Battle of Chupas in 1542.

‡ This culminated in Gonzalo Pizarro's rebellion two years later.

LUIS SÁNCHEZ: At the time I was in the city of Cusco and witnessed Alonso de Toro, Lieutenant Governor of Gonzalo Pizarro, take Mansio Serra prisoner and do him much injury, and it was believed that he would kill him for being his enemy, and that is what I remember.

FRANCISCO DE ILLESCAS: I was in Cusco and witnessed Gonzalo Pizarro take Mansio Serra's Indians in the city for refusing to be one of his followers, and he gave them to a certain Guerrero, who was a native of his land, who I saw make use of their service and of their tribute, of gold, silver, crops and clothing, sending his factor for their collection; and I also witnessed that when Gonzalo Pizarro came to Cusco he wanted Mansio Serra and his woman thrown out of his house, and because of people's reaction he did not do so; and he allowed Mansio Serra to retain a section of it, the rest he gave to his ally Guerrero, to whom he had given his Indians; and other than this, I believe they took from him many other things in his house, also his cattle and farms he had in his villages; and this I heard, and also that he lost a great quantity of gold and that he had been unable to leave Cusco, being in virtual custody until Gonzalo Pizarro himself left the city: for no one fled without being brought back a prisoner and hanged; and only after Gonzalo Pizarro and his men had left Cusco was he able to make his escape from his confinement and flee the city on horseback. After which I saw him in the encampment of the President Don Pedro de la Gasca in the battle against Gonzalo Pizarro's army, in which he served as an hidalgo and vassal of His Majesty, and took part in the imprisonment of Gonzalo Pizarro.

HERNANDO DE CESPEDES: Mansio Serra suffered much ill-treatment and torture for his stance, and for not wishing to go with Gonzalo to the Battle of Huarina; and this is known to me for I had been taken prisoner at the battle and brought to Cusco by Gonzalo Pizarro, when he had come there carrying the royal standard of the Captain Diego de Centeno. I know that Mansio

Serra has always been opposed to the opinion of the rebels and I do not know, nor have I heard it said he was involved with them against His Majesty's service; and I have witnessed him treated with great honour, and as an hidalgo, maintaining a house and a family and supporting many soldiers and servants of Your Majesty; and I was especially witness to this when many prisoners were taken to Cusco after the Battle of Huarina, whom Gonzalo Pizarro sold.

CONQUISTADOR: I served in His Majesty's army of the President Gasca and did all that was commanded of me as a gentleman and person of honour until the Battle of Jaquijahuana, in which I fought with my arms and horses until Gonzalo Pizarro and his allies were made prisoner.

DIEGO CAMACHO: Having joined the royal camp of the President Gasca in the province of Huaylas, I saw Mansio Serra later join us and fight under the royal standard at the Battle of Jaquijahuana until Gonzalo Pizarro and his followers were taken prisoner; and I witnessed him serve in the battle, going there in good order with his horses, arms, slaves and servants, like an encomendero and man of great standing.

CONQUISTADOR: I was to serve His Majesty on the orders of the Licentiate Gasca in the capture of a number of Gonzalo Pizarro's partisans who had fled to the provinces of Cuntisuyo and Charcas, among them the Captain Diego Guillen and the priest Vizcaino. And seeing how zealous I was in the service of His Majesty, the Licentiate confided in me various commissions of great importance.

PEDRO SÚAREZ DE ILLANES: After the battle the Captain Guillen and other followers of Gonzalo Pizarro fled to the provinces of Callao and Cuntisuyo, and I heard it publicly said that the President Gasca had commissioned Mansio Serra to find them and capture them, and that this he did.

FRANCISCO DE ILLESCAS: This witness saw Mansio Serra bring from Cusco to this City of the Kings, and from Huamanga, certain prisoners who had been followers of Gonzalo Pizarro, and who had been sentenced to serve their punishment.*

CONQUISTADOR: At the time of Francisco Girón's rebellion,† only by the use of my sword was I able to prevent him harming Gil Ramírez Dávalos, who was the Governor of Cusco, and I helped him flee the city and took him to my villages, and fed and cared for him, and did all that I could in His Majesty's service. When the Marshal Alonso de Alvarado came from Charcas to assist His Majesty against Francisco Girón I went to receive him, well armed with my men and horses. And being ordered to go to the enemy's camp near Nazca and to the plains of the province of Parinacochas,‡ taking with me some Spaniards, I went there to discover the movements and intentions of the enemy. And I carried out my mission with much care, inspecting the enemy encampment and scouting its movements, as a good caudillo and captain; and I informed the Marshal of what exactly was taking place in the rebel's camp; all of which was of great difficulty, for the land there is very rocky, and impossible to reach by horse without being detected.

HERNÁN GÓMEZ: When the Marshal Alonso de Alvarado brought his army against Francisco Girón, he sent Mansio Serra to the province of Cuntisuyo with a number of soldiers to scout the land and discover the state of the rebel's army and its movements, and to ascertain the road His Majesty's army should take, which was of great importance; and after this he went to the province of Parinacochas to scout out its land, and when our army reached that province I saw him there, and he had with him the caciques of all that province, whom he had brought with him,

---

* Most had been sentenced to serve in the royal galleys.
† The encomendero Francisco Girón's rebellion in 1553–4.
‡ Site of the pre-Colombian Nazca lines.

so that their men could serve us as scouts, and in carrying information; and it is known to me that he experienced great difficulty in his mission because of the barrenness of the land, much of which he crossed on foot, and that he surveyed the vicinity of the enemy camp at great risk to his life.

JUAN DE RIVAMARTÍN: As one of the commanders of the royal army of the Marshal, I know that Mansio Serra took with him a number of soldiers to the lands of his Indians, which are between the provinces of Cuntisuyo and Parinacochas, and near the road the rebel Girón was to take his army, and that the Marshal was informed of their movements. And because he was known by the natives of that province and respected by them, he was also sent to organize provisions for the royal encampment; and this he complied in doing, with those men he had taken with him to a native fortress in Parinacochas, which is today the encomienda of Alonso de Hinojosa, citizen of Cusco, and which had previously belonged to Don Baltazar de Castilla; and on the orders of the Marshal I went there to organize the provisions, and one night, at midnight, a night of terrible cold, I met Mansio Serra, who was returning to inform the Marshal of what he had learnt. The land was barren and rocky, and most of it could only be crossed on foot.

CONQUISTADOR: I gave favour to many soldiers, supplying them with muskets and powder and horses, and other articles of war for the service of His Majesty, and all at great cost to myself in pesos of gold; and by order of the Marshal, taking with me some hundred soldiers, I then went to cut off certain mountain passes and bridges where the enemy would march. And in the company of the Marshal Alonso de Alvarado I entered in the Battle of Chuquinga, well armed, with my horses and my servants, and I was one of the vanguard in the battle and urged the soldiers to fight, and I fought there as a gentleman and servitor of Your Majesty until we were defeated, being one of the last to leave the field on foot; there I lost a great sum of gold, of some ten thousand pesos.

HERNÁN GÓMEZ: It is true the Marshal sent Mansio Serra with certain soldiers to cut off the passes of that part of Chuquinga, where the army of the rebels would have to flee through, if it were defeated in the valley: a mission he accomplished at great risk; but as the rebels won the battle it was to no avail though a great service, and this I know for I was in the army of the Marshal. That very night after our defeat, leaving the field of battle in the upper valley and fleeing the enemy, I saw Mansio Serra, who was himself fleeing on foot with only a naked sword in his hand, and robbed of all his possessions, and we walked together the whole of that night until day-break, when we each went our own way; and I know he lost a great deal of his wealth in the battle, for I had seen him in our encampment well provisioned with his horses, arms and his servants, with his dining plate and tents.

FRANCISCO DE ILLESCAS: Each of us escaped as best he could, and on reaching the Cuntisuyo, some ten days later, I learned that Mansio Serra was there, and that he had left the battlefield on foot. I later saw him on horseback with his men, and I heard it said that he had borrowed the horse, or purchased it; and his losses would have been great, because when he entered the battle he was well armed with horses, slaves and provisions, all of which he lost, and when I met him again all he possessed was the clothes he wore. In the province of Cuntisuyo, where Mansio Serra had his Indians, I saw that he shared what he could to enable others to go with him in search of the royal army of the lord judges; and from there, he and I and other soldiers walked across the most arid and desolate land in order to evade the enemy, in all some 150 leagues, until we found the royal encampment at Huamanga, having taken with us some ounces of gunpowder and other arms we had made for us in Cuntisuyo.

CONQUISTADOR: In order to avoid being captured by Francisco Girón and his followers I walked for some 200 leagues in search of the lord judges, and these I later joined, bringing with me many Spaniards and provisions for the royal service and some 10 ounces of gunpowder. And I later served under His Majesty's royal standard at the Battle of Pucará in the front line of cavalry, with my horses and servants, like a good soldier and gentleman, leading my men forward until Francisco Girón and his followers were captured and brought to justice.

FRANCISCO DE ILLESCAS: In the morning, in the retreat of the enemy, I saw him give them chase, and I saw that his horse had lost an eye, gorged by either a lance or by musket shot.

PEDRO DE ALCONCHEL: Throughout the whole of the Conquest, as also in the battle, I witnessed Mansio Serra serve as a nobleman and a valiant gentleman, always doing his duty and putting himself in danger and at risk, and at his own cost and expense; for we all served in like manner, and he could not but have spent a great deal of his wealth.

NICOLÁS DE RIBERA: Having known Mansio Serra some thirty-one years, more or less, I always saw him serve at his own expense as a good soldier and hidalgo, and he could not have failed to have spent a great deal of his wealth; for which he never received any repayment or aid, because at the time of the conquest of this realm this was the custom, though it is now no longer so among encomenderos.

CONQUISTADOR: I declare I have been in these realms thirty-one years, in which time I have served Your Majesty with all diligence and honour and at my own expense, as a gentleman of ancient lineage, having expended in such service and in the past wars and rebellions of these kingdoms more than fifty thousand pesos of gold, and having always complied with Your Majesty's summons, in times of both peace and of war, with my person, arms and wealth, my servants and soldiers, whom I have always maintained, though I am at present poor and in debt. And though the Marquis Don Francisco Pizarro awarded me two encomiendas, one in the Cuntisuyo called Alca, and the other in the Antisuyo, which to reward Don Paullu Inca* he took from me and gave him, which was the encomienda of Callanga. And to this day I have only had one of these encomiendas to maintain myself.

HERNÁN GÓMEZ: In war and in times of peace I have always seen Mansio Serra treated with great respect and honour, as a gentleman and hidalgo and a man of great quality, supporting as he did his family and many soldiers whom he often had with him in his house; maintaining also horses, mules, slaves and arms, and always giving aid to whosoever was in need: and because of this he did indeed spend greatly and because of this it is natural that he has debts and now lives in need of sustenance.

FRANCISCO DE ILLESCAS: The township where Mansio Serra was born is but a league in distance from my own, and when meeting people from his homeland I have always heard it said that his parents were hidalgos, and that as such they enjoyed the privileges of hidalgos in the township of Pinto,† and as such I have always held him. Because of his great expenditure over the years in His Majesty's service, for which he received neither aid nor recompense, and because of the little value of his encomienda, Mansio Serra lives in great need and possesses many debts, for I myself have seen his creditors visit him.

HERNANDO DE CESPEDES: In the years I have known Mansio Serra I have always seen him treated and esteemed as a gentleman and hidalgo, and in such rank he is held, and this is not only portrayed in his manners and behaviour, but is publicly known; for there are many persons in this realm from his native land, and the lineages of Spain are equally well known in these realms.

---

* Paullu Inca, a son of the Emperor Huayna Cápac and ally of the Spaniards.
† The Castilian township of Pinto, south of Madrid.

LUCAS MARTÍNEZ VEGAZO: I have always regarded Mansio Serra as an hidalgo, and as such he has lived. I saw that he was married to the daughter of Mazuelas in Cusco, and that a number of children were left him from his marriage, though I do not know how many, and that the income he receives from his Indians is little and not in accordance with his rank, for he is now in much need and in debt.

EIGHT

The Haunting

The Peruvian folklorist Ricardo Palma, writing in the nineteenth century, recalled some of the events that took place in Lima's Plaza Mayor on a particular night in the year 1565.[1] Much of his information was derived from the chronicler Garcilaso de la Vega's history of Peru, which itself relied on first-hand accounts from an Indies colonist and a Franciscan friar, both of whom Garcilaso had met in Spain. As Palma records, the story concerned the theft of the skulls of Gonzalo Pizarro, Francisco de Carbajal and Francisco Girón, which were kept in the city's main square.

Public documents record that during the four years of his rebel government of Peru Gonzalo had been formally addressed not only by his courtiers but by the bishops of the colony as the 'Glorious Gonzalo' and the 'Very Magnificent Lord'. Tall and black-bearded like all his brothers, he was thirty-six years old at the time of his execution, and presided over the most opulent court the colony had ever seen, where Spanish and Indian women alike wore the finest costumes and jewels.

In 1544 he had rebelled against the Spanish Crown's New Laws, and proclaimed himself Lord Protector of Peru. These harsh Laws would have deprived the veterans of Cajamarca of their lands and Indian vassals. Every single conquistador or encomendero who tried to oppose him faced hanging or imprisonment. Not surprisingly, not a single one of them spoke in his defence four years later after the battle at Jaquijahuana, just north of Cusco; deserted by his officers and men, he had surrendered to the priest governor Pedro de la Gasca, who had been sent by the Emperor to crush the rebellion.

The tunic Gonzalo wore over his coat of mail that day was made of yellow velvet, covered with gold metal discs; his helmet and head

81

strap were also of gold. He tried to justify his rebellion by reminding Gasca that it was he and his brothers who had originally won the Inca Empire for the Spanish Crown. A chronicler recorded that the diminutive priest, himself dressed in full coat armour, answered 'that although His Majesty had granted his brother the Marquis all he had given him, which was sufficient to raise him and his brothers from a life of poverty to that of great wealth, lifting them from the very dust, they had shown no gratitude, especially as he himself had done nothing toward the discovery of Peru, and his brother, who had done everything, had always demonstrated his gratitude, loyalty and respect. He did not wait for a reply but ordered his marshal to take him away.'[2]

All that night Gonzalo was kept in a tent, guarded by men who only a few months previously had knelt to him in obeisance as his courtiers. His tall figure was silhouetted by the light of a lamp as he restlessly paced up and down, and only before dawn did he sleep for a while.

In the morning he was taken on a mule, his naked body wrapped in a black cloak, to the scaffold that had been hastily erected on the battlefield. In his hands he held a crucifix. Through the silent ranks of men he was led by the priest Gasca's marshal and a crier who recalled his crimes, until the little procession reached the small wooden gallows. There, Gonzalo himself made a short speech, once more repeating what he had told the priest Gasca, and then he knelt on the block and addressed the executioner, the mulatto Juan Enríquez: 'Do your work well, brother Juan.'[3] And with one stroke of the axe, his head was struck off.

The priest Gasca then ordered that Gonzalo's body be taken to the convent of La Merced at Cusco, where the decapitated corpses of the Adelantado Diego de Almagro and his mestizo son also lay buried, and that his head be fried in oil and sent to Lima, and placed there on display in a cage at the end of a pole in the main square. Among the papers found in his abandoned camp was a letter he had received several years before from the commander of his army. It was sent shortly after the killing of the colony's first Viceroy, Don Blasco Núñez Vela, and the defeat of his army at the battle of

Añaquito. Núñez Vela's naked corpse had been mutilated by Gonzalo's foot-soldiers, and for weeks afterwards his bloodstained beard was worn as an adornment on the helmets of his captains:

My Lord, when a viceroy is killed in a pitched battle and his head is struck off and placed on a gibbet, and the battle was against the royal standard, and where there have been many deaths and as much looting, there is no pardon hoped for, and no compromise to be made; even though your lordship makes ample excuses and proves himself more innocent than a suckling babe. Nor can you trust in words or promises, nor whatever assurances be given you, unless that is you declare yourself king; and seize the government yourself without waiting for another to offer it to you, and place the crown on your head: allocating whatever land is unoccupied among your friends and adherents; creating them dukes and marquises and counts, such as there are in all the countries of the world, so that they will defend your lordship in order to defend their own estates; and pay no heed if it is said that you are a traitor to the King of Spain; you are not, for as the saying goes, no king is a traitor. I beg your lordship to consider carefully my words, and of what I have said about ruling the empire in perpetuity, so that all those who live here will follow you. Finally, I urge you again to crown yourself king. Die a king, I repeat, and not a vassal, for whosoever accepts servitude can merit no better. . . .[4]

The second head to be placed in a separate cage on the same day in Lima's main square was that of the eighty-year-old Francisco de Carbajal, the author of Gonzalo Pizarro's letter, who was known as the 'Devil of the Andes' because of his legendary brutality. Born Francisco López Gascón, as a young man he had studied for the priesthood in his native Castile, adopting the name of his patron Cardinal Bernardino de Carbajal. A veteran of the Italian Wars, he boasted he had left Seville for the Indies with only the clothes on his back, and owing 'half a real to a woman who kept a tavern in the Puerta de Arenal'.[5]

His reputation for cruelty and banter followed him even to his execution, and many of the onlookers who had experienced years of abuse and torture at his hands must have revelled at the sight. Some of them had even been present when he had taken three of Cusco's fugitive conquistadores, naked and on mules, to the outskirts of Lima where he had hanged them from a tree, each according to his rank, selecting the highest branch for the hidalgo and conquistador Pedro del Barco.

As a young boy Garcilaso de la Vega met Carbajal in Cusco and described him as a corpulent and ruddy-cheeked man 'who always wore a purple Moorish burnous with a hood, and on his head a hat of black taffeta with a plain silk band adorned with black and white chicken feathers'. He also recalled the caustic wit for which he was renowned. On one occasion Carbajal, coming across a new recruit whom he sarcastically addressed as 'Your Grace', asked the man his name; on being told that it was 'Hurtado' [stealing], he commented: 'Not worth finding, let alone stealing!' On another occasion, having taken prisoner a loyalist encomendero who pretended not to know why he was being hanged, he said to him: 'I perceive you wish to establish a pedigree for your martyrdom, so that you can point to it as an heirloom for your descendants. So be it, and now, Adíos!'[6]

Carbajal's capture had soon followed Gonzalo's and he was taken to the headquarters of the royalist commander Diego de Centeno. A year previously Carbajal had defeated him in battle, and on several occasions had pursued him across the Andes, but now he pretended not to know him. Visibly irritated, Centeno demanded whether in fact he did recall him. 'My God, Sir!' Carbajal exclaimed, 'having only ever seen your buttocks in retreat, I can say I do not!'[7]

Carbajal was to receive little mercy from the priest Gasca, who could hardly forget the letters he had received from him, urging him to return to Spain:

With what genius does a priest, of the intelligence some say you to possess, involve himself in an enterprise not even the king with all his forces is able to suppress, nor is capable of, if not by your worthless decrees and letters filled with lies? What you may consider is that the inducements which made the traitors surrender to you the fleet, selling their lord for money, as did Judas, was only so that they could themselves become lords, and you, their priest . . . and let us hope that your sins will in time bring you safely into my hands. . . .[8]

Stripped of his armour, Carbajal was placed naked in a wicker basket which was dragged by several mules to the scaffold. Before his execution he was asked by his confessor to say the Our Father and the Hail Mary. Defiant to the end, and to the amusement of even his enemies who crowded around the gallows, he simply repeated the words 'Our father, hail Mary'.[9] Hanged like a common criminal, his body was subsequently quartered and his head placed in the very same saddlebag that had carried his master's head to Lima.

Five years later Peru was again plunged into civil war through a rebellion led by the encomendero Francisco Girón. For almost a year he had held the colony in his grasp as a populist caudillo, before being apprehended and executed, raising the first squadron of Negro slaves as his personal bodyguard. Interestingly, his principal adviser was an astrologer.

Some eleven years after Girón's head had been placed in the third iron cage in Lima's Plaza Mayor, Ricardo Palma wrote that a newly arrived colonist, shocked by the gruesome spectacle which most of Lima's citizens took for granted, met Girón's Castilian widow, Mencia de Sosa, and offered to retrieve her husband's skull so that it could receive a Christian burial. On the night in question, he took a ladder to the Plaza Mayor and, with the assistance of an Indian servant, removed one of the skulls from its cage and carried it to the widow's house. To her dismay she recognized it as that of Carbajal. The colonist returned to the square and removed another of the skulls, but the widow identified it as Gonzalo Pizarro's. Finally, just before daybreak, he once more went back to the square and removed the remaining skull.

Garcilaso de la Vega recorded that one of his informants, the Franciscan Luis Jerónimo de Oré, had seen the skulls years later in a wooden box in his convent at Lima, but by then no one was able to identify them. His other informant, Luis de Cañaveral, claimed that all three skulls had been buried by the colonist on the instructions of Girón's widow, though the site was never discovered. Whatever the truth of the story, the popular belief that the Devil had taken his own was never denied by the priests who later officiated at a ceremony held to purify the square. The poles were felled, salt and Holy Water were sprinkled on the ground and the three men's crimes of treason and tyranny were publicly recalled for the last time by the city's crier.

NINE

The Requiem

In the year 1549 the Emperor Huayna Cápac's son Paullu Inca died at Cusco. He was thirty-one years old. Only six years previously he had been baptised a Christian and had taken the name and title Don Cristóbal in honour of the colony's governor, Don Cristóbal Vaca de Castro, his godfather. For several days his body lay in mourning, barefoot but otherwise clothed in all the finery of Spanish court dress, in the palace of Colcampata, the ruined façade of which can still be seen above the northern hills of the city. On his head rested the plumed Inca headdress and on his chest lay the standard of the coat-of-arms that the Spanish Emperor had awarded him for his loyalty and service. For hours on end the wailing of the five hundred or so armed warriors who had surrounded the palace walls could be heard; they were to remain guarding his body until his burial in the adjoining chapel that he had built and named in honour of his Christian saint.

An insight into the treatment Paullu Inca endured at the hands of the conquistadores is given by the friar Vicente de Valverde in a letter to the Emperor Charles V, dated 2 April 1539, in which he describes how on Diego de Almagro's expedition to Chile the Inca prince had been chained by the neck.[1] Later the priest Luis de Morales recorded:

In regard to Paullu Inca, Your Majesty's vassal and servitor, he has been truly a good friend of the Christians and of Your Majesty, as he has shown by his deeds, and in the war and battles against his brother Manco Inca, who remains in rebellion; and but for his aid most of the Spaniards who now live here would have been killed; and regardless of this he receives the cruellest abuse and treatment at their hands, but being of an astute and prudent disposition he has suffered them: breaking into his house and stealing his belongings, and taking from him his women. And wishing to become a Christian he has resided in my own house these five months, in which time I have instructed him in the Faith.[2]

At his christening his mother, a cacique's daughter, and his sister-wife had also been baptised; he had obliged them to wear Spanish clothes and take the Christian title names the Governor Vaca de Castro had awarded them as hidalgos. Though he was able to make a mark for his name he had never learnt to speak Castilian.

The incense and gentle candlelight seemed to shroud his body and all that could be heard was the weeping of the women kneeling around the wooden casket. The requiem was sung by the bishop of the city in the chapel Paullu Inca had founded and was attended by all the members of the Inca royal house. But only his young son Don Carlos Inca understood what was being said, as the chanting voices rose and fell and incense drifted through the wooden rafters of the small chapel.

TEN

The Blind Man of La Mota

The stranger had little to show for the years he had spent in the Indies. He was dressed in the sombre-coloured breeches and threadbare woollen smocks of his fellow townsmen, and adorned only with the gold Indian chain he wore round his neck. The young woman, an orphan seventeen years old, watched him walk across the town's central square, where the great annual trading fairs of Medina del Campo took place, a solitary and dishevelled figure, his reddish beard full grown and lined with grey. She never saw him again, nor did anyone speak of him. Only once did she hear someone remark that his name was Bernal Díaz, and that he had accompanied the great Cortéz on his conquest of Mexico. Nor would she ever know that in the poverty of his new-found life in the Indies, to which he would one day return, he would write one of the greatest chronicles of the New World, *Historia Verdadera de la Conquista de la Nueva España*.

It was almost noon by the time she crossed the square, accompanied by her aunt, with whom she lived. Born a nobleman's daughter, over the years she had been reduced to taking in washing from the newly rich merchant families of the town, many of whom now inhabited the old palaces whose carved escutcheons were proud reminders of a world to which she no longer belonged. It was a summer's morning like any other in the arid plain of Castile, the sun warming the pink-tiled houses and market stalls, as the two figures walked out of the town's southern gate towards the river, the younger of the women carrying in her arms a bundle of clothing.

Ahead of them stood the castle of La Mota, which lies across the River Zapardiel on the outskirts of the town, its massive grey stone and red brick crenellated walls and tower visible for miles around.

Forbidding and austere, it had served as both a royal residence and a prison since the days when the Dukes of Alba bequeathed the fortress to Queen Isabella, and its walls were haunted by the faded memories and ghosts of its former captives. They included the exiled Cesare Borgia, son of the Pope, who escaped by leaping into the moat and then fled to the mountain kingdom of Navarre for refuge, and Juana the 'Mad Queen of Spain', mother of the Emperor Charles V, whose cries it was said could still be heard as she clung for days to the castle's portcullis, in the hope of once more seeing her wastrel of a husband. She would spend the rest of her life a captive to her insanity.

The two women walked on towards the castle, for the elder of the two had obtained permission to visit a new prisoner, only recently arrived from Madrid, who was to be confined for an indefinite period in the castle. Everyone in the town knew the purpose of her visit, and the shame it would bring her impoverished relatives. Even her orphaned niece who walked by her side had at first doubted her intentions, but after a while chose to ignore the gossip and innuendo of the townswomen, who had always taken pleasure in observing the daily humiliation of their lives.

The interview took place shortly after two o'clock that afternoon, after the prisoner had attended Mass in the castle's chapel. The chamber in which he met the two women was furnished with tapestries and decorative armour lined its walls. The oak table, laid for a meal, was adorned with gold plate, and a Negro slave woman was busily putting the finishing touches to the preparations, bringing in silver salvers of fruit and the sweet pastries she had purchased that morning at the town's bakery.

The prisoner was in his middle years and partially blind. On the breast of his short cape he wore the scarlet cross of the knightly Order of Santiago. The chronicler Gonzalo Fernández de Oviedo, who had once met him on the Caribbean island of Hispaniola, described him as 'a huge and tall man, with thick lips and tongue, his nose bulbous and covered with sores'.[1] The understanding he reached that day with the elder of the two women was referred to many years later in the evidence given in a testimonial, the manuscript of which is at the Biblioteca Nacional in Madrid.[2] One of the witnesses recorded that 'the said Doña Francisca de Mercado, aunt of Doña Isabel de Mercado, whom she had raised as her niece, forced by her extreme poverty did take her to the fortress, the prisoner being a man of great fortune'. Another witness recalled that 'the young woman was very beautiful', and that he had once seen her 'occupying one of the two beds of the prisoner's bedchamber'.

For nine years the orphan Doña Isabel was to remain the mistress of Spain's most celebrated captive, a man accused of murder and genocide, yet possibly the richest subject in the realm. He had been publicly disgraced for having ordered the execution of the elderly Adelantado Don Diego de Almagro after the Battle of Salinas, in the first of Peru's civil wars.

Only twice in the years the two women shared his imprisonment did they leave the castle, 'for fear that their relatives would kill them'. Other witnesses recorded that minstrels used to visit the castle to entertain the prisoner and his mistress, and that musical instruments had been purchased by him for this purpose, 'including a harpsichord and viola'.

In the years of her captivity Doña Isabel gave birth to four children, two of whom died young. Her future, and that of her surviving children, a boy and a girl, would be decided not by the Crown, which had chosen to ignore her existence, nor by the constant condemnation of the town's clergy, who derided her as little better than a whore, but by events that took place thousands of miles away in Peru.

On 15 March 1551 a seventeen-year-old mestiza girl bade farewell to her Indian mother at Peru's port of Callao and boarded a barque bound for Panama. She was accompanied by her Spanish stepfather and her twelve-year-old half-brother, the son of her dead father's other Indian mistress. For as long as she could remember she had dreamt of Spain: a land about which she had heard so many extraordinary and remarkable tales, of its wealth and great cities, its lords and princes, and its emperor, who ruled most of Europe and the New World. He himself had now ordered her to her father's homeland.

She did not trust, nor did she care for, her stepfather; she knew that he had offered to escort her only to try to make as much money as possible from the expenses her guardian had given him for the voyage. Nor did she much care for her mother, whose existence only served to remind her of her mixed blood.[3]

By early May the small group of passengers had reached the Pacific port of Panama, where they remained for almost a month before travelling by mule across the isthmus to the Atlantic port of Nombre de Dios, described by many of the travellers who passed through its inns and lodging houses as one of the most desolate and disease-ridden townships in the tropics. A month later they sailed to Cuba, from where they made the final crossing by galleon to the port of Seville.

Though Seville's appearance had altered little since the days when her stepfather had sailed to the Indies, the city had almost doubled in population to some eighty thousand inhabitants. Its merchants dominated the Indies trade, and many of them had established commercial houses at Lima, whose architecture and culture more than any other colonial city reflected the Andalusian capital. Some six thousand African and Moorish slaves are recorded as the property of Sevillians, whose opulence in dress and brashness were eagerly imitated by the returning colonists.[4]

The Spaniard Francisco de Ampuero recorded in the book of expenses he kept that his stepdaughter bought a great number of items of jewellery and silver plate in the city, and that her young half-brother also purchased large quantities of velvet and taffeta clothing.[5] It is not known how long they remained in Seville, but they were received there by one of the Emperor Charles V's officials, who agreed to the young woman's request to visit her father's native township.

No record has survived to indicate exactly when Pizarro's daughter arrived at Medina del Campo. What is known, however, is that before her arrival Doña Isabel de Mercado left the castle of La Mota and entered the town's Dominican convent of Santa Clara.[6] Before the end of that year the young mestiza heiress Doña Francisca Pizarro knelt before La Mota's blind prisoner, a man old enough to be her grandfather, and accepted him as her husband and lord.

What is known of her marriage to her uncle Hernando Pizarro is derived principally from the various court cases and petitions the couple made to the Crown as they tried to secure her vast inheritance as her father's sole heir, and from the protracted court case in which Hernando defended himself against the charge of ordering the execution of the elderly Adelantado Almagro. It was for this offence that he had been imprisoned for so many years.

The couple also asked some of the surviving conquistadores in Cusco to give evidence on their behalf in a testimonial that Hernando compiled of his brother's service in the conquest of Peru: 'from these realms has been taken such an infinity of gold and silver and pearls and riches to Spain', one of the conquistadores recorded, 'which are daily sent to Your Majesty and his kingdom, all of which has been made possible by the discovery, conquest and pacification of these realms by the Marquis Don Francisco Pizarro and those who accompanied him, and the greatest service ever recorded in either ancient or modern history any vassals have ever rendered a monarch; all at their own cost and endeavour and without any expenditure of Don Carlos, our emperor and lord, as is well known, and for which the Crowns of Castile and León have been so greatly endowed . . .'.[7]

In the nine years the couple lived in the castle – the same period of time Doña Isabel de Mercado had lived there, almost to the day – five children were born to them.

In the summer of 1561 Hernando Pizarro was finally released from La Mota by order of King Philip II. Accompanied by his young wife and children, and a large entourage of servants and slaves, he finally left the shadow of the great castle and set off on the westerly road to Estremadura and his native township of Trujillo. The column of carriages, escorted by outriders and liveried footmen, soon approached the battlemented medieval town, rising above a bleak and endless skyline. Horses and men climbed slowly up the town's winding cobbled streets, halting from time to time to receive the applause and garlands of the townspeople who had come to see

Pizarro's daughter. Finally they reached the town's small square, where Hernando Pizarro raised his bejewelled hand in salute to the cheering crowd.

Supported by a footman and by his wife, he walked into the very same square where as a young man he had been the first to pledge support to his bastard brother. He stood to greet each of the town's officials with the authority inbred in him, his gilded coat armour adorned with emeralds and pearls, and his face partly hidden by the velvet mask that covered his eyes. Within the hour the couple left the town for their country estate, their steward scattering the last few coins of silver among the crowd of beggars and onlookers.

Later that day another carriage passed through the gates of the town and headed towards the convent of Santa Clara, where the heavily veiled figure of Doña Isabel de Mercado was seen entering its precincts. For almost forty years she was to live out her life as a nun here.

In August 1578 the Knight of Santiago Hernando Pizarro died at Trujillo and was buried in the Franciscan monastery there, leaving a fortune derived from the spoils of Peru, as recorded by the Inca Prince Don Diego Cayo, Atahualpa's cousin, in a testimonial. It gives a vivid insight into the first days of the Conquest and his obsessive quest for gold:

I had heard it said and it was commonly known at the time throughout all the villages of the coast that the sons of the sea had come from the waters, conquering and fighting with the natives of these realms, and that they overcame them, taking from them their gold and silver; and that in the valley of Tangarara they had founded a village, and that from there they had climbed to the valley of Cajamarca where they found Atahualpa with his army; and that without any resistance they had made him their prisoner: for it was said that their horses and their bodies were of the same body, and that when their horses lifted their tails they killed the Indians with the fire of their arquebuses, and they did with their swords . . .

I also heard it said that after the Spaniards captured Atahualpa they took from him and from his lords more than two million pesos of gold and silver, the majority of which was given to Don Francisco and his brothers Hernando Pizarro, Juan Pizarro and Gonzalo Pizarro. And at that time it was known that Don Francisco Pizarro and Hernando Pizarro asked Atahualpa to give them and their brothers, and all those who came with them, gold and silver, and that if he would comply with this they would free him. And Atahualpa, believing in Don Francisco's word, sent messengers to all the regions of his empire to gather such a treasure, and also to bring with them the mamacuna. And this I witnessed, and the great multitudes of Indians laden with gold, silver and jewels, who took them to Cajamarca, and two large chambers were filled with the treasure; and this was given to Don Francisco and his brothers, and they did with it what they wished. . . .

I also heard it said that Atahualpa offered to give to the Spanish king many of his caciques and lords for his service, together with a further amount of some six million pesos of gold and silver, on condition he be taken to Spain; and this Don Francisco promised him. And I was present and witnessed the words of Atahualpa. But without any cause or reason Don Francisco ordered his killing.

And I know that Atahualpa would have been able to provide the six million pesos of gold and silver he had promised, for there were great amounts of other treasures in the temples and among the mamacuna throughout the realm; but once it was known he had been killed all these remained hidden, and no one has ever been able to discover them because of the hatred the Indians had and still have for the Spaniards who came to these kingdoms, and who still continue to come. . . .

I saw that after Don Francisco ordered the killing of Atahualpa, he also ordered the killing of many of his warrior lords and relatives, and many other Indians, some ten thousand in number, and this is known among my people.

It is also known that many caciques and Indian lords informed Don Francisco of the great treasure at the temple of Pachacamac, some 4 leagues in distance from the City of the Kings, and that he ordered his brother Hernando Pizarro to go there; and I was one of those who accompanied Hernando Pizarro and I met and saw him at Cajamarca, and I was told that messengers had been sent to all the principal provinces to collect gold, silver, jugs, the jewels of the mamacuna and of other women; all of which was to be given to Hernando Pizarro; and I saw that from all the regions some twenty thousand Indians brought treasure to Pachacamac: gold and silver adornments and sculptures of birds, frogs, men and women, birds, llamas, mamacuna, all of much value, and some of which had also come from the temple of the sun at Pachacamac, all of which was assembled together, and carried by some ten thousand Indians to Cajamarca, accompanied by Hernando Pizarro.

Much later, when I was in the city of Cusco, Hernando Pizarro imprisoned Don Diego de Almagro and ordered his head cut off. At this time he was Don Francisco's governor of Cusco. And I witnessed him also imprison Manco Inca Yupanqui, Atahualpa's brother, and he held him captive in the fortress of the city and treated him cruelly, taking from him his women and servants, and he kept him prisoner in order to obtain more gold and treasure from him. And as I have said, he took from him his women and servants, placing him in a darkened cell, and I witnessed him at various times try to obtain gold and silver from him, telling him that he would free him and name him successor as Inca. I also saw that in order to end the abuses and tortures to which he had been subjected, Manco Inca promised to give Hernando Pizarro two life-sized figures in gold of a man and of a woman, which it was said weighed more than forty thousand pesos, or the same as one hundred baskets of gold. And I saw him give Hernando Pizarro these treasures, for my father was responsible for seeing them taken to Hernando Pizarro, believing that Manco Inca would be freed.

But he did not free him. He demanded from him even more gold and silver, which he said he desired to take to His Majesty in Spain. And I witnessed Manco Inca order some three thousand Indians to bring each week gold powder to Hernando Pizarro, and this they did for a space of five moons, each Sunday, even before Hernando Pizarro had risen and dressed to go to Mass.[8]

Within three years of his death Hernando's young widow was to marry the penniless son of the Count of Puñonrostro, a grandson of Don Pedro Arias Dávila, the infamous Pedrarias, who had been Hernando de Soto's father-in-law, and whose hatred for the Pizarros had almost cost them the Conquest.

For the rest of her life Pizarro's daughter was to dissipate the vast fortune she had inherited from her father and from her husband. In the few years he had been in Peru the latter had accumulated more wealth from her mother's people than any other conquistador. She died in Madrid in 1598.

In that same year Doña Isabel de Mercado herself died in the convent at Trujillo, unaware that one day, through the extinction of Doña Francisca's line, her own descendants would eventually inherit the marquisate awarded to the Pizarros, together with the grand palace her lover had established in the town's main square. In the cemetery, in what is now an abandoned and roofless chapel, stands a life-sized sculpture of Hernando Pizarro in armour, but the little that can still be recognized of his features certainly resembles the grotesque description of him left by the chronicler Fernández de Oviedo.

ELEVEN

The Emperor's Daughter

For the third day running Cusco's town crier, the mestizo Pedro de Valdelomar, announced the forthcoming auction of the old Indian woman's goods, her clothing, furniture and personal belongings. The grey stone-walled mansion, where she had lived with her now dead husband, the Spaniard Diego Hernández, was also to be auctioned, by order of the city's court. The mansion had been built by the conquistador Vasco de Guevara, and some twenty years previously his orphaned heirs had sold it to the woman. As its finely cut Inca masonry glowed in the early morning sunshine, supporting the lavish Moorish columns and galleries, none of the crowd of people gathered in the small square of the convent of San Francisco had any idea that the woman was still inside the building. Defiant to the last, earlier that morning she had told her elderly Negro slave to barricade not only the main entrance door but all the side doors and the metal-grilled windows.

Bidding was brisk and soon a young Spanish nobleman had purchased the mansion from the city's bailiffs. Some time later the woman's slave, who had been brought to the colony by Pizarro's brother Hernando, told her that her two sons had finally left the building, climbing over the roof tops to make their escape. Only then did she finally weaken. Pulling her shawl over her face, she ordered him to unbar the great door. The ransacking of the mansion took several hours, and what the bailiffs did not steal for themselves was thrown into a pile in the square. The woman said nothing and simply walked out into the street, a sad and lonely figure, nor did she even look up when her slave was also sold by the mestizo.

For the rest of that day she sat alone among the garbage in the street, like the Indian beggars who lined the porch of the square's

98

convent church, and it was here that Martín, the lawyer the court had appointed for her, and who spoke her language, eventually found her. He had, he told her, done everything in his power to prevent the auctioning of her home and her belongings, appealing on a number of occasions even to her neighbour, the Alderman de los Ríos, in whose house she had been married so many years before, but he too had refused her his help. She listened to his words in silence. She knew that he too would try to betray and rob her, and persuade her to make her mark on documents she neither understood nor would ever be able to read. But he was a kind man at heart and offered her a bed for the night.

In the darkness of Martín's house, in the little room he had given her to sleep in, she remembered how she had accompanied him to the city's court, dressed in the Spanish garments her husband had always forced her to wear, but with her precious Indian shawl covering her frail figure. Her once black hair now grained with white, she had stood impassively in the court's main chamber as she had waited for the mayor of the city to address the court. She recalled how she had shuddered when Martín had informed her of the mayor's identity, wondering how many of the persons assembled there that day knew that she had once been his concubine and had been abandoned by him, and that he was the father of her eldest son.

For over an hour he listened to the various petitioners who had brought charges against her for money they claimed she owed them, and then to her lawyer Martín, who explained to the court that after the death of her husband Hernández she had discovered that he had mortgaged all her property for the sum of 1,700 pesos of silver, and this he had done without her knowledge. She admitted, he told the court, making her mark on several documents acknowledging her husband's action, but claimed that she had been deceived by him, and that at his death she had been forced to purchase her own house from his heirs, together with various other properties. Unfortunately, she had been unable to secure any financial recompense from any of them because of the debts he had left her, and so she was now being sued for payment not only by the litigants, who were unknown to her, but by her husband's illegitimate son.

It was then that the mayor addressed her in her own language, telling her that the evidence against her was irrefutable. He had, however, decided to deny any demand to auction her possessions until her appeal to the Crown had been heard. He then repeated his judgment in Castilian, but neither his fairness nor the petitions she later sent to the Viceroy had prevented the humiliation she suffered that day.

In the summer of 1571 the old Indian woman died. She was only fifty years old but she had looked much older. A thousand or so of her people followed her coffin along the winding cobbled streets of the city to the monastery of Santo Domingo, for she had asked to be buried in the same tomb as her eldest son, laid to rest seven years previously.

Her abject poverty and the years of litigation she had endured at the hands of her husband's creditors are recorded in a previously unpublished manuscript in the Archivo General de la Nación at Lima, and would doubtless be of little historical interest were it not for her identity.[1] Among the manuscript's various documents, including her will, which she dictated 'in poor health, but sound mind', is a royal decree of King Philip II, dated 20 August 1570, which reached the viceroyalty after all her belongings and goods had been auctioned:

Don Felipe, by the Grace of God, King of Castile, León and of the Indies. Be it known to all and sundry that Miguel Ruiz, advocate in the name of Doña Beatriz Manco Cápac Coya, daughter of Huayna Cápac, once lord of these realms of Peru, to whom by royal warrant the encomiendas of Urcos and Juliaca were awarded, in the petition presented to us, stated that she was in dire need of sustenance, and that each day her creditors sold her farmlands and belongings, extracting the revenues from her Indians, and taking possession of her house; and that not only because she is the daughter of Huayna Cápac, but as an encomendera she asks and begs of us our royal decree: that no single individual, under any circumstance, or in lieu of any debt, be entitled to take possession of her house, nor of one single slave or slave woman of hers, nor of the revenues of her encomiendas, and that what has been taken from her be repossessed . . . including whatever clothes and other belongings of hers. . . .

The woman who was buried that day at Cusco was known in her native tongue as the Coya Quispiquipi Manco Cápac and she was the last surviving daughter of the Inca Emperor Huayna Cápac and his queen the Coya Rahua Ocllo.[2] Little is known of her life but she was surely one of the most remarkable and tragic figures of the conquered Inca dynasty. Her eldest son Juan, beside whom she had been buried in the monastery of Santo Domingo, was the illegitimate son of the conquistador Mansio Serra de Leguizamón, who, as the city's mayor, had presided at her trial a year before her death.

She was born in the northern city of Surampalli, capital of the Cañari people (the site of the present-day Ecuadorian city of Cuenca), which he later named after his panaca of Tumibamba. At her birth, as was the Inca custom, she was given for her guardian and protector one of her father's most powerful warrior chiefs, the Cacique Cariapasa, lord of the Lupaca nation, whose lands lay on the northern and western shores of Lake Titicaca.[3]

As a child the princess had suffered the loss of her father, and only a few years later her mother and her brother, the Emperor Huáscar, were killed by her half-brother Atahualpa's warrior chiefs. Together with her only surviving full sister Marca Chimbo, she was spared because of her youth, and, as the chronicler Juan Díez de Betanzos recorded, because she 'had known no man'.[4] Both princesses were kept prisoner in Cusco to await Atahualpa's triumphal entry into the city; they had been selected for his personal harem, possibly as a way of further humiliating the memory of Huáscar. Nothing is known of the role of her guardian Cariapasa during her captivity, and it seems likely that, like so many of her father's old warrior chiefs, he had sided with Atahualpa's rebel army. Once Cusco fell to the Spaniards, he is reported to have urged his bondaged Lupaca tribesmen to return to their ancestral lands: 'When Don Francisco Pizarro entered Cusco there came to the city the principal lord of the province of Chuquito called Cariapasa, an elderly Indian who was governor of that province, and he arrived at the village of Muina where his tribesmen were bondaged by the Incas, and said to them: "My brothers, we are no longer living in the time of the Inca, for each and every one of you can go home to your lands".'[5]

The conquistador Juan de Pancorbo recalled having first seen the princess 'a few days after the capture of Cusco', when she would have been perhaps only twelve years old.[6] The presbyter Sánchez de Olave also mentions having seen her after the fall of the city, remarking that she was one of the women accompanying her half-brother Manco Inca, who had sworn fealty to the Spaniards and had duly been appointed native ruler by Pizarro.[7]

It is more than likely that she only became the conquistador Mansio Serra de Leguizamón's mistress some two years later, by which time her half-brother Manco was a prisoner of the Spaniards. Her cousin Cayo Inca stated that 'it had been known to him and witnessed by him, that when Hernando Pizarro held Manco Inca prisoner he took from him his women and servants'.[8] Another manuscript records that the guards allotted to hold the young Inca prince prisoner, and who tortured him quite mercilessly, were the conquistadores Diego Maldonado, Pizarro's young kinsman and future chronicler Pedro Pizarro, Alonso de Mesa and Mansio Serra de Leguizamón, and implies that each took one of the royal princesses for his concubine.[9] The chronicler Gonzalo Fernández de Oviedo wrote that Hernando Pizarro, his two brothers Juan and Gonzalo and their intimate companions 'left not one single woman or sister of his unviolated'.[10]

The conquistador Juan de Pancorbo recalled that a short while later the young princess 'informed her master, in whose house she lived, and who was Mansio Serra de Leguizamón, about the rebellion her brother had planned, and he informed Hernando Pizarro'.[11] This rebellion was the great Inca uprising led by Manco that would leave Cusco besieged for almost fourteen months, during which period the princess remained with her lover in the fortified Inca palace in the city, where the two hundred Spaniards and their Indian auxiliaries had barricaded themselves. The subsequent retreat of Manco's forces into the Andes and the seizure of Cusco by the Adelantado Diego de

1. Inca Princess. Cusco School, eighteenth century. (*Museo Inka, Unsaac, Cusco/Author*)

2. Inca Túpac Amaru. Cusco School, eighteenth century. (*Museo Inka, Unsaac, Cusco/ Author*)

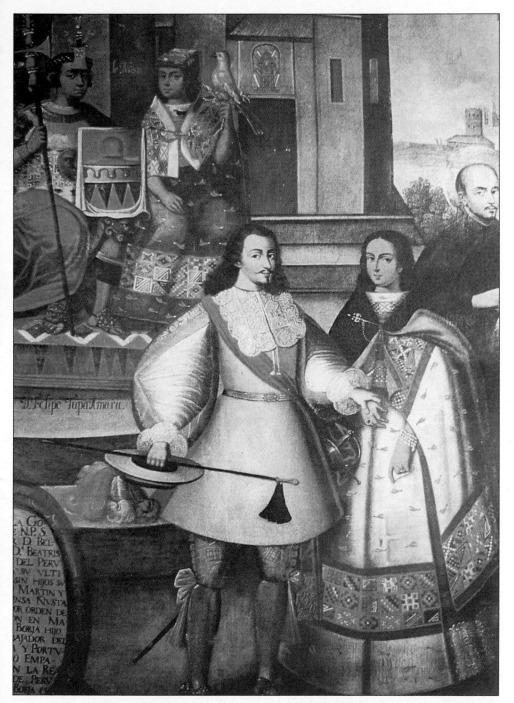

3. The Union and Imperial Inca Descent of the Houses of Loyola and Borja. Don Martín de Loyola and the Princess Doña Beatriz Clara. Top left: Doña Beatriz, Clara's uncle, the Inca Túpac Amaru, and her mother, the Princess Doña María. Cusco School, eighteenth century. (*Church of the Compañía, Cusco/Author*)

4. Inca Tupa Yupanqui. One of the sons of the Emperor Huayna Cápac. (*Archivo General de Indias, Seville/Author*)

5. Archangel. Painted by the Master of Calamarca, *c.* 1680. (*Museo Nacional de Arte, La Paz, Bolivia/Author*)

Labels within the image:

D̃ Diego Ant.º Iupa. D̃ ₉el pe Tupañare

Martin de Lo...
...vernador de Cⁱh...
de N PŚ Ignacio
fermᵃⁿ mayⁱ D. Beł
...ola caſo con D. Bear...
heredʳ y Prin.ˣ delſe
ja de D Diego y una
...ffere miſᵗo...
...que yuga de D Marⁱ...
...o D Lorenſa nula del...
...Eſpõponden de mŝ Ga...
la Caſaron con N̄. con e...
...uan de Borja hijo d...
...nha. del SŔ D Fͪⁿ...
...ydˣʳⁿ con eſte Ma...
...te en parentⁱ con
...Caſa de los V³ˢ²⁵
...te E V B²⁵

...ae 1718

Admius Regu...
tem Ieſu...
Dei
...Guriaã liSV.

D̃ Lorenſa nulla de
Loiola.

D. Iuan d Borja.

6. The Union and Imperial Inca Descent of the Houses of Loyola and Borja. From left to right: Don Martín de Loyola, the Princess Doña Beatriz Clara, their son-in-law Don Juan de Borja and their daughter Doña Ana María Lorenza de Loyola. In the background are the bride's and groom's ancestors, St Ignatius de Loyola and St Francisco de Borja. Cusco School, 1718. (*Museo Pedro de Osma, Lima/Author*)

7. Don Marcos Chiquathopa. Cacique and Inca descendant. Cusco School, eighteenth century. (*Museo Inka, Unsaac, Cusco/Author*)

8. The feast of Corpus Christi. Detail of Inca nobles of Cusco. Cusco School, eighteenth century. (*Museo de Arte Religioso, Cusco/Author*)

9. Virgen del Rosario. Painted by Luis Niño, *c.* 1750. (*Museo de la Casa de la Moneda, Potosí, Bolivia/Author*)

10. The Church of San Lorenzo, Potosí, Bolivia (1728–44). (*Author*)

11. Coat-of-Arms of the Conquistador Mansio Serra de Leguizamón. It incorporates the head of the Villaoma, the Inca High Priest of the Sun. Awarded by the Emperor Charles V. Wall sculpture, early seventeenth century. (*Ayuntamiento de Pinto/Author*)

12. Virgen de la Candelaría. Painted by Luis Niño, *c.* 1730. Medallion miniature. (*Private Collection/Author*)

13. The Palacio Díez de Medina. (*The present-day Museo Nacional de Arte, La Paz, Bolivia/Alexander Stirling*)

14. Coat-of-Arms of the Inca Tupa Yupanqui. Awarded by the Emperor Charles V in 1545. (*Archivo General de Indias, Seville/Author*)

15. The Castle of La Mota, Medina del Campo. Nineteenth-century engraving by Parcerisa. (*Private Collection/Author*)

16. Francisco Pizarro and the Princess Doña Inés. (*Palacio de la Conquista, Trujillo, Estremadura/Author*)

Almagro, who imprisoned Pizarro's brothers and supporters, among them the 22-year-old Serra de Leguizamón. This left the princess, who was carrying his child, at the mercy of his captors.

Francisco de Illescas, one of Almagro's prisoners, stated that in July 1537 he was present at the birth of the princess's son Juan, though it is more than likely that by then she would have been seized as booty by one of Almagro's captains.[12] The subsequent defeat of Almagro at the Battle of Salinas by Hernando Pizarro led to the release of her son's father after almost a year of captivity, chained up with the other leading Pizarrist prisoners in the belfry of one of the city's Inca towers. But his release brought her little consolation: it was probably the humiliation he must have felt at her enforced concubinage that led him to abandon her.

The city in which the seventeen-year-old princess was forced to find a home for herself and her young son was entirely in the hands of its conquerors, its great palaces and temples contemptuously converted into their stables and living quarters; here they kept their numerous Indian mistresses, many of them daughters of the caciques of their encomiendas. The princess could not even seek shelter in the former temples in the city, as they were now serving as storehouses or private chapels.

The plight of numerous destitute and abused Inca women, many of them suffering from syphilis and malnutrition, was highlighted by the Dominican friar Vicente de Valverde, by then serving as Cusco's bishop after a brief sojourn in Spain. In a letter to the Emperor Charles V, he explained that many of the princesses were being forced into prostitution:

Your Majesty has the obligation to grant them the means to eat, for they wander this city abandoned, which is a great shame to witness: and what I feel is that the women, after being instructed, will become Christians, for there will be no lack of men who would wish to marry them if Your Majesty were to reward them.[13]

Another letter in similar vein was written to the Spanish Emperor by the priest Luis de Morales: 'There are many who have nothing to eat and who die of hunger, and who go from house to house, carrying in their hands a mendicant's candle and bowl, begging for food in the name of God and of his Holy Mother.'[14] A year later he wrote:

> There are many princesses, especially in the city of Cusco, daughters of Huayna Cápac, whom many a fine hidalgo would marry, for some demand them; though for lack of their dowries they refuse to betroth them, especially as all of them previously possessed dowries and much land that was left them by their father. Your Majesty: I beg that you decree they be given dowries and lands so that they may live decently and marry, and so they will be secure to live honestly and in the service of God. And that Pedro de Bustinza, a poor hidalgo and citizen of Cusco, who has married a daughter of Huayna Cápac, who is called Doña Beatriz, and who by the Grace of God has children, and who live in great poverty, be given an encomienda so that they may be able to sustain themselves, and, in so doing, render God great service, by which much joy will be given to the natives.[15]

The Basque Pedro de Bustinza was a minor treasury official who had come to Peru in the train of Hernando Pizarro on his return to the colony. The marriage probably took place some two years after the princess's abandonment by Serra de Leguizamón, and it was possibly then that she was baptised and given the Christian name Doña Beatriz. She was named after her godmother, the former Moorish slave Beatriz de Salcedo, who had befriended many of the princesses at both Cajamarca and Cusco, and who later established herself in Lima and became one of the most influential and wealthy women in the viceroyalty.

In response to Morales's letter the Emperor Charles V granted Princess Doña Beatriz the encomienda of Urcos, lying to the south-east of Cusco in the ancestral lands of her mother, the Coya Rahua Ocllo, part of which had previously belonged to Hernando Pizarro. The award was to alter dramatically the lives of the couple and their children: her five-year-old son Juan, and her two younger sons by Bustinza, Pedro and Martín.

The rebellion of Gonzalo Pizarro in the years 1544–8 was to bring even greater prosperity to the princess and her husband, who was one of Gonzalo's most prominent supporters. He was also one of the witnesses Cusco's rebel governor Diego Maldonado called upon to justify the rebellion, recording in the city's council that Gonzalo's army had been raised solely to defend the city from attack by the Inca Manco:

It is known to me that Manco Inca, native lord of these realms, has rebelled against His Majesty and that he had publicly declared that he intends to bring his warriors to this city of Cusco and to seize it. I know of this because I am married with a lady who is a daughter of Huayna Cápac, once native lord of these realms and sister of Manco Inca, and that since the day Gonzalo Pizarro and his men left the city, which is a month, more or less, each single day, my wife, who is greatly frightened, has implored me that we leave the city with our belongings, for she fears that Manco Inca will come here with many of his warriors and take her prisoner, and kill every single Spaniard . . . and through another messenger sent by a sister of my wife, she has learnt that the Inca has stated that he is not angry with her: for she is his sister whom he most loves . . . but still she wishes to flee the city . . . for there are few of us left here and no more than twenty horses.[16]

Another witness stated: 'Manco Inca has sworn by the sun and by the moon, and by the earth, that within a few days he will stand in the main square of Cusco, and that his sisters, who are in this city and married to Spaniards, have also informed me of this, and they have each begged me to implore their husbands to leave the city for Arequipa, for if the Inca finds them he will kill them, for they had once been his women.'[17]

However, Manco Inca was never to besiege Cusco again. A few months later he was murdered by a Spanish renegade soldier who had sought shelter in his mountain retreat at Vilcos, near his subtropical fortress city of Vilcabamba, known to this day as the 'Lost City of the Incas'. Whatever the differences Doña Beatriz may have had with her half-brother, she demonstrated her love for him by looking after two of his daughters, the Princesses Usezino and Ancacica, whom he had left behind in Cusco after fleeing the city eight years previously.[18]

Doña Beatriz's nephew, the mestizo chronicler Garcilaso de la Vega, records the death of her husband Bustinza, whom Gonzalo Pizarro had appointed Mayor of Cusco after his victory at the Battle of Huarina in 1547. Betrayed by her cousin Cayo Inca, Bustinza was captured by loyalists while raising Indian auxiliaries from her lands; he was taken to the Governor Pedro de la Gasca's encampment at Jauja, where he was garrotted.

Now twenty-seven years old and a widow with three sons, Doña Beatriz's future, like that of so many other wives and mistresses of rebels, depended on the outcome of the Battle of Jaquijahuana, which was brought to a speedy conclusion by the mass desertion by Gonzalo Pizarro's once invincible army of several thousand men. The news of his subsequent beheading was brought to her at Cusco. Her prospects looked gloomy, since her husband had been one of Gonzalo's principal supporters. Nevertheless she awaited her fate with a mixture of patience and defiance, as Garcilaso de la Vega recorded:

The wife of Pedro de Bustinza, who was a daughter of Huayna Cápac, and whose Indians of her encomienda had belonged to her and not to her husband, the governors gave in marriage to a fine soldier of good character called Diego Hernández, who it was said – more from malice than truth – in his youth had been a tailor. And when this was known to the princess she refused to marry him, saying that it was not right that a daughter of Huayna Cápac should be married to a tailor; and though the Bishop of Cusco begged her to reconsider and the Captain Centeno and other personages tried to persuade her, none was able to do so. It was then they called upon Don Cristóbal Paullu, her brother, who on visiting her, took her aside to a corner of a room and told her that it was not in their interest that she refuse the marriage, for it would only bring hardship to the royal family and the Spaniards would regard them as their enemies and never more offer them their friendship. She then agreed to accept her brother's command, though not in very good humour, and thus she went before the bishop and the altar. And being asked by an interpreter if she would accept to be the wife of the soldier, she replied in her language: 'íchach munani, íchach manamuni', which means, 'perhaps I do, perhaps I don't'. And so was concluded the betrothal, which was celebrated in the house of Diego de los Ríos, encomendero of Cusco.[19]

The princess's new husband was a native of Talavera; an elderly soldier of fortune, he was probably twice her age. The dowry she brought him was substantial. In addition to her mansion at Cusco, her encomienda of Urcos had an annual tribute of some four hundred male Indians and their families. She also possessed substantial holdings in the region of Cusco, including several mills, estates and coca plantations.[20] The Indian Mazma recalled: 'I have seen the Indians of all the regions and nations show her their obedience and respect as daughter of the lord and king.'[21]

The total Andean population by then consisted of probably no more than 2 million Indians and some 8,000 colonists; 346 of the latter were encomenderos, but only four encomiendas were held by members of the Inca royal house.[22] All the other relatives of the princess were landless and had no income, and were obliged to make a living as virtual servants of the colonists. The wealthiest of the encomendero Inca princes was her half-brother Paullu Inca, after whose death she assumed the nominal leadership of the royal house at Cusco. Her elder sister Doña Juana, whose husband the conquistador Francisco de Villacastín had been exiled for life by Gasca for his part in Gonzalo's rebellion, may also have died by this time. 'In Cusco where she resided,' the chronicler Diego Fernández recorded, 'there was no lord, male or female, greater than she.'[23]

The small court over which the princess presided at her mansion in Cusco would have been Indian in appearance and custom, for neither she nor any of her close relatives ever learnt to speak Castilian. Like other encomenderos, by then restricted to residing in the cities from which their encomiendas were held, she would nevertheless have been obliged from time to time to make a tour of her lands and tributary Indians, travelling in a litter and accompanied by her husband and sons and her yanacona servants. The administration of her encomienda would have been in the hands of Spanish stewards: these landless colonists were in general renowned for their cruelty and blatant dishonesty as foremen, and in later years most were replaced by mestizos, although these were equally despised by the Indians of the encomiendas. The stewards were responsible for gathering the tribute and supervising the agricultural produce of the caciques which twice yearly – on the feast of St John the Baptist (24 June) and at Christmas – would be brought to the city of the encomienda's jurisdiction for sale in its markets. Produce included coca, maize and potatoes, clothing and livestock (llamas, alpacas and vicuñas), together with whatever gold or silver had been mined in the tributary lands.

The princess's marriage to an almost unknown conscript of Gasca's army was indicative of the general reluctance of the more prominent conquistadores and Spaniards of hidalgo rank to marry the Indian mothers of their children. Such racism was bred in the psychology of Spanish men, irrespective of their own humble origins; their sense of racial purity, *Limpieza de sangre*, dominated their attitude to the lineages they wished to establish as grandees of a new social order. Such attitudes were widespread even in Spain, where their countrymen took pains to distance themselves from any stigma of mixed Jewish or Moorish blood. (Indeed, this anomaly was still evident in Spain until as late as 1859 for entrance to the corps of officer cadets.)[24]

The early years of the Conquest, when the veterans of Cajamarca had lived openly with their Indian mistresses, had given way to a semblance of moral conformity imposed on the colony by successive missionaries and by the Crown itself. The Crown publicly criticized the failure of the now middle-aged conquistadores to marry and set an example to both colonists and Indians alike: an attitude it had previously overlooked during Pizarro's governorship. He himself had refused to marry either of the two Inca princesses who were the mothers of his four children.

The reluctance of the conquistadores to marry their Indian concubines led to a 'gold-rush' of female fortune-hunters from Spain and the isthmus, women who were more than willing to trade their youth and pale skins for the fortunes of the gout-ridden and battle-scarred soldiers, most of whom were disfigured by syphilis or by the facial warts often contracted in the tropics; the elder Almagro among others was recorded to have suffered from such warts. The influx of women, ranging from the noblest families of Castile to the humblest prostitutes, laid the foundations for the future creole aristocracy of the colony. It also deprived the conquistadores' illegitimate mestizo children of any legal right to their elderly fathers' fortunes, and most were regarded by their young Spanish stepmothers as a threat to their own children. Few conquistadores escaped this cycle. The elderly Lucas Martínez Vegazo, for example, married a creole young enough to be his granddaughter, and it was she who would eventually inherit his encomienda.

As mestizos, all three of the Princess Doña Beatriz's sons were deprived of the legal rights granted to even the humblest colonist, in accordance with a decree issued at Valladolid in 1549 by the Emperor Charles V. This not only prohibited mestizos from holding public office, it also denied them the right of inheriting their fathers' encomiendas or of carrying arms.

The mestiza daughters of the veterans of Cajamarca were in many cases much better off. Most were given considerable dowries for their marriages, or for their endowment to the city's convents. There is little evidence to suggest that the majority of the conquistadores regarded their mestizo children with anything other than affection, as is evident in the will of Alonso de Mesa, who paid a considerable fortune for his daughters' admission to Toledo's most prominent convent. Those less fortunate children whose Spanish fathers were of lower rank either married fellow mestizos or Spanish peasant immigrants, or reverted to their Indian heritage, many of them making alliances with families of their former cacique subjects. This practice was followed by the pure-blooded daughters of the Inca princely nobility of Cusco for several generations.

After years of cohabiting with their Indian women many of the conquistadores were regarded by the newly arrived Spanish colonists as little more than natives themselves, speaking with fluency both quéchua and aimára, the principal languages of their tributary vassals, and like medieval barons maintaining their native armies from their encomiendas. Nevertheless, as many of the testimonials of the Inca princesses demonstrate, it was the elderly conquistadores more than any others who defended the princesses' privileges and supported them in their petitions to the Crown.

One of the princesses living in Cusco at the time of Doña Beatriz's marriage to Diego Hernández was Doña Angelina, Atahualpa's niece and favourite wife, whom Pizarro had briefly taken for his concubine. She had borne him two sons. She was, however, regarded with hostility by Doña Beatriz and other members of her panaca, who never forgave her for her association with Atahualpa and his bloody massacre of the imperial family, graphically described by the conquistador Juan de Pancorbo: 'I saw on a hill above the city more than 150 corpses hanging from poles, and I was told that they were Inca lords, who had been killed by Chalcuchima, Atahualpa's warrior chief, and placed there for all to see.'[25]

This hostility was evident in the writings of Garcilaso de la Vega (whose mother belonged to Doña Beatriz's panaca), who was responsible for maligning the origins of Atahualpa's mother by claiming quite falsely that she was a subject princess from Quito. A counter-assertion can be found in the chronicle of Doña Angelina's Spanish husband Juan Díez de Betanzos, who omitted Huáscar from his list of Inca monarchs and referred to Doña Beatriz's mother, the Empress Rahua Ocllo, as a concubine. (A similar allegation was made by the Inca Titu Cusi Yupanqui, an illegitimate son of the Inca Manco, many years later in his attempt to impress the Spaniards as to his right to the Inca throne.) Betanzos, however, on the strength of his wife being the mother of Pizarro's sons, obtained for her an encomienda in the Yucay valley, which he later appropriated for himself.

In October 1555 the Spanish Emperor Charles V announced his abdication in the great hall of the palace at Brussels, bestowing the crowns of Spain and of the Indies on his son Philip II. By this time the Princess Doña Beatriz was thirty-four years old.

One of the last decrees the emperor had signed before travelling into self-imposed exile in Estremadura had been the appointment of a new viceroy for his Peruvian territories. The Marquis of Cañete arrived in Lima in 1556, bringing with him one of the largest retinues of officials and attendants ever seen. By this time the only resistance to Spain's absolute sovereignty of her colony was in the Andean region of Vilcabamba, which was now virtually an independent Inca kingdom. Since the Inca Manco's death his son Sayri Túpac, aged twenty-one in 1556, had ruled the remnants of his army of warriors in the fortified mountain enclave, and had repeatedly refused to negotiate a peace agreement with the Spaniards. The presence of his warriors in the vicinity of Cusco led to unease among the colonists, and a number of travellers on the road from the city to Lima were physically attacked.

One of the Marquis of Cañete's first acts was to write to the Princess Doña Beatriz asking for her help in persuading her nephew Sayri Túpac to receive his envoys. The delegation which subsequently left Cusco for Vilcabamba included her husband Diego Hernández, the chronicler Betanzos and two Dominican friars, and was led by her twenty-year-old son Juan. After three separate journeys to his cousin's sub-tropical Andean refuge, Juan finally managed to persuade Sayri Túpac to surrender to the Crown.

In October 1557, leaving behind at Vilcabamba his younger full brother Túpac Amaru and his half-brother Titu Cusi Yupanqui, the Inca chief began his journey from the Andes, accompanied by his daughter and his young sister-wife Cusi Huarcay, and several hundred of his warriors. The caravan of litters that carried him and his family to the valley of Andahuaylas was escorted by his cousin on horseback and by Doña Beatriz's husband Diego Hernández. At the gates of Lima they were met by the city's councillors. The Viceroy received the Inca with equal honour, seating him by his side in the audience chamber of his palace.

Describing a banquet staged by the Archbishop of Lima, at which Sayri Túpac was presented with documents awarding him a pardon and the grant of his encomiendas of Indians, Garcilaso de la Vega observed that the Inca had traded what had once been his empire for the equivalent of a thread of the cloth that covered the dining table.

The encomiendas awarded to the Inca and his descendants in perpetuity included much of the Yucay valley, known as the 'Sacred Valley', which had once formed part of the lands of his grandfather the Emperor Huayna Cápac's panaca of Tumibamba. His transformation into a Castilian encomendero would be completed after his arrival in the ancient capital of his ancestors with his baptism and Christian marriage to his sister-wife Cusi Huarcay, for which a special dispensation from Rome would eventually be secured by King Philip II. The Inca and Cusi Huarcay were given the Christian names Don Diego and Doña María in honour of the Viceroy and his wife. Their daughter Beatriz Clara was named after their aunt, the Princess Doña Beatriz.

On their entry into Cusco, carried in litters, they made a tour of the few remaining native monuments in the city in the company of their cousin Juan, towards whom, as the conquistador Juan de Pancorbo recalled, the Inca 'showed great love'.[26] Thousands of the Inca's subjects from across the former empire made pilgrimages to the city to render him homage during the weeks he and his young wife stayed as guests of their aunt in her mansion. Among their relatives who came to pay homage was the nineteen-year-old Garcilaso de la Vega.

Before departing for his encomienda in the Yucay the Inca gave his cousin Juan the sole legal right to administer his lands and wealth, and also dictated a will, witnessed by Doña Beatriz's husband Diego Hernández, in which he left Juan a thousand pesos of gold in gratitude 'for the work he has done for me and for his service to me'.[27]

A few days after the couple left the city, the Governor of Cusco Juan Polo de Ondegardo decided to display for public viewing in his mansion the mummies of Doña Beatriz's father and grandmother. This was without doubt one of the most insensitive acts of the later colonists and Crown officials, and illustrated all too clearly their attitude to the remnants of the Inca royal family. Nevertheless, it was an event the governor proudly recorded several years later in a letter to the Viceroy Don Francisco de Toledo:

> As I was at the time in charge of the government of these provinces, some twelve or thirteen years ago, with much diligence and through various sources I was able to discover the bodies . . . some of them were so well embalmed and so well maintained they appeared as if they had only recently died; and four of them, which were those of Huayna Cápac and Amaru Topa Inca and Pachacuti Inca, and that of the mother of Huayna Cápac, who was called Mama Ocllo, and the others, I discovered in bronze cages that had been secretly buried; and also among them I discovered the ashes of Túpac Inca Yupanqui in a small earthen jar, wrapped in rich cloth and with his insignia; for it was this mummy, I had heard, Juan Pizarro burnt, believing that treasure had been buried with it.[28]

The whereabouts of the mummies may have been revealed to Polo de Ondegardo by the Inca on the advice of the Dominican Melchor de los Reyes, who had instructed his conversion. They were to remain in the governor's mansion until the Viceroy ordered their removal to Lima, where they would eventually be buried in the grounds of the city's hospital of San Andrés. In silent resignation Doña Beatriz accepted the sacrilege. Her only consolation was the reward the Viceroy granted her in return for her collaboration: the encomienda of Juliaca, which lay on the northern shores of Lake Titicaca. This area had once belonged to her childhood guardian Cariapasa, lord of the Lupaca nation. Her son Juan was also rewarded by the Viceroy for the part he played in the negotiations with the Inca, but only with the grant of an insignificant encomienda at Písac in the Yucay, valued at less than four hundred pesos of silver annually. It was a pitiful recognition of his services, and is clear evidence of the prevalent discrimination against those of mestizo origin.

The Princess Doña Beatriz's principal heir, as her will records, was her eldest legitimate son Pedro de Bustinza, who succeeded to her encomienda of Juliaca, although at his death it would revert to the Crown.[29] His descendants through marriage became caciques of the encomienda, a title they held until the early nineteenth-century War of Independence. The heirs of Doña Beatriz's youngest son, Martín de Bustinza, would in their turn become caciques of her former encomienda of Urcos, and would also play a prominent role supporting the Spaniards in the final days of their rule.

The Emperor Huayna Cápac's daughter was buried beside her son Juan in the monastery of Santo Domingo, on the site where the Inca temple of the Sun had once stood; here, as a child, she had been venerated as the daughter of a living god. Her life and death are reflected in the words of a contemporary Inca memory poem:

> I was born as a flower of the field,
> As a flower I was cherished in my youth,
> I came to full age, I grew old;
> Now I am withered and die.[30]

The Will of Doña Beatriz

In the name of God, amen, let it be known that by this will, I, Doña Beatriz Manco Cápac Coya, daughter of Huayna Cápac, who was lord of these kingdoms and provinces of Peru, encomendera of this great city of Cusco, capital of these realms, being as I am ill of body but of clear mind and judgement, as Our Lord has willed, and believing as I do most firmly in the truth of the Holy Trinity, Father, Son and Holy Ghost, and in one true God, and in all that the Holy Mother Church preaches, being at the point of my death, and wishing to save my soul, I order this my will and testament in the following order:

Firstly, I commend my soul to Our Lord and God, and that when finally my body expires it be buried in the monastery of Santo Domingo of this city of Cusco, in the tomb where my son Juan Serra de Leguizamón is buried, and that the masses for my repose and the alms given be paid for by my executors.

I declare that due to the persuasion of Martín and Cristóbal de Bustinza and Juan Palacios, I agreed to various deeds and documents in favour of the brothers and heirs and debtors of Diego Hernández, my second husband, now deceased; and that in all this I was deceived, and which I did against my will; and because of which to this day certain court cases are outstanding, and I declare that I owe them nothing, and that my heirs defend my property.

I declare that Juan Palacios owes me 800 pesos, more or less, from the time he collected the tribute of my Indians, and for which he has never given me an account, and I order that this be obtained from him.

I declare that the houses of my dwelling, where I now am, were paid for with my money, and that the letter of ownership of Diego Hernández is not valid, for they are mine, and of my heirs.

I declare that at the time of my marriage to Diego Hernández we possessed and purchased the farm and estate of Pancarbamba, which lies below the old fortress of Urcos, between the river and the road, and also the farms of Yaguaci and those of Mollebamba and Cachebamba, the one at Urcos, which we bought, and the others that were given to us by the Crown; and during our marriage we constructed the mill at Yaguaci, which was paid for by me, and the half ownership of which I granted my husband, and which is now the property of his heirs, and worth some eight or nine thousand pesos; for that is what the letters of payment made by Diego Pérez Ballesteros and Cristóbal de Lugones demonstrate, and which I was forced to re-pay because of the debts of Diego Hernández and the demands made upon me by his sisters and relatives, due to the promises he had made them for their dowries. And I order that what can be retrieved from them be held for my heirs.

I declare it is my wish that all the Indians of my distribution, as named in the seals of my encomienda, be inherited according to the law by my eldest legitimate son Pedro de Bustinza, son of Pedro de Bustinza, my first husband, and whom I name my heir and successor to all my Indians.

I order that the farmlands and vineyards I possess in the ravine of Urcos in the Yucay, and all that it comprises, be inherited by my son Martín de Bustinza, the son of my first husband.

I order that the farms of Quipevarpata and Guachas Puquio that I own in the valley of Yucay be inherited by my son Pedro de Bustinza.

I order that the farmlands of coca I own at Paucarbamba and at Las Salinas be inherited by Martín de Bustinza, my younger son.[31]

Ill-health prevented Doña Beatriz from finishing her will, which she had dictated in quéchua to her nephew Alonso Martín de Ampuero, the son of her half-sister Doña Inés. One of the witnesses was her other nephew Juan Balsa, the son of her sister Doña Juana. She died shortly afterwards. All her possessions, other than her encomienda of Juliaca, were in the hands of her former husband's creditors, as demonstrated in the court case brought by Martín García de Licona against her two sons and heirs, which would drag on for several years.[32]

TWELVE

The Mestizo Prince

In the Archives of the Indies at Seville is the testimonial of the Emperor Huayna Cápac's grandson Don Juan Serra de Leguizamón, who died in 1564.[1] It gives a remarkable insight into the veneration in which his mother the Princess Doña Beatriz was held by her people, and describes the negotiations he entered into with his cousin the Inca Sayri Túpac at the lost city of Vilcabamba, the site of which has never been fully established. The manuscript also depicts his often sad and impoverished existence at Cusco after the death of Sayri Túpac, whose encomiendas he had managed, but which reverted to the Crown in its role as guardian of the Inca's young heiress daughter Doña Beatriz Clara.

Unlike his childhood companions Pedro del Barco, who headed an abortive rebellion by the mestizos of Cusco in 1560 (for which he was exiled to Chile), and the chronicler Garcilaso de la Vega, Juan Serra de Leguizamón led a virtually reclusive life. At his small encomienda at Písac, in the Sacred Valley of the Incas near Cusco, below the ruins that marked the site of his grandfather's country retreat, he built his lodging beside the Vilcanota River in one of the most beautiful regions of the Andes. For five years he remained Písac's encomendero, living there with his wife Doña María Ramírez and their two children, Don Juan, who inherited his encomienda and was awarded by the Crown the governorship of the Yucay, and Doña Bernardina, who became a nun in the convent of Santa Catalina at Cusco.

The small colonial township of Písac, built in the seventeenth century by Jesuit missionaries, is all that remains of his legacy. Today, the town's colourful Sunday market and Inca ruins are among Cusco's most popular tourist attractions.

117

Between the years 1559 and 1561 he presented his testimonial to the Royal Chancery Court at Lima, and it was duly forwarded to King Philip II by the Viceroy the Marquis of Cañete. Six conquistadores from Lima and Cusco appeared as his witnesses, together with several Inca nobles, caciques and bondaged Indians, mostly elderly men, who swore to the truth of their testimony in accordance with their native rites.

The Testimony

JUAN SERRA DE LEGUIZAMÓN: Most powerful Lord, I, Juan Serra de Leguizamón, declare I am the grandson of Huayna Cápac, once lord and king of these realms, and son of Doña Beatriz Yupanqui,* his legitimate daughter, and desiring as I do to beg your royal person to favour me in my need. And I ask of Your Highness that in accordance with your royal ordinances the following questions be put to the witnesses I present: If it be known to them that Huayna Cápac Yupanqui was king and lord of these realms of Peru, of its mountains and valleys, from Chile as far as the lands of Pastu,† and that among his many children born to him was my mother Doña Beatriz Yupanqui. And that at the time of her birth at Surampalli‡ in his domain of Tumibamba, he gave her for her guardian and service the Cacique Cariapasa, Lord of the Lupaca, for being his legitimate daughter of his queen, mother of Huáscar Inca,§ who was later to succeed him as king and lord of Cusco; and that ever since the death of Huayna Cápac she has been obeyed and honoured as his legitimate daughter by all the Indians and native lords of these realms. And that she inherited the rank of his legitimate wife, her mother, who was also the mother of Huáscar Inca, who was later king.

---

* Yupanqui – Inca title denoting royalty.

† Pastu – northern Ecuador.

‡ Surampalli – ancient capital of the Cañari people, later given the name of the emperor's panaca of Tumibamba. Site of the present-day Ecuadorian city of Cuenca.

§ The Emperor Huáscar's mother, the Coya Rahua Ocllo.

DON GARCÍA SUMA YUPANQUI, INCA: It is known to all the Indian people that Huayna Cápac was king and lord of these realms, from the lands of Chile to those of Pastu, and that all his laws and commands were obeyed by his subjects, for it is what I know and witnessed. And in my presence his daughter Doña Beatriz Yupanqui was born in Surampalli in the lands of Tumibamba, and to mark her birth many feasts were held. And I myself was present when Huayna Cápac acknowledged her as his daughter, which I heard him repeat many times; for I had accompanied him to Tumibamba from Cusco, and had served him there as a warrior in his wars. And from the day of her birth to the present time she has been honoured and obeyed by all the natives of these realms.

PASTAC, INDIAN OF CUSCO: It is as it is said that she was born in the lodgings at Surampalli and that she is the daughter of Huayna Cápac: for I witnessed her birth, because of which great feasting was ordered, being as she was the daughter of so great a lord and king, the feasting lasting for ten days and ten nights. And from that time to this very day she has been obeyed and revered because of her birth which I witnessed, having accompanied and served Huayna Cápac in his wars from this city of Cusco to his seat of Surampalli.*

DON DIEGO CAYO, INCA: Since her birth until the present time she has always been obeyed and respected, as I have always obeyed her and respected her.

MAZMA, INDIAN OF MAYO: I went with Huayna Cápac from this city to his seat of Surampalli at the time of the wars, in which I served the Inca; and there I witnessed her birth among the other daughters born to him at that season; and I was present when Huayna Cápac commanded Cariapasa to serve her and to

* The northern conquests of Huayna Cápac.

119

be her guardian; for Cariapasa was a warrior chief of many people. After the death of her mother I saw that she inherited her rank, and I have seen the Indians of all the regions and nations show her their obedience and respect as daughter of the lord and king.

DON JUAN APANGA, INCA: Being as she was the daughter of so great a king, great rejoicing was commanded at her birth, and I witnessed the warrior chief Cariapasa render her homage.

JUAN DE PANCORBO: I first saw her a few days after we Spaniards entered Cusco, and it was made known to me that she was the daughter of Huayna Cápac. And I saw then as I still do now that the Indians of these realms obey her and show her reverence.

DIEGO DE TRUJILLO: The Indians of this city of Cusco and of other regions show her their homage and obedience.

JUAN SERRA DE LEGUIZAMÓN: If it is known to them that in her house Doña Beatriz Yupanqui sheltered and raised several granddaughters of Huayna Cápac, among them the daughters of Manco Inca, the father of Sayri Túpac; because of which a great many calamities were averted at the time Manco Inca was in rebellion.

DON MARTÍN NAPTI YUPANQUI, INCA: I have seen her raise two daughters of Manco Inca, her brother, the one called Usezino and the other Ancacica.

FRANCISCO DE ILLESCAS: I saw two Indian princesses, who it was said were daughters of Manco Inca, living in her house, who at the time was in rebellion and in the Andes; and I also saw other relatives of hers, to whom she had given shelter in her house, being as she was such an important personage among the natives; and because of which many attacks by the rebel Indians were avoided. And it was she who informed Hernando Pizarro of Manco Inca's planned rebellion.

BERNABÉ PICÓN: I have known her since the year 1533, when the Marquis Don Francisco Pizarro, Governor of these realms, entered with the Spaniards this city of Cusco, and I have heard it said that she had living in her house some daughters of Manco Inca, who were her nieces, sisters of Sayri Túpac, who has since sworn fealty to the lord Viceroy; and that at the time that the Villaoma returned to the city from where the Adelantado Don Diego de Almagro had taken him on his way to the discovery of Chile, and from which he fled, I heard it said that it was she who informed her master Mansio Serra de Leguizamón, with whom she lived, that Villaoma had returned to take Manco Inca with him because he wished to escape from the city; and that it was Mansio Serra de Leguizamón who made this known to Hernando Pizarro, telling him that it was Doña Beatriz who had informed him of how Villaoma and Manco Inca planned to flee the city.

JUAN SERRA DE LEGUIZAMÓN: If it be known to them that the Licentiate Vaca de Castro, Governor of these realms, like all the other governors before and after him, attempted in every manner to entice the Inca Manco to make peace, and this they were not able to do because of the Inca's death; and that his son Sayri Túpac was his heir, and that he remained in the Andes with all the people and the warrior chiefs of his father.

DIEGO MARTÍN: On a number of occasions I witnessed various persons go to the Andes of Vilcabamba at the time of Don Diego de Almagro and of his son, and also during the governorship of Vaca de Castro, each attempting to persuade Manco Inca to leave there in peace; and among those I saw go there were Pedro de Oñate, Juan Gómez Malaver and the Captain Rui Díaz, and several others whose names I can no longer recall. I myself in the company of Sancho de Canda went there, and none of us was ever able to persuade him to leave, and his people would not let us see him, and only brought us word that he would not leave.

JUAN SERRA DE LEGUIZAMÓN: After the death of Manco Inca no Spaniard was able to enter Inca Sayri Túpac's domain other than Francisco de Pino, guardian of the sons of Don Paullu Inca, and then only with a safe-conduct and accompanied by Martín, the translator, at the time of the President Gasca. Neither was he able to achieve anything.

CHASCA, INDIAN WARRIOR: The Inca sent me and other chiefs of his to the President Gasca to tell him that he would come in peace, and to ask of him where he would live; and this witness and the other chiefs spoke to the president who told us that if he left there within three months he would give him the Indians that had belonged to Huayna Cápac and some houses and estates in Pomacorca in the valley of Písac and lands in Mayo, in this valley called Guancaro. And I told the Inca of what the president had ordered me to say, and the Inca was then about to leave with all his people but for one captain of his, who was a Christian, who told him that he was too young, and that he should not leave until he was much older, and for that reason he did not leave.*

BERNABÉ PICÓN: Francisco de Pino told me in person that if they offered him the whole of Peru he would never return there.

JUAN SERRA DE LEGUIZAMÓN: The Lord Viceroy the Marquis of Cañete sent many persons to the Andes to persuade Sayri Túpac to leave there in peace, and no one wished to go there except for two friars of Santo Domingo and Juan de Betanzos, the translator; but no one was allowed to enter there other than myself.

---

* This Christian captain was possibly a renegade Spaniard and supporter of the defeated Gonzalo Pizarro.

JUAN DE PANCORBO: I saw Juan de Betanzos leave the city for the reason given, and it is commonly known he was not allowed to enter Vilcabamba to see the Inca. I myself at another time left this city with a number of horsemen as a reprisal against the Indians of Sayri Túpac, who had killed several Negroes and burnt farmhouses, and carried out other attacks on the road near the Apurímac River. And I rode on to one of the landmarks of the region that was snowbound, and where I learnt that Sayri Túpac had some eight hundred warriors at his command, and that the attack on the farmhouses we saw had been made by two hundred of his warriors, who were well armed; and having no commission from the justices of the city I had no recourse but to return to the road, where I remained there in guard for several days.

JUAN SERRA DE LEGUIZAMÓN: I was involved in the treaties and negotiations with the Lord Viceroy and the Inca, and I came and went three times to the viceroy, until after much persuasion on my part I was able to bring the Inca from there in peace, together with his warrior chiefs and lords: because of which the roads and regions of that part of the Andes are now tranquil and free from war.

FRANCISCO DE VILLAFUERTE: What I know of this is that I saw Juan Serra de Leguizamón pass the door of my house and he told me that he was going into the Andes to bring Sayri Túpac out from there in peace.

PAUCAR YUPANQUI, INCA: As a warrior in the service of the Inca Sayri Túpac, in his company I witnessed him enter Vilcabamba, and as he was his first cousin the Inca received him well, and also out of respect to his mother Doña Beatriz Yupanqui, his aunt. And he was accompanied by the friar Melchor. And I heard him say to Sayri Túpac that if he left Vilcabamba the Viceroy the Marquis of Cañete would give him many Indians and lands for his people and many clothes and other goods, so that he would be content; and all this he told him many times and in my presence, and I also heard him say the same to his warrior chiefs. I further witnessed him take part in the treaty and discussions with Sayri Túpac; and the Inca sent him twice to the Lord Marquis with regard to his leaving Vilcabamba, and he came twice to see the Inca, bringing with him payment and presents.

DON MARTÍN NAPTI YUPANQUI, INCA: On a number of occasions I heard Sayri Túpac say after he left the tambo* of Vilcas where I had gone from this city, that it was his cousin who had brought him there in peace; and this is known to me because I raised Sayri Túpac when he was a young child and because I saw Juan Serra de Leguizamón go to the City of the Kings, and then return to where the Inca was, bringing with him dispatches and safe-conducts for him to leave in peace.

DIEGO MARTÍN: I know of this because on the road to Vilcas I came across Sayri Túpac, coming with a great number of Indians, and accompanying them was Diego Hernández,† encomendero of this city, and Juan Serra de Leguizamón.

DIEGO DE TRUJILLO: It is publicly known that Diego Hernández, encomendero of Cusco, and Juan Serra de Leguizamón brought the Inca out of Vilcabamba in peace and took him to meet the Lord Viceroy, and I witnessed them afterwards enter this city of Cusco, where I reside. And that since that time the roads and farm lands of the region have been safe from attack.

JUAN DE PANCORBO: I witnessed Juan Serra de Leguizamón walking about this city in the company of Sayri Túpac, who showed him great love.

---

*   Tambo – Inca fortress, stockade.
†   Diego Hernández Escobar – Doña Beatriz's husband.

JUAN SERRA DE LEGUIZAMÓN: If it is known to them that I am the natural son of Doña Beatriz Yupanqui and of Mansio Serra de Leguizamón, and as such I am held by all those who know me, and that I was born before either of my parents were married. And that I am at present married by the rites of our Holy Mother Church to Doña María Ramírez. And that my father Mansio Serra de Leguizamón is a hidalgo and a person of great distinction, and one of the first conquistadores of this kingdom, who by his deeds and actions has always revered Your Royal Majesty. And if it be known to them that I only possess a small village of Indians, called Písac, which has an annual income of some three to four hundred pesos of silver, because of which I live in great poverty and need, dependent as I am on the kindness of my father and mother to feed and care for me. And that when Sayri Túpac met with the Viceroy, he believed as I did that I would be rewarded; something which my cousin begged him on a number of occasions.

PASTAC, INDIAN OF CUSCO: It is known to me he is the son of Doña Beatriz Yupanqui, daughter of Huayna Cápac, because I was in this city of Cusco when she gave birth to him; and from that time to the present I have always seen him live in her house. And it is also known to me that Mansio Serra de Leguizamón is his father. And being as I am an old man, I have known his father for a great many years.

FRANCISCO DE ILLESCAS: This is so, for I have known him since the day he was born. And his father I hold for a hidalgo, and as such he was held and known in the township of Pinto in the kingdoms of Spain, where he was born.

ALONSO DE MESA: I have known his father Mansio Serra de Leguizamón for more than thirty years, and also his relatives, and I have known him as a conquistador whom the Marquis Don Francisco Pizarro rewarded with an encomienda of Indians, and that he has served Your Majesty in the siege of this city by the

Indians and in the rebellions of this realm. And I know that if it were not for the assistance given him by his parents he would not be able to maintain himself or his family, for his village of Písac is of little merit.

DON DIEGO CAYO, INCA: I have seen him live a married life with his wife Doña María Ramírez, for I know that they were married by the rites of the Holy Church in the City of the Kings at Lima.

DIEGO DE TRUJILLO: It is known to me and witnessed by me that he lives in great poverty with his mother, and that the Indians he possesses are few in number and equally poor, and the rent they give him may well be what he says. And I have seen him mostly in his mother Doña Beatriz's house, and it is there that he eats and drinks and sustains himself.

FRANCISCO DE VILLAFUERTE: I know him to possess a small encomienda at Písac that was given to him by the Viceroy the Marquis of Cañete, and which has few Indians. I have also seen him in prison, in the jail at Cusco, for being unable to pay a debt of seventy pesos.

THIRTEEN

The Bride of Santa Clara

All that evening at Cusco the bells tolled. In the darkness of her cell at the convent of Santa Clara, the young daughter of the dead Inca Sayri Túpac imagined the sound to be announcing the birth of some great emperor or lord. In fact the bells were to mark the capture of a young man she had never known, who was being brought under guard from the forests of the Andes. Only later would she learn that he was her uncle.

She was fourteen years old and had spent more than half her life in the convent, having been taken there by her mother, the Inca Princess Doña María, at the age of five. Her crime – for the little girl believed she must have offended grievously in some way to warrant so many years of confinement – had never been made known to her. Occasionally her mother and her Spanish stepfather, a man regarded by his own people as of little worth, were allowed to speak to her in the visitors' gallery, and on certain days she was given permission to play in the convent's small garden, enclosed within the quadrangle of cloisters erected by the first abbess, Doña Francisca Ortíz. The convent stood on a site once occupied by part of the mansion of the conquistador Alonso Díaz, who had been hanged for his part in the encomendero Girón's rebellion.[1]

The girl was never to see her uncle, nor witness his entry into the city that day, but the townspeople flocked into the streets to watch as column after column of armed Spaniards made their way through the northern Carmenca gate, which had been decorated with flowers. Among them were elderly veterans of the Conquest, dressed in their antiquated armour and morrión helmets, their heraldic pennons held aloft by their Indian caciques, and line after line of armed soldiers led by the city's clergy, Augustinians, Dominicans

127

and Mercederians, in their distinctive black, white and brown habits. Behind them marched the 1,500 Indian auxiliaries of the elderly Inca Prince Cayo, dressed in Spanish breeches and velvet doublet, and finally, enthusiastically applauded by the townsfolk, came the young captain of the Viceroy's guard who had captured the Inca, and now led his prisoner along by a gold chain attached to his neck. Several eyewitnesses recall that as Loyola approached the Viceroy Don Francisco de Toledo's balcony he gestured to the Inca to remove his headdress and bow his head; when the young man refused, Loyola struck him several times in the face.

Thirty-eight years later Baltasar de Ocampo, one of the Spanish conscripts in the Vilcabamba expeditionary army, wrote a description of the Inca's execution at Cusco, based on the eyewitness account given him by a Mercederian friar:

> The Inca was dressed in a mantle and doublet of crimson velvet. His shoes were made of wool of the country, of several colours. The crown or headdress called mascapaicha was on his head with a fringe over his forehead, this being the royal insignia of the Inca.
>
> After His Excellency the Viceroy had savoured his conquest, he ordered that the Inca and his chieftains be taken to the fortress which is in the parish of San Cristóbal, of Colcampata . . . at the end of two or three days, after being taught and catechized, Túpac Amaru was baptised.
>
> He was then taken from the fortress through the public streets of the city with a guard of four hundred Cañaris armed with lances . . . accompanied by the priests Alonso de Barzana, of the Company of Jesus, and by Father Molina, one on either side of him . . . the open spaces, roofs and windows in the parishes of Carmenca and San Cristóbal were so crowded with spectators that if an orange had been thrown down it could not have reached the ground anywhere, so closely were the people packed.
>
> As the executioner, who was a Cañari Indian, brought out his knife with which he was to behead the Inca, an extraordinary occurrence took place. The whole crowd of natives raised such a cry of grief that it seemed as if the Day of Judgement had come,

and all those of the Spanish race did not fail to show their feelings by shedding tears of grief and pain. When the Inca beheld the scene, he only raised his right hand on high and let it fall. With a noble mind he alone remained calm, and all the noise was followed by a silence so profound that no living soul moved, either among those who were in the square or among those at a distance.

The Bishop of Popayán, the Provincial of the Order of Merced, the Prior of the Order of San Agustín, the Prior of Santo Domingo, the Provincial of San Francisco, the Rector of the Company of Jesus . . . all went to the Viceroy. They went down on their knees and besought him to show mercy and spare the life of the Inca. They urged he should be sent to Spain to be judged by the king in person. But no prayers could prevail with the Viceroy.

Juan de Soto, chief officer of the court, was sent on horseback with a lance to clear the way, galloping furiously and riding down all kinds of people. He ordered the Inca's head to be cut off at once in the name of the Viceroy . . . the executioner then came forward and, taking the hair in his left hand, he severed the head with a knife at one blow, and held it high for all to see. As the head was severed the bells of the cathedral began to ring, followed by those of all the monasteries and parish churches in the city . . . when the head was cut off it was put on a pole and set up on the same scaffold in the great square . . . there it became each day more beautiful . . . and the Indians came by night to worship the head of their Inca.[2]

The Inca Túpac Amaru was just twenty-eight years old. As he walked to his death on that September morning, a Spaniard recalled that his sister the Princess Doña María, witnessing the spectacle from the window of a house, cried out to him: 'Where are they taking you, my brother, prince and sole king of Tahuantinsuyo?'[3] The soldier Ocampo's informant was also to recall that several nights after the execution the Princess Doña Beatriz's young grandson Don Juan Serra de Leguizamón, having woken at dawn, gazed down from his bedroom window and witnessed thousands of Indians kneeling as they worshipped the bloody remains of his cousin.[4]

A few weeks later a messenger from the Viceroy Toledo arrived at the convent door, requesting the abbess to prepare the young Indian novice for her betrothal, which, she was informed, would take place that night in his presence in the mansion of the encomendero Diego de Silva. Still wearing her native clothes, the girl was hurriedly escorted by two nuns to the mansion, where she was informed of the identity of the man she was to marry. Accompanied by her mother and her stepfather, who had been obliged to attend the ceremony, she made her way to the small private chapel of the mansion, where the Viceroy and her future husband awaited her. Within the hour the Princess Doña Beatriz Clara was betrothed to the Knight of Calatrava Martín García de Loyola, great-nephew of St Ignatius Loyola, the founder of the Jesuit Order – and the captor of her dead uncle. That evening she returned to the convent, where she would remain for a further eighteen years.

In a letter to King Philip II the Viceroy Toledo informed him that Loyola, who was then in his early thirties, had agreed to marry the princess, 'even though she was an Indian and still wore her native dress, in order to serve the Crown'.[5] No one in the Council of the Indies who read the Viceroy's dispatch when it arrived in Madrid was in any doubt as to the motive of the young guardsman, or of the patronage he enjoyed. A subsequent dispatch from Peru informed the Council of Toledo's allocation to Loyola of all the princess's encomiendas and lands in the rich Yucay valley, north of Cusco, which the Crown had held in trust for her since the death of her father, the Inca Sayri Túpac.

Two years after their betrothal Loyola returned to Spain for a brief visit, during which period he obtained from the king an annual pension, adding to his already vast income. He also asked permission to amend the Loyola coat-of-arms, depicting two wolves holding a cauldron, to incorporate a decapitated head, but this request was turned down. Five years later he was appointed governor of the city of Potosí.

Whether Loyola's reluctance to consummate his union with the young princess was due to his probable homosexuality or to his aversion to marrying an Indian will never be known. But such a union was anyway impossible for a very long period of time because of the return to Peru of the man who claimed to be her lawful husband. The mestizo Cristóbal Maldonado, a nephew of Peru's wealthiest encomendero, had been exiled from the colony for several years for his part in an abortive rebellion. Now he not only declared Loyola's betrothal illegal, and any such marriage as bigamy, but claimed from him all the revenues he had received from the princess's dowry. Loyola's enemies added to the problem by appealing to an ecclesiastical court on Maldonado's behalf. In his declaration before its tribunal, Maldonado disclosed that at the age of seven the princess had been removed from the convent of Santa Clara by her mother, and that she had lived with him as his mistress for almost two years – but that he had also married her. He also informed the court that the princess's mother had at the time been his brother's mistress, and that she had borne him two illegitimate daughters. The revelations continued on a daily basis, adding ever greater notoriety to the scandal.

During the years of the trial Doña Beatriz Clara was kept a virtual prisoner at Santa Clara, for fear that one party or other would abduct her. The revenues of her vast wealth meanwhile continued to be collected by Loyola's agents, who denied her any share of the money; mostly in gold and silver pesos, it was paid twice yearly by her Indian vassals.

In 1591 the long-disputed trial was finally resolved in Loyola's favour. By the time of their marriage later that year Doña Beatriz Clara was thirty-three years old but she knew little more of the world than the walls of her convent. The following year the princess left Cusco never to return and joined her husband in the colony of Chile, where he had been appointed governor-general. At the township of Concepción she gave birth to their only child, Doña Ana María. Not long afterwards Loyola met his death leading an expedition of reprisal against the Araucanian Indians. Within a few weeks the princess left the governorship for Lima, where she lived with one of her sisters until her death two years later.

The marriage of her daughter to a descendant of St Francis de Borja was commemorated by Peru's Jesuits in a series of paintings depicting St Ignatius Loyola, her husband's famous ancestor. Loyola, who had suffered the same fate as the princess's uncle twenty-six years previously, would make one final appearance on history's stage: when the Araucanian Indians eventually surrendered to the Spanish authorities, they brought with them his skull, which they had kept as a trophy.

In Doña Beatriz Clara's will, dated 3 March 1600, she left her entire fortune and all her possessions to her daughter. Among the items listed were her three Negro slaves and her jewellery 'of gold chains, pearls, rubies and diamonds'; these she ordered to be retrieved from Cusco's pawnbrokers, where they had been taken by her husband.[6] The Viceroy Don García Hurtado de Mendoza, himself a former Governor of Chile, left a rather unflattering description of Loyola, with the words: 'he was a fine merchant, but miserly, and certainly not a soldier'.[7]

FOURTEEN

The Lost Treasure

On 24 July 1911, almost 340 years after the burning of the Inca city of Vilcabamba by the Viceroy Don Francisco de Toledo's army of conquest, a tall and lanky American history professor, dressed in jodhpurs and wearing a battered fedora, gradually clambered up through the dense sub-tropical undergrowth that covered the razor-sharp cliffs of an Andean mountain ridge, a thousand feet or so above a dirt road 60 miles north-west of Cusco. His purpose was to discover Vilcabamba's location, and to this end he was armed with the accounts of several chroniclers, principally that of the seventeenth-century Augustinian friar Antonio de la Calancha y Benavides, who had left a description of the region in his history of his Order. Though the Viceroy Toledo had later founded a city with the same name, the actual site of the 'Lost City of the Incas' that was burnt to the ground by the conquistadores had been swallowed up over the centuries by the dense undergrowth, though its treasures and fame lived on in the legends and stories of the Andes.

The American was accompanied by two men, a Peruvian army sergeant and the owner of a local bar, who had told him about some stone buildings he had seen near a small plot of land he owned. As they climbed, the two Peruvians began moving at a faster pace, their machetes hacking a path for the American, who, against their advice, had brought along a cumbersome camera and tripod, which only added to the weight of the packs they carried. Descending again, they entered the canyon of the fast-flowing River Urubamba, and crossed its bridge of logs. At about noon they reached a hut belonging to an Indian peasant family, who worked for the bar owner as wood cutters. The American noted in his diary that it was 12.07 p.m., and that the Indians invited them to a meal of sweet potatoes.

After they had eaten it was decided that the bar owner would remain behind in the hut, and that the young son of the family would accompany the American and the army sergeant. They walked on for a while in silence, following a long path hidden by forest, until they came across what appeared to be a rocky promontory sticking out of the undergrowth. It was then the American realized they were actually standing on a flight of stone terraces, beyond which he could see the outline of finely cut stone buildings. Some distance away, perched above the mountain canyons, bathed in a low hanging mist, was the ruined city of Machu Picchu. It was perhaps the single greatest archaeological discovery of the twentieth century.[1]

As he gazed in awe at the ruins, thirty-year-old Hiram Bingham believed he was looking at the lost city of Vilcabamba, but in fact he had discovered an Inca temple city of far greater antiquity: Machu Picchu. Ironically, 24 July was also the birthday of the liberator Simón Bolívar, the study of whose military campaigns had first brought Bingham to the Andes.

Only in recent years have archaeologists established the probable location of Vilcabamba at Espíritu Pampa, a sub-tropical valley in the neighbouring region of the Andes, to the west of Machu Picchu. Astonishingly, no single Spanish chronicler or contemporary Inca witness ever made any reference to the existence of this temple city, which lay not far from either Vilcabamba or Cusco; nor was its identification made any easier by the fact that the city's original name remains unknown. It was given the name Machu Picchu, meaning the old mountain, by Bingham's companions.

In all probability Machu Picchu was built a hundred years before the Conquest, in the reign of the Emperor Huayna Cápac's father Pachacuti, and remained in the possession of his panaca after his death.[2] Contemporary colonial records show that the land in the vicinity of the city was known to the conquistadores, as an encomienda here was granted by Pizarro to his brother Hernando; this encomienda, which included a township also called Vilcabamba, was later awarded to the Inca collaborator Paullu in 1539.

It seems very unlikely that Manco Inca, who had fled into the region during Cusco's occupation by Atahualpa's generals and had constructed Vilcabamba as a fortress refuge, could have been unaware of Machu Picchu's existence. Nor does it seem credible that so sacred a temple site would have remained unknown to his sons and successors. It is more than likely that it was still being used as a temple and place of worship in the early years of the Conquest, and that its treasure was secretly removed either by the Incas themselves or by any one of the conquistadores who held encomiendas in the region; their Indians would have undoubtedly informed them of its existence, in order to win favour. Certainly Hernando Pizarro, the principal encomendero of the province, would have had no qualms about looting the city and then taking his secret to the grave, thus evading payment of the Crown's tax on treasures.

Few of the great Inca treasures were ever declared to the Crown by the conquistadores. Gold had been the primary purpose of their conquest and it would remain so over many years. The lake of Urcos, south-east of Cusco, had been repeatedly searched for the giant gold chain in the shape of a snake, which the Emperor Huayna Cápac had ordered to be made to mark the birth of his son Huáscar. The chain was known to have been used during religious festivals at Cusco and had stretched the entire length of the city's square. The Inca war huaca known as the Muru Urco, a square stone of great size that once stood in Cusco's main square, encased in gold and emeralds, had also never been found. Nor had the undoubted treasures of the Inca temple at Copacabana at Lake Titicaca, which had probably been thrown into its waters.

One of the commanders of the 1572 sacking of Vilcabamba was the historian Pedro Sarmiento de Gamboa, regarded by the Viceroy Toledo as the most learned man he had met in the Indies. He appeared to be convinced of the existence of a city of great riches in the Andes, built by one of the sons of the Emperor Huayna Cápac. Whether his information was based on some particular evidence or was the result of necromancy – for which practice he had been imprisoned on two separate occasions by Lima's Church authorities

– will never be known. Fourteen years later, while en route to Spain, he was captured by an English corsair and taken prisoner to London, where he was granted an audience with Queen Elizabeth I. In his later testimonial to the Spanish Crown he recalled that he spoke to her in Latin, and she, at the behest of Sir Walter Raleigh, ordered his release.[3]

Raleigh acquired a great deal of knowledge about Peru from Sarmiento de Gamboa, and this influenced his misguided search for the legendary Inca kingdom of El Dorado and his exploration of Guyana, the name of which was a misspelling of the Emperor Huayna Cápac's name. If any Spaniard was aware of the existence of Machu Picchu it would have been Sarmiento de Gamboa, for he had spent a considerable period of time in Vilcabamba and its surrounding region, and also led the main interrogation of the Inca witnesses to the Viceroy Toledo's enquiry at Cusco and in the neighbouring valley of the Yucay.

Another possible reference to a treasure in the Andes is found in a letter written by the Princess Doña Beatriz's grandson Don Juan Serra de Leguizamón, the Governor of the Yucay, who as a young boy had witnessed the execution of his father's cousin the Inca Túpac Amaru. He wrote to King Philip III's chief minister, the Duke of Lerma, in Madrid:

Your Excellency, Our Lord and King is greatly served, due to the honour shown me by certain Indian elders because of my ancestry, I have been informed by them that they will show me the location of the great treasure of the Incas, hidden near Cusco, the fruits of which I wish His Majesty to be the first to enjoy; and for this reason I am sending the Reverend friar Antonio Martínez, my companion, who is also aware of the treasure's existence, to inform His Majesty of this in person, and which I plan to find. May God grant Your Excellency good health. And with regard to my petitions of my past service, I hope Your Excellency will show them favour and justice, at Cusco, April 15 1614, I kiss Your Excellency's hands. Signed. Don Juan Serra de Leguizamón.[4]

At the bottom of the document the Friar Martínez added the words: 'This letter was written by Juan Serra de Leguizamón at Písac in his house and in my presence, though it is postmarked Cusco.'

Whether Juan Serra de Leguizamón had invented this 'great treasure' simply to further his petitions to the Spanish court, or whether he later decided to keep for himself what the Indians had shown him, remains a mystery. What is evident is that the Augustinian Friar Martínez was left ignorant of the matter, as his later correspondence with King Philip III shows:

Some years ago I went from Cusco to Spain on behalf of Don Juan Serra de Leguizamón, encomendero of Cusco, to give Your Majesty an account of the greatest treasures of the World, for as such they are described by him in the letters I enclose; assisting him also in sending him the various royal decrees he had asked for; and as Your Majesty saw that he did not comply with what he had professed, Your Majesty gave me permission to return to Peru. On my arrival at Cusco, on three occasions, and without any other's company, he again assured me of the truth of everything he had told me, and that it was only a question of time before he would discover the treasure. However, seeing that he did nothing, I wrote to the Viceroy the Prince of Esquilache, requesting that he summon both of us before his presence, and as he did nothing either, I wrote to the Royal Chancery of Lima, who in the presence of the Viceroy read my letter; and as a result he ordered that we both appear before him. I, for my part, made the journey. Don Juan fled to the mountains and there hid in various churches, and as he did not come to Lima, several royal mandates were ordered for him to comply with the summons.[5]

But Juan Serra de Leguizamón never complied with the Viceroy's summons. Other than a few bequests he later made to the convent of Santa Catalina at Cusco, nothing more is recorded of his life. We shall never know if he ever saw the riches he claimed to have discovered, or if they truly existed; if they did, is it possible that they had ever formed part of the great treasure of Machu Picchu or Vilcabamba?

FIFTEEN

The Sacristan of Córdoba

The mestizo Garcilaso de la Vega is referred to more than any other chronicler in the early history of colonial Peru, and his writing was to influence much of Europe's later conception of the New World, giving birth to Rousseau's romantic image of the 'noble savage'. He was born at Cusco in 1539, the illegitimate son of an Estremaduran conquistador and the Inca Princess Doña Isabel, a niece of the Emperor Huayna Cápac. Brought up in his father's house in the city, together with his cousin Juan Serra de Leguizamón and other mestizo sons of the conquistadores, he attended the small school opened at Cusco in 1552 by the Canon Juan de Cuéllar, a native of Medina del Campo. So proud was the canon of his charges, Garcilaso recalled years later, that he wished he could have sent each of them to the University of Salamanca.

For most of his life, however, Garcilaso would suffer the stigma of his mixed blood. 'The children of Spaniards and Indians are called mestizos,' he wrote in his old age, 'which is to say we are of mixed race, and the term [was] invented by the early Spaniards who had children by Indians; and as it was a name given us by our fathers I was proud to call myself as such . . . though now in the Indies it is regarded as a term of inferiority.'[1] It was, however, the humiliation of seeing his mother reduced almost to the role of a servant by his father's wife that most influenced his desire to leave Peru.

Garcilaso's father, a former Governor of Cusco, was one of the richest encomenderos of Peru. He died in 1558 and in his will he left his son 'four thousand pesos of gold and silver, so that he may travel to Castile for his studies', adding, 'this I desire because of the love I have for him as he is my natural son, and as such I name and acknowledge him'.[2] The following year Garcilaso, now aged nineteen, left Cusco for Spain; he was never to return.

138

The early years of his Spanish exile were cruel and disappointing. Having failed to persuade the Council of the Indies to award him a pension, he was completely reliant on the charity of his father's relatives, few of whom were willing to see him, and on his talent for breaking and schooling horses, which for a while brought him a small income. He joined the army of Don Juan of Austria and took part in the fighting against the Morisco uprising in Andalusia, and then settled in the township of Montilla (later moving on to Córdoba), and dedicated himself to the study of literature and the chronicles that had been published about the New World. Far removed from his homeland, the former pupil of Canon Cuéllar's small school at Cusco wrote one of the greatest narrative histories of the Americas, *Comentarios Reales de los Incas, Historia General del Perú*, which would influence thinking about Inca civilization for centuries to come.

Though at times unreliable in anything that might detract from his projection of a heroic and almost utopian Inca society – he denied, for instance, the Inca practice of human sacrifice – his history nevertheless presents an epic account of a people, their religion and customs in a prose style unequalled by any of Peru's chroniclers.

Much of what he wrote was based on the stories and legends he had heard as a child from his mother's relatives, and from what he had himself observed during his adolescence among the conquistadores, whose homes he frequented. One of his more lasting errors, which was followed by numerous historians, was his portrayal of Hernando de Soto and Pedro del Barco as the first conquistadores to enter Cusco before its capture; carried into the city in hammocks, and marvelling at the treasures of the city, they were treated by the Incas as gods. This story was invented by del Barco's orphaned mestizo son, Garcilaso's boyhood companion, who later repeated the story in his testimonial to the Crown, perhaps in an attempt to glorify his father's role in the Conquest. The elder del Barco, who was not even at Cajamarca at the time, makes no such claim in his own testimonial.[3] Contemporary chroniclers who also believed the story included Agustín de Zárate, whose account of the history of Peru was read and approved by King Philip II during his voyage to England to marry Queen Mary Tudor; in the following year this account was published in the Netherlands.

In 1603 Garcilaso was presented with one of the more painful requests he was to receive over the years from his royal kinsmen in Cusco. They had also written to his mestizo cousins Alonso de Mesa and Don Melchor Carlos Inca, both of whom lived at the time in Valladolid. The young Melchor Carlos was the grandson of the Inca Paullu, the most prominent Inca collaborator with the Spaniards. His father, Don Carlos Inca, had inherited not only Paullu's extensive encomiendas but also his palace of Colcampata above Cusco, and to further his status he had married the daughter of a Spaniard. The family's fortune, however, had been virtually lost after Don Melchor Carlos's supposed involvement with a mestizo rebellion at Cusco.

It was soon after Melchor Carlos's arrival in Spain that Garcilaso received their kinsmen's request to present their petition on their behalf to the king, 'enclosing with their letter to all three of us [Garcilaso, Melchor Carlos and Alonso de Mesa] their pedigrees and royal descent, together with a family tree painted on white silk . . . and with the portraits of their sovereign ancestors'.[4]

Garcilaso adds that he sent the petition and accompanying papers to Melchor Carlos, 'but he was unwilling to present the papers so as not to reveal how many persons there were of royal blood, thinking that if he did so, it would prejudice his own claims'.[5] In truth, there was little any of them could have done to alleviate the suffering and hardship faced by their kinsmen, whose privileges and right to exemption from servitude had been discarded, and some of whom were publicly flogged in Cusco for refusing to work as bondsmen.

Garcilaso's own mother, defrauded by the Spanish husband she had later married, had died leaving the little that remained of her possessions to her daughter Ana, the wife of Garcilaso's cousin Martín de Bustinza, the youngest son of the Princess Doña Beatriz.

Don Melchor Carlos died seven years later in a monastery guest-house at Alcalá de Henares, Cervantes's birthplace. He was thirty-nine years old. In his will he records that his household consisted of nine servants, a slave and a dwarf.

One of Garcilaso's later sources for the writing of his history was the elderly soldier of fortune Gonzalo Silvestre, who had taken part in Hernando de Soto's disastrous expedition into the southern United States. His entry into Garcilaso's adopted Andalusian township of Montilla, where he had first lived during his Spanish exile, was described by one of its inhabitants: 'An obese and swollen old man, nursing his venereal disease and drawn in a cart by a lumbering ox. An aged crone, touched by his sight, came out to enquire as to the source of his misery, and on being informed, directed him to the neighbouring township of Las Posadas, where in the spring of each year a plant could be found to alleviate his affliction, and where he was to settle.'[6]

In 1605 Garcilaso's account of Soto's conquest of Florida, *La Florida del Inca*, was published, and four years later the first part of his history of the Andes, *Comentarios Reales de los Incas*, was released, seven years before his death at Córdoba in 1616 at the age of seventy-seven. He bequeathed a small legacy to the chapel dedicated to the Holy Souls of Purgatory in the city's cathedral mosque. He had served in the cathedral as a sacristan, and his remains were buried here. In his will he left his Negro slave Marina de Córdoba an annuity of 50 ducats and a mandate for her freedom. To his own illegitimate son he left the remainder of his belongings.[7]

To the end he remained ignorant of the universal fame the history of his mother's people would bring him, and he would surely never have imagined that some three centuries after his death his ashes would be brought back to the city of his birth by his sovereign's descendant King Juan Carlos of Spain, to be buried in state at Cusco's church of el Triunfo.

SIXTEEN

The Last of the Conquistadores

Two years after the defeat of the Spanish Armada the last witness of the Inca Empire of Peru died at Cusco in the first days of the year 1590.[1] In the preamble to his will and testament he left the only known apologia for the empire's conquest and subsequent destruction, addressing his words to his sovereign King Philip II. The conquistador Mansio Serra de Leguizamón had been born in 1515, the same year as St Teresa of Ávila, and at the age of fourteen he had left his widowed mother and set out to make his fortune in the Indies, initially serving as a page in the conquest of Veragua in Nicaragua. Four years later he accompanied Diego de Almagro's cavalry to Cajamarca.

For several months before his death he had lain bedridden at his mansion in Cusco, which was built on the foundations of the Inca palace of Yacha Huasi; it would later be known as the House of the Serpents because of the giant sculpted snakes supporting his coat-of-arms above the portico. The Jesuit chronicler Bernabé Cobo recorded that several huaca stones, some of them bearing emblems of snakes (denoting wisdom, and the fact that the palace had been used as a schoolhouse by the Inca nobles in pre-Colombian times), formed part of the mansion's masonry. Built some ten years after the Conquest, the house was one of the few buildings to survive the earthquake that demolished most of Cusco in 1650. Its story was not always a happy one. From one corner upper window Gonzalo Pizarro's commander Francisco de Carbajal had hanged María Calderón, the wife of the astrologer Jerónimo de Villegas, for slandering him.

Mansio Serra de Leguizamón was born in his mother's native Castilian township of Pinto, south of Madrid, although his family was from Vizcaya, where they served as one of the *parientes mayores*, the thirty-five seigneurial families that governed its *fueros*, which the Kings of Spain traditionally swore to uphold at Guernica.[2] The Victorian writer Richard Ford, who travelled widely across the province, described the Vizcayan people as obsessed by their independence and their lineage: '[Their] armorial shields, as large as the pride of their owners, are sculptured over the portals of their houses, and contain more quarterings than there are chairs in the drawing rooms or eatables in the larder . . . well did Don Quijote know how to annoy a Vizcayan by telling him he was no gentleman.'[3]

According to the fifteenth-century Spanish chronicler and genealogist Lope García de Salazar, the Leguizamón family were descended from Álvar Fáñez de Minaya, a cousin of Rodrigo Díaz de Vivar, known to history and legend by his Moorish title el Cid, the Lord, whose name would embellish the ballads of the Middle Ages and inspire the epic *Poema de Mio Cid*. Salazar wrote:

> Of the lineage of Álvar Fáñez de Minaya, cousin of the Cid of Vivar, succeeded a knight who came to settle the lands known as Leguizamón, and there founded the House of Leguizamón the old many years before Bilbao was populated, and from father to son was succeeded by Diego Pérez de Leguizamón, a fine knight and held as the noblest of his name, who bore for arms horizontal bars as borne by the said Álvar Fáñez de Minaya in his sepulchre at San Pedro de Gumiel de Hízan where he is buried, and which this lineage bears, and who in turn was succeeded by Sancho Díaz de Leguizamón who was killed in the vega of Granada.[4]

It was a lineage the old soldier displayed proudly, not only in the coat-of-arms awarded him by the Emperor Charles V, which surmounted the portal of his mansion in Cusco, but also in the woven tapestries he had commissioned from Seville: these depicted the Cross of Calatrava of Serra, the three bars of the Leguizamón, and the gold chains and crowned head of the Villaoma, the Inca High Priest of the Sun, whom he had taken prisoner so many years before.

The most remarkable aspect of Leguizamón's character is shown by the attitude he demonstrated in his later years towards the Indians of his encomienda, and by the restitution he offered them in both of his wills: an act few European colonists would even contemplate. A small number of other conquistadores were also to make certain restitutions to their Indians, and there is little reason to deny their sincerity, even if such sentiments were influenced by the prospect of impending death and the prompting of their confessors. Many made no such gestures. Nor did any of the later encomenderos, who were responsible for much greater exploitation and ill-treatment of the Indians of their encomiendas.

In his first will, written several years before his death, when he was virtually destitute because of his gambling debts, Mansio Serra de Leguizamón ordered his executors to return to his Indian vassals almost all of the produce and livestock of his encomienda, which by right should have been inherited by his children:

> I declare that the produce and inheritance of my encomienda at Alca* belongs to the Indians of its encomienda because it was they who planted it, and they who built its hacienda, because of which it is theirs and they are to keep and own it, as it was once their own. I declare that all the horse mares, goats, Castilian sheep, belong to the Indians of my encomienda . . . and this I give them so that it be distributed among them . . . I declare that I have received over the years in tribute from my Indians some 50,000 pesos of gold, and it is what I owe them.[5]

Old age had calmed the old conquistador, and for solace he had turned to religion and one of the city's confraternities. His wife had been dead thirty years. In the fifteen years of their marriage she had borne him two daughters and five sons. The eldest of their children was Doña María, who had been born at Cusco in the closing years

---

* Alca – an encomienda in the Cuntisuyo province of Arequipa, site of the present-day town of Alca de Hontiveros.

of Gonzalo Pizarro's rebellion; at the age of eleven she had been placed in the city's Franciscan convent of Santa Clara, located in the same square as her parents' mansion, then known as Santa Clara la vieja. Founded in 1550, this was the first such institution in Peru, and here the young Princess Doña Beatriz Clara spent much of her life. The first abbess had charge of twenty-four nuns of Spanish parentage, twelve mestizas and forty creole girl students who were educated until they reached marriageable age. Among the founding nuns were the daughters and granddaughters of the conquistadores Bernabé Picón and Francisco de Villafuerte.

In defiance of her parents Doña María chose to enter the convent's novitiate. Her action led to a lengthy dispute between her father and the nuns, but eventually he was forced to donate to the convent a dowry of jewels and vestments, valued at 2,000 pesos of gold, together with 700 cattle for the convent's farms. His refusal to give any further donations on behalf of his daughter may explain the wording of much of the Franciscan chronicler Diego de Mendoza's account of the young novice:

> Among the glories of this life was Sister María de Leguizamón, one of the twenty-four founding nuns of this convent, daughter of the valorous conquistador Mansio Serra de Leguizamón and of his wife Doña Lucía, encomenderos of Cusco, who were well known in this realm for their nobility and wealth, and who at the age of eleven left the home of her parents, and fleeing from there, and from the vanities of the world, entered the convent of Santa Clara . . . and from where not all the influence of her parents would make her leave; neither by enticements nor promises; until they disinherited her, denying her their refuge and her maintenance . . . yet at so tender an age she commended herself to God . . . and the more her parents denied her vocation the more she accepted her spiritual sisters as her family . . . bringing her from the confusion and captivity of Babylon to the doors of Sion.[6]

Taking the name of Sister María of the Visitation, Doña María was to become one of the most prominent figures in Cusco, devoting much of her life to the care of Indians in the native hospital of the city, and eventually she was elected Abbess of Santa Clara. In his history the friar Mendoza refers to her many demonstrations of sanctity and mortifications. At her death, at the age of sixty, he recalls that a choir of angels was heard singing Vespers in the chapel of the convent, and that some days later she appeared to one of the nuns. Four years after her death, when the convent was transferred to its present site, the friar described how her coffin was opened and her body was found to be incorrupted; he added that the nuns wanted to place her remains in a smaller coffin to be taken for burial in their new church; in order to do so they broke her legs, and 'blood flowed freely from the wounds'.

The maternal grandfather of Leguizamón's legitimate children, the conquistador Gómez de Mazuelas, had been one of the wealthiest encomenderos of Cusco, outliving his companion Gonzalo Pizarro. A letter he sent to Gonzalo shortly after his daughter's marriage demonstrates the troubled relationship between him and his new son-in-law, who had abandoned his bride for the gaming tables of Lima – having lost the Inca gold figure of the sun in a night of gambling after the sacking of Cusco, he could well be regarded as the patron saint of gamblers:

My Illustrious lord, by other letters I have sent you and which you have not answered, I have already informed your excellency of the events that have taken place here [in Cusco]. In this letter I will only touch on what has wasted me away, with the little that I possess, which is ever at your excellency's disposal and service . . . as your excellency is aware, Mansio Serra de Leguizamón, encomendero of this city, married my daughter; I would have imagined he would have best served your excellency in this city or in the domain of his encomienda, and if he be there, and that be the case, I breathe freely in accepting his departure . . . however, as I know him to be so obsessed with this business of his gambling, I believe he has gone to that city [of Lima] which offers him greater opportunity to be among people of that persuasion; yet not content in merely gambling what he possesses and what he does not possess, he has sold the dwelling of his mansion in this city, which has caused us all here a great deal of trouble, and being informed of this, my daughter, his wife, has petitioned the justices of this city for the tribute he receives from his Indians . . . the justices, nevertheless, have informed me that your excellency has ordered that the tribute be sent to Lima. If your excellency has no need of it for your service, I beg it be sent to his wife, even if it be only for her food and sustenance. And this I beg as your servant, for other than it being just, I will also receive some mercy. Our lord, most illustrious excellency, may health and prosperity be yours, whose illustrious hands I kiss.[7]

Mazuelas's ability to survive the purges against the former Gonzalist rebels is evident in his later appointment by the Crown as an alderman of Cusco, an office he held for life. His testimonial records that in 1550 he sent to Spain 2,000 pesos of gold for the construction of a church in his native village of Valdetorres, near Medellín.[8] It also records the lengthy interrogation of several witnesses in the village to prove his father's hidalgo lineage. Some confirmed his nobility, others simply said he was an Old Christian and nothing more. In his old age Mazuelas, a widower, like so many other conquistadores fell victim to a marriage with a young Spanish adventuress. Doña María Arias Castillejo was the sister of Cusco's cathedral dean, and shortly after his death she married a much younger man, Martín de Olmos, who eventually inherited Mazuelas's encomiendas at both Cusco and in the region of La Paz.

Few records survive of the conquistador's other children. His son Jerónimo also entered the religious life in the Dominican monastery of Santo Domingo at Cusco, built on the foundations of the Inca temple of Coricancha. Perhaps his decision was influenced by the fact that his mother Doña Lucía had been buried there. The licentiate Cepeda sent a letter to King Philip II from the city of La Plata, dated 14 February 1585, enclosing a missive from the Jesuit Alonso de Barzana: 'In order to comply with my office in approving the native speech of the Indians among the clergy who reside within this Bishopric of Charcas, I can testify that the

Reverend Father Jerónimo de Leguizamón, curate of the parish of San Pedro de Potosí, speaks with great propriety the quéchua language.'[9] Ten years later Jerónimo was elected prior of the monastery of Santo Domingo in Huamanga.

Only two of the conquistador's legitimate children married. His eldest son Mansio, heir to his encomienda of Alca, married Doña Francisca de Cabezuelas against his wishes, as he recorded in a letter in 1586, two years after his son's death:

> I wish to place as a matter of record to His Majesty the King and to the Mayors of this city of Cusco, that my eldest son, Mansio Serra de Leguizamón, abandoned my house against my will and against all reason, being though a person of much quality and intelligence . . . and that the Archbishop of Lima seeing the disorder and inequality of the marriage my son proposed, imprisoned him for his own good, but on his release he went to the city of Arequipa and there married all the same.[10]

Whatever the reason, the conquistador strongly disapproved of the marriage, and because of it he disinherited his son and spent years in litigation fighting the demands of his granddaughters, the eventual heirs to his encomienda. His younger son Francisco, whom he had twice sent to Spain at the cost of 10,000 pesos of gold to seek a reward for his services from the king, would equally disappoint the old conquistador by his marriage to a young woman from Seville, who could neither read nor write, and whose claim to hidalgo nobility was only verified by several illiterate witnesses, one of whom described her as 'fair haired, with aquiline features and a mole on the right side of her face'.[11] His mestizo son Don Juan, whose mother was the Princess Doña Beatriz, had been dead some twenty years, leaving the old man with two grandchildren, Don Juan and the nun Doña Bernardina, both of whom were present at his death.

Ghosts and memories were all that now remained to the old man. He remembered his youth in Castile, and his crossing of the Atlantic; his exploits in Nicaragua and Cajamarca; the killings, and the tortures he had himself endured; he conjured up images of war and of love, orphaned faces and voices, all now lost for ever in the silence of old age. Finally, in the darkness of his bedchamber, its walls hung with the armour and arms he had worn as a young man, the elderly conquistador breathed his last. He was seventy-five years old, and the last of the conquistadores of Peru.

The Will

I, the Captain Mansio Serra de Leguizamón, encomendero of this great city of Cusco, capital of these realms of Peru, and the first who entered it in the time of its conquest: being as I am infirm and bedridden yet of sound mind, judgement and memory, and fearful of death as is natural, and which comes when one least expects it, authorize and let it be known that I make this my last will and testament of my own free volition, listing its legacies and codicils in the following order:

Firstly, for the peace of my soul and before beginning my testament I declare that for many years now I have desired to address the Catholic Majesty of Don Felipe, our lord, knowing how Catholic and Most Christian he is, and zealous for the service of God, Our Lord, seeing that I took part in the name of the Crown in the discovery, conquest and settlement of these kingdoms when we deprived those who were the lords Incas, who had ruled them as their own. And it should be known to His Most Catholic Majesty that we found these realms in such order that there was not a thief, nor a vicious man, nor an adulteress, nor were there fallen women admitted among them, nor were they an immoral people, being content and honest in their labour. And that their lands, forests, mines, pastures, dwellings and all kinds of produce were regulated and distributed among them in such a manner that each person possessed his own property without any other seizing or occupying it. And that nor were lawsuits known in respect of such things, and that neither their wars, of which there were many, interfered with the commerce and agriculture of their people. All things, from the greatest to the smallest, had their place and order. And that the Incas were feared, obeyed and respected by their subjects as being very capable and skilled in their rule, as were their governors.

149

And as we were to dispossess them of their authority in order to subjugate them in the service of God, Our Lord, and take from them their lands and place them under the protection of Your Crown, it was necessary to deprive them entirely of any command over their goods and lands which we seized by force of arms. And as God, Our Lord, had permitted this, it was possible to subjugate this kingdom of so great a multitude of peoples and riches, even though we Spaniards were so few in number, and to make their lords our servants and subjects, as is known.

I wish Your Catholic Majesty to understand that the motive that moves me to make this statement is the peace of my conscience and because of the guilt I share. For we have destroyed by our evil behaviour such a government as was enjoyed by these natives. They were so free from the committal of crimes and exorbitance, both men and women, that the Indian who possessed one hundred thousand pesos worth of gold or silver in his house left it open by merely placing a small stick across the door, as a sign he was out. And according to their custom no one could enter nor take anything that was there. And when they saw we put locks and keys on our doors they imagined it was from fear of them that they might not kill us, but not because they believed anyone would steal the property of another. So that when they discovered we had thieves among us, and men who sought to force their wives and daughters to commit sin with them, they despised us.

But now they have come to such a pass in offence of God, owing to the bad example we have set them in all things, that these natives from doing no evil have changed into people who now do no good, or very little; something which must touch Your Majesty's conscience as it does mine, as one of the first conquistadores and discoverers, and something that requires to be remedied. For now those who were once obeyed as kings and lords of these realms, as Incas with power and riches, have fallen to such poverty and necessity that they are the poorest of this kingdom and forced to perform the lowest and most menial of tasks, as porters of our goods and servants of our houses and as sweepers of our streets. And in accordance with the Viceroy Don Francisco de Toledo's order, exempting them from such service if they acquired a trade, some of them are now shoe-makers and work in similar such lowly occupations.

And because many such things are permitted it is necessary for Your Majesty to be made aware of this for the sake of his conscience, and of the conscience of those who are guilty of such offences. I inform Your Majesty that there is no more I can do to alleviate these injustices other than by my words, in which I beg God to pardon me, for I am moved to say this, seeing that I am the last to die of the conquistadores and discoverers, as is well known, and that there is no one left but myself, in this kingdom or out of it. And now I have unburdened my conscience of this, I declare and order my will and testament in the following order:

Firstly, I wish to offer my soul to God, Our Lord, who gave it life and who replenished it through His Passion and with His Most Precious Blood, and order that my body be placed in the earth from where it was formed.

I order my body be buried in the convent of San Agustín of this city, in the chapel of the Brotherhood of San Nicolás and Santa Lucía, and that my executors conform to this and donate to the convent a sum apart from the one thousand pesos of gold I have already donated for the offering of Masses for my soul, and which I order they adhere and comply with.

I order my body be buried in the habit of San Agustín and that it be clothed in an old habit of one of the friars, and that a new habit be paid for and given him.

I order on the day of my burial all the priests of the city offer a Mass for my soul, and that the Council of the Holy Church accompany my body, together with all the confraternities of which I am a member, with four religious from each of the monasteries; and that they all offer Masses for my soul, and that their expenses be paid.

I order a further two hundred Masses be offered for my soul, a hundred in San Nicolás de Tolentino and the other hundred as a requiem, and that the expenses of these be also paid.

I order that when my body be interred a stone monument be placed with my coat-of-arms and with a large cross, and that a lighted taper be hung over it in perpetuity, and that it will also be the burial place of my heirs.

I order fifty Masses be offered for the conversion of the natives of this realm.

I order twenty Masses be said for the souls of those for whom I have been responsible, and for those who are unknown to me.

I order the said Masses to be said in the monastery of San Agustín, and that fifty of the Masses be said in the monastery of Santo Domingo, and that all the expenses be paid.

I order thirty pieces of eight be given to the poor of the hospital of the natives of this city.

I order the caciques, Indians and community of Alca, my encomienda, be neither asked for nor pay any tribute during the Feast of San Juan to that of Christmas at the end of the year, and I relieve them of this obligation.

I declare that at the time of Cajamarca and of the distribution of treasures among the conquistadores that I, as one of them, was awarded two thousand pesos of gold, and that in the distribution in Cusco, some eight thousand pesos, more or less. And that I was given the figure of the sun which was of gold and kept by the Incas in the house of the Sun, which is now the monastery of Santo Domingo and where they practised their idolatry, which I believe was worth some two thousand pesos; all of which being some twelve thousand pesos of gold. And I wish my executors to record this sum for the peace of my conscience and to pay this exact sum from my estate.

I declare the doctor Alegría treated me in my house for almost a year, even though for short periods of time, and I order his heirs be paid whatever my executors deem fit.

I order if any debts of mine by deed be made known they be paid, and that if anyone will swear I owe him even ten pesos he be also paid.

I declare the lawyer Galín de Robles owes me one thousand pieces of eight I lent him.

I order that what is owed me by the Governor of Cuntisuyo, in which province my encomienda is situated, be collected from him, for I believe he is still in debt to me for my having overpaid him for the evangelization at Alca and Potosí, and what he already owed me in the past.

I declare that at the time my daughter Doña María de Leguizamón entered the convent of Santa Clara of this city, my wife and I bequeathed her with many jewels and finery, and later some seven hundred cattle, all of the greatest value and worth some two thousand pesos of gold; this I record so that the said convent will make no further demands on my estate.

I declare that Gómez de Mazuelas, my father-in-law, made a gift to his grandchildren, my children, of twelve cows and a bull, and that I myself gave them cows and bulls for the purpose of breeding, and that I paid for their maintenance; and that of these cattle, part were gifted to the convent of Santa Clara because of the said Doña María, my daughter, and part to the monastery of Santo Domingo, where my son Jerónimo de Leguizamón was a friar. And that a part was also given to Mansio Serra de Leguizamón, my eldest son, together with other cattle I gave him. I record this so it be understood that their estate has received more than enough, and that the said Mansio received from me some two thousand pesos until his death, and that I provided for him and for his wife and children from the time of his marriage, which is some twenty years, so that his heirs be denied any further claim to my estate; for they have already received more than they were entitled.

I declare my landed estates comprise of my house of abode and the other houses surrounding it, to the value of some eight thousand pesos of gold, more or less; some lands and fields of alfalfa in the valley of Tubembaque; in the township of Alca in my encomienda several houses, plantations and lands; and in the valley of this city and in that of Huanacauri a small estate for the breeding of goats and the manufacture of timber wood.

I declare I own five bars of gold, three large and two of medium size, marked and stamped, that I believe are worth some three thousand pesos and which I order be taken and deposited in the monastery of San Agustín, where they are to be kept safe until they be divided among my heirs.

I declare I own in silver a large decorated urn and a smaller one, a serving dish and two bottles, also thirteen small plates and two jars, three spoons, a chamber pot, three salt-cellars, a candelabra, a figure of the Saviour, all in silver, which I also entrust to the care of the Reverend Friar Juan Pacheco, Prior of the monastery of San Agustín.

I declare I am still owed the tribute of my Indians of Alca, which is their payment for the Feast of San Juan of this year.

I declare I own a tapestry, trunks, chairs, tables, beds, linen, a jewel case, a Negress, a horse, a coat-of-mail, a sword, a helmet of steel, and much other furniture and furnishings.

I declare that a year after my death the slave Filipa, in the service of my daughter Doña Petronila de Leguizamón, shall be granted her freedom in perpetuity, and this I order by deed.

I order Juan Fernández, mulatto, who has served me for many years, be given two hundred pieces of eight.

I declare that for the time she has served me Francisca Montañesca be given from my estate one hundred and fifty pieces of eight.

I declare Doña Paula de Leguizamón is my natural daughter, whom I recognise as such and who lives in my house, and order she be given two thousand pieces of eight from my estate for her welfare.

I declare that in the time of my youth I had a natural son Don Juan Serra de Leguizamón, now deceased, whose mother was Doña Beatriz Manco Cápac, youngest daughter of Huayna Cápac, once king of these realms, and that I provided for his marriage and household, and that the Viceroy of those times the Marquis of Cañete awarded him the encomienda of the valley of Písac, for being my son and for having brought his cousin Diego Sayri Inca from the mountain of Vilcabamba. And that the Indians of the said encomienda now enjoy the lordship of Juan Serra de Leguizamón, my grandson, his son, and help in the maintenance of Doña Bernardina de Leguizamón, his sister and legitimate daughter of my son, who are my grandchildren. I beg them to pardon me, as I beg Your Catholic Majesty because of my past service to reward them in their lifetime, and this I ask humbly of so Catholic a king and lord.

I declare my legitimate children from my marriage to Doña Lucía de Mazuelas, now deceased, to be Francisco Serra de Leguizamón, Doña Petronila de Leguizamón, Pablo Serra de Leguizamón, and Miguel de Leguizamón, all unmarried. And the said Doña María de Leguizamón, who is a nun, and Jerónimo de Leguizamón, Dominican friar, and Mansio Serra de Leguizamón, my eldest son, who has been dead now many years and married against my orders and wishes; leaving three legitimate children, the eldest of whom, Doña Lucía, succeeds her father in accordance with the laws of our lord the king as my heir to the encomienda of Alca. And that regardless of my present state of poverty she has brought a lawsuit against me, and knowing as I do she will never look after my other children I have no recourse but to plead my past service to the Crown for their benefit.

This I now plead in this hour of my death, as one of the discoverers and conquistadores of these realms whose service was of great value in those early days when we were lost in the hands of the natives, and much later at the time of their rebellions, as is well known; and who through his diligence and actions contributed to the pacification of this kingdom, and for which in that first year of the conquest I was granted by the Marquis Don Francisco Pizarro the encomienda of Alca; and that the province of Catanga and Callanga, being the richest in the realm and which he also granted me, he later found necessary to take from me and award to Paullu Inca, as successor of the Incas and lords of this realm, for siding against his brothers and family in the pacification of this kingdom. And that neither I, nor my children, have ever benefited from its surrender which I made for the good of the realm. And because of it I have been left poor with only the town of Alca of my province of Cuntisuyo, with which I have maintained my children, and from which income I helped pay towards the wars between the Spaniards, even though my province was on three occasions taken from me for my loyalty to Your Majesty, and of which the traitors enjoyed the tributes. So I have been forced to place one daughter in a convent, and the other, yet unmarried, in my house; for neither can I leave them or my other legitimate children enough to feed them for a year.

Thus, I humbly beg His Royal Catholic Majesty the King Don Felipe, our lord, to take into his consideration my legitimate children, whom I name as my universal heirs. And exclude from my estate my son Francisco, whom on two occasions I have sent to Spain with expenses of ten thousand pesos in gold, and Mansio, my eldest son. And this I approve and ratify in the hope Your Majesty will consider these children of so loyal a vassal, who for the benefit of the Crown surrendered his provinces and who was never to benefit from the rewards of his efforts; this I beg Your Majesty for the peace of his conscience.

I name as my executors the Reverend friar the Prior of San Agustín, Don Bernardino de Lozada and Pablo Serra de Leguizamón, my legitimate son, whom I give full power to sell or keep whatever goods for the compliance of this my will. And I declare it be my wish that the house of my abode be not sold by my executors and that my said children live there for the rest of their lives, and without anyone depriving them of that right.

And by this will I make null and void a previous will I authorized before Antonio Sánchez, public notary, and any other testaments and agreements, either verbal or written; and that only this be recognized, written on nine pages, including this one, the first two in one hand, and the other six, and this page, in another, and I wish they be recognized as my last will and testament . . . and this I authorize before the public notary and witnesses in this city of Cusco, in this my dwelling where I lie bedridden, this Eighteenth day of September, in the year of Our Lord, Fifteen Hundred and Eighty Nine.[12]

SEVENTEEN

The Torture of Doña Catalina

The screams could be heard for over an hour coming from the city's jail. It was dark by the time they stopped, and only a woman's sobbing came from the small barred window that looked out on the street. The crowd of Indians and Spaniards who had assembled outside the jail could be seen in small groups, discussing the events of that day late into the night. Only a few of them had seen the Licentiate Paredes enter the jail with his prisoners and armed guards earlier that morning. Some said the young woman had been interrogated beforehand in her own house, others that she had also been tortured there first. But no one really knew the truth; only that her screams began to be heard shortly after ten o'clock that night.

The crime the 26-year-old Doña Catalina de Urbina and her husband Gregorio de Gamarra had been accused of committing, and for which the Viceroy Don Francisco de Toledo had been instrumental in ordering their torture had been the secret discovery, as recorded by several witnesses, of a huaca of Inca treasure. The elderly conquistador Alonso de Mesa recalled that 'it was said Gamarra had taken a certain treasure from a huaca, and that when the Licentiate Paredes, who had been accompanied by the Bishop, came to Cusco, he ordered the arrest of Gamarra and his wife, and he instructed that she be tortured by several Negroes, without the least respect for her, being one of the principal ladies of this city'.

Another witness, Antonio Marchena, stated that

the Licentiate Paredes at first had held Doña Catalina prisoner in a small and darkened room in her house, not allowing her to speak to anyone, and eight days later, when her husband Gamarra

157

returned to the city, he also had him arrested and put in irons, in a separate room of the house. And then he once more began his interrogation with great rigour, and ordering their torture, and the arrest and torture of many of their friends and servants. Among these were some elderly Indians, some of whom died from sheer terror, and one of whom, a young pregnant woman, miscarried her child and later died in the hospital of the natives. And after everything that happened the Licentiate Paredes freed Gamarra and his wife from the public jail, declaring that he had not been able to find any proof of their guilt, but in order to pay for his own salary and that of his guards he ordered that all their possessions, slaves and haciendas be sold; and because of this Doña Catalina has remained poor all her life, and with one of her arms crippled. . . .

The sad fate and poverty of Doña Catalina is recorded in an unpublished manuscript in the Archive of the Indies, and forms part of a testimonial she made to the Crown almost a quarter of a century later in 1602. This reveals that her mother, Doña Teresa de Mazuelas, was the illegitimate daughter of the conquistador Gómez de Mazuelas and of an unnamed woman.* Her grandfather had been one of the wealthiest encomenderos of Cusco and of the Collasuyo of Bolivia, numbering some 'thirty repartimientos',† among them Gonzalo Pizarro's former encomienda of Puno and the lands on which most of the city of La Paz today stands – all of which, because of the laws of inheritance, on his death had become the property of his widow, Doña María Arias, and eventually of her second husband, the Captain Martín de Olmos.

I, Doña Catalina de Urbina, widow of the Licentiate Gregorio de Gamarra,' she declared in her evidence, 'record that the Captain

---

* It is more than likely because of the date of Doña Teresa's birth that her mother was one of the Inca princesses Mazuelas and several other conquistadores were recorded to have raped during the imprisonment of Manco Inca.
† Repartimientos – distributions of Indians and encomienda lands.

Gómez de Mazuelas, my grandfather, was one of the discoverers and conquistadores of the Island of Hispaniola and of the province of Tierra Firme. And that from there he passed to Peru in the company of the Marquis Don Francisco Pizarro, and that he was also a conquistador and settler of these provinces. And being a valiant soldier he was charged with many missions, in which he served Your Majesty with his arms, horses and servants, and in reward of which the Marquis awarded him thirty repartimientos of Indians in the region of Cusco, of which he was made alderman for life.

And that Diego de Urbina, my father, was a later conquistador of Peru. He was a soldier of great courage and zealous in the service of Your Majesty. And at the time of the rebellion of Francisco Hernández Girón against the Crown he gathered about him many relatives and friends under the royal standard. He was later captured by the rebels and garrotted. His house was sacked and he was robbed of all his silver, jewels and valuables that belonged to him and his wife. My father was the nephew of the Captain Diego de Urbina, Maestro de Campo of the royal army that fought against Gonzalo Pizarro, and in which he was wounded by a shot of an harquebus, and from which he later died. He was the brother of Juan de Urbina, Maestro de Campo of the Emperor's army.[*]

And that Gregorio de Gamarra, my husband, served for more than twelve years in the army of the Adelantado Pedro Meléndez de Valdés and also in His Majesty King Philip's service in Flanders and in England, and also in the conquest and settlement of the provinces of Florida, and in the war against the French Lutherans who had settled there. And on the pacification of that land he went to Cartagena at the time the English pirate Francisco Draque [Sir Francis Drake] wished to sack the city, and he was one of those who fought in its defence, and because of which the pirate could not enter its walls. . . .[1]

[*] Juan de Urbina served as an infantry captain in the army of the Emperor Charles V in Italy. He came to Peru in the service of the Viceroy Don Blasco Núñez Vela in 1544, accompanied by his brother and nephew.

EIGHTEEN

The Bishop's Legacy

On 1 August 1619 a small caravan of horses and mules, in company with several wagons and escorted by outriders, could be seen making its way across the mountains to the city of Arequipa, its whitewashed buildings, monasteries and churches lying at the foot of the snow-capped volcano of the Misti. On that morning His Grace the Friar Bishop Don Pedro de Perea y Díez de Medina finally entered his see and formally took possession of the newest of all the bishoprics of the Indies of Peru.[1] Aged sixty-three, and worn down by the years of political intrigue that had robbed him of the great episcopates of Spain, he was a scholarly and austere figure. His only known work was a treatise supporting the contention of the Immaculate Conception, which he dedicated to the theologian Agustín Antolínez, Archbishop of Santiago de Compostela.

The Friar Bishop's talents, so greatly admired in his youth at the University of Pavia and in Rome, meant nothing to the men who greeted him in Arequipa's council chamber – but he would soon earn their distrust and condemnation by his high-handed and authoritarian manner, notably in a dispute concerning the building of his cathedral church. The king himself was forced to intervene in this matter. In a letter to King Philip IV dated 30 March 1622, the Friar Bishop wrote: 'I once more beg Your Majesty to give me your permission to leave Arequipa as soon as possible, for I truly fear for my life.'[2]

Among the presbyters who had supported the Friar Bishop was the Andalusian Miguel Pérez Romero, whom he appointed to administer his diocese when he was later forced to travel to the viceregal capital at Lima to face the censure of both the Viceroy and the colony's archbishop. The relationship had been further strengthened by the subsequent marriage of Romero's daughter to the bishop's nephew Don Pablo Díez de Medina, a hidalgo and lawyer from Briones, in the Rioja of Old Castile.

On 28 May 1630 the Friar Bishop died at Lima. His will shows that he left much of his considerable fortune to the Augustinian convent at Burgos and to the church at Briones for the founding of a chapel. Here his sculptured features can still be seen under a grill awning of his coat-of-arms, bearing ten Moors' heads and the title name of his family. This was awarded to his ancestor for killing single-handed ten Moors in the medina, or citadel, of the castle of Tíscar, during the reconquest of Andalusia.[3]

Shortly before the Friar Bishop's death a valuable manuscript had come into his possession. Aware of its antiquity and historical interest, he entrusted it to the care of his fellow Augustinian Antonio de la Calancha y Benavides, who had written a preface to his book on the Immaculate Conception, printed in Lima a year previously by the publisher Jerónimo de Contreras.* A Creole from the city of La Plata, Calancha had spent several years researching Inca history and traditions, together with his Order's missionary role in Peru. The manuscript he now received from the Friar Bishop was the last will and testament of the conquistador Mansio Serra de Leguizamón, the grandfather of the presbyter Romero's wife. Calancha included the preamble to the will in his history *Corónica Moralizada del Ordén de San Agustín en el Perú*, published in Barcelona in 1638, but erroneously attributed the will to a 'Mancio Sierra Lejesema' – an error that was later copied by the nineteenth-century American historian William Prescott, author of *The History of the Conquest of Peru*.

A curious development is recorded in another manuscript, dated 1631. It is signed by the conquistador's youngest son, and in it he appoints the bishop's nephew Don Pablo Díez de Medina and his wife as the heirs of his father:

* *De Immaculate Virginis Mariae conceptionis certitudine*, Lima, 1629.

I, Miguel Serra de Leguizamón, resident of this township, legitimate son of the Captain Mansio Serra de Leguizamón and of Doña Lucía de Mazuelas, his wife, both deceased, being as I am the legal heir of my father, of his goods and rights, and his only surviving son; and that having retired to this township of Alca,* where I have lived for almost thirty years now, I have been cared for and looked after by Miguel Pérez Romero, the husband of my niece Doña María de Leguizamón, daughter of my eldest brother Mansio, and also with equal kindness by Don Pablo Díez de Medina, the husband of my niece's daughter and heir, Doña Lucía Romero de Leguizamón, with whom I at present live. And in appreciation of their kindness by this instrument of inheritance I bestow on them, their children and successors, all my rights and legacies, being as I am the sole and last heir of the said Captain Mansio Serra de Leguizamón.[4]

This document was later sent to King Philip IV as part of a petition made by Don Pablo Díez de Medina in the name of his wife, describing the poverty to which she had been reduced, and pleading for recompense in respect of her great-grandfather's past service to the Crown.[5] The king duly awarded Don Pablo the governorship of the province of Parinacochas (where the Nazca lines are located), and a few years later granted him the wealthy governorship of Larecaja, near the city of La Paz. Here his descendants in due course built the Díez de Medina Palace, one of the finest eighteenth-century mestizo rococo buildings in the Americas, which today houses Bolivia's National Museum of Art.[6]

One of Don Pablo's descendants was Don Francisco Tadeo Díez de Medina, who was responsible for the completion of the Díez de Medina Palace in 1775. A bachelor and lawyer, for thirteen years he presided as one of Chile's Chief Justices at Santiago, assuming interim control of the government there on several occasions. His

---

* Alca – the township of the conquistador's encomienda, which by the laws of succession of encomiendas had by then reverted to the Crown.

name is, however, most widely remembered for his infamous sentencing of the Indian rebel leader Túpac Catari and his followers, who besieged the city of La Paz for a year in 1781. The diary he wrote of the day-to-day events of the siege is now preserved in the Archive of the Indies at Seville. He died in Santiago in 1803.

Another of Don Pablo's descendants was Don Clemente Díez de Medina. A school companion of Simón Bolívar in Madrid and a former Guards officer and aide-de-camp to General Ricardos during the siege of Roussillon, on his return from Spain he enlisted in the liberator San Martín's army of the Andes at Buenos Aires and commanded a squadron of mounted grenadiers at the battles of Maipu and Ayacucho, which brought to an end Spanish rule in Andean America. His cousin Don Crispín Díez de Medina, who had been involved in a failed uprising in La Paz in 1809, was imprisoned for several years by the Spanish authorities in the Falkland Islands.

NINETEEN

The Imperial City

In all the chronicles of the Indies no other city symbolizes more dramatically than Potosí the fabulous wealth of the New World. Even the renowned sixteenth-century Jesuit missionary Matteo Ricci included it in his map of the world commissioned by the emperors of China.

Potosí's fame derived from a mountain lying in the foothills of the Andes. Known as the Cerro Rico, the rich mountain, for almost a century it was to supply half the world's silver – enough, it was said, to build a bridge of solid silver to the very gates of Seville. Rising to some 2,000 feet, the mountain had once been a huaca, an Inca magic site, and several chroniclers record that it was visited by the Emperor Huayna Cápac during his conquest of the southern provinces of the Charcas. Its silver was made known to the Spaniards by an Indian named Hualpa in 1545; in his will he recorded that he had been sent to its summit by four Spanish soldiers at the time of Gonzalo Pizarro's rebellion. At the top he found a native shrine, and discovered that pure silver ran in the mountain's veins.

By 1611 the city that had developed at the foot of the mountain boasted some 160,000 inhabitants – by far the largest population of any city in the Americas and most of the capitals of Europe. The Emperor Charles V was to award it the title 'Imperial' and his own coat-of-arms, and his son Philip II would later add to its royal arms the motto: 'For the Powerful Emperor, for the wise King, this lofty mountain shall conquer the world.'

Men and women from every region of Spain and the Indies crossed the cordillera of the Andes to reach Potosí's windswept and desolate landscape. Some eighty churches were built in the city, among them San Lorenzo, one of the finest examples of Spanish

164

colonial architecture in the Americas. Miguel de Cervantes, creator of Don Quijote, who would many years later fail to secure an appointment as governor of the Andean city of La Paz, described Potosí as 'a sanctuary for bandits, a safeguard for assassins, a cloak and mask for card sharpers, the aspiration of courtesans, the common disappointment of many, and the special remedy of a few'.[1]

Duelling and tourneys became fashionable among the rich miners. Eight fencing schools were opened. The city's chronicler Bartolomé Arzáns de Orúa y Vela records that some students wore red ermine taffeta shirts so that the blood from their wounds would not be noticeable, while others put on chain mail or metal breastplates, and 'some fought with pistols, they fought on horseback, on their knees or any other position'.[2] In one of its tourneys, Arzáns recalled, 'in the street of the Mercedarians Don Estebán de Luna, a Creole of Potosí, made his entry, armed and mounted on a black horse, its bridle of gold chains and pearls; on his helmet he wore a crest of a gold serpent, its eyes adorned with rubies, with blue and yellow ostrich plumes, in his right arm he held his lance, in his other his shield emblazoned with his arms of a single moon, and the motto: "Not even the sun shall eclipse me" . . . then entered the square Don Severino Colón, citizen of Potosí, and great-grandson of Don Cristóbal Colón,* who gave the New World to Spain, his crest a giant globe of the world'.

The patronage of Potosí's wealthy miners also helped to create one of colonial America's finest periods of baroque mestizo architecture and painting, influencing both the La Paz and Cusco regions. Splendid stone carvings adorn the façades of the city's minting house, Casa de la Moneda, and the Church of San Lorenzo, sculpted by the Indian Juan de la Cruz. The city's painters were equally prominent in the decoration of its sanctuaries, among them the Creole Melchor Pérez Holguín, who depicted the Viceroy Archbishop Morcillo de Auñon's entry into the city in 1716, and the Indian Luis Niño, who sent several of his paintings to Europe.

---

* The Spanish spelling of Columbus.

An earlier Indian artist who was drawn to Potosí was Tito Yupanqui. He came from the hamlet of Copacabana, on the south-eastern shore of Lake Titicaca. While working as an apprentice to one of the city's artists in about 1582, he is credited with carving an image of the Virgin, which was later venerated in the Augustinian sanctuary built at Copacabana. The history of this sanctuary was recorded in the early seventeenth century by the friar Ramos Gavilán in his work *Historia del celebre santuario de Nuestra Señora de Copacabana*.

But it was the glorious paintings of an anonymous artist known only as the Master of Calamarca that were the most original and stylish of all Potosí's religious works, and his style was imitated throughout the Cusco and Bolivian Andean region.[3] He takes his name from the small village of Calamarca, some 28 miles from the city of La Paz; this was founded by Pedro de la Gasca to celebrate the end of Gonzalo Pizarro's rebellion, and initially it served as a staging post for travellers and merchandise between Cusco and Potosí.

The paintings in the small church at Calamarca, where the Master's best work is to be found, show a series of angels, depicted in their distinctive Orders and Choirs in all the finery of seventeenth-century Spanish court dress, some of them armed with rifles or holding musical instruments. They include the Seraphim, the spirits of adoration, symbolized by the fiery red of love; the Cherubim, the angels of wisdom, portrayed with the blue wings of knowledge; the Thrones, the angels of majesty, spirits of contemplation and justice, depicted with emerald-coloured wings and fiery aureoles, each bearing a throne in one hand. Also shown are the Dominions, Virtues and Powers, governors and regents of the stars and elements of nature, with their orbs and sceptres of office, and the Principalities, Archangels and Angels, carrying various wands, swords, rifles or lilies. Most glorious, though, are the seven Archangels of the Presence, depicted in all their glory: the armoured Michael, the warrior Viceroy of Heaven who defeated the fallen Lucifer; Gabriel, the angel of the Annunciation, holding a lily, the symbol of the Virgin; Raphael, the angel healer of the Book of

Tobit, with a casket of ointment; Uriel, the angel who stood at the gate of the lost Eden, his open hand surmounted by a flame; Chamuel, the angel of Gethsemane, holding a sacred chalice; Jophiel, the angel who drove Adam and Eve from Paradise, symbolized by a fiery sword; and Zadkiel, the angel of mercy, who stayed the hand of Abraham and whose emblem is a knife.

These beautiful paintings formed part of a wider Christian iconography evident throughout the Andean region, often intermingled with the indigenous emblems of nature, whose deities the Indians continued to venerate, adapting their own interpretation of the religion of their conquerors in the stone carvings of their churches, where Christ and the Virgin are synonymous with the Inca Sun and Moon.

By the end of the sixteenth century the Imperial City possessed more churches than any other city in the Americas – but it also boasted thirty-six gambling houses, where some eight hundred professional gamblers and prostitutes plied their trades. Arzáns recalled Potosí's celebrations to mark the Feast of Corpus Christi, describing how its miners lavished their new-found wealth on 'fountains sprouting the finest European wines, the men with chains of gold around their necks, and their dark-skinned mestizo and Indian women wearing slippers tied with strings of silk and pearls, their hair adorned with rubies and precious stones'.[4] And as a final demonstration of their allegiance to their God 'they would cover the streets with bars of solid silver, from one end to another'.

Goods of every type were to be found in the city's markets: 'embroidery of silk, gold and silver from France, tapestries and mirrors from Flanders, religious paintings from Rome, crystal and glass from Venice, vanilla and cocoa from the Caribbean islands and pearls from Panama'. Portuguese traders also brought illicit merchandise across the selvas and cordillera of the Andes from the Brazilian port of Rio de Janeiro, whose golden beaches they named in honour of Potosí's Church of the Virgin of Copacabana.

Describing another of Potosí's religious festivals Arzáns wrote that the city's nobility, numbering thirty counts of Castile, 'were to form themselves into bands of men and women, wearing their costumes, with jewels and plumes and waving flags, and just to wrench these flags from one another they knifed and killed each other, leaving more than a hundred dead, men and women'.

The Dominican Domingo de Santo Tomás, in his interview with the Council of the Indies, was to refer to the Cerro Rico as 'a mouth of hell consuming thousands of innocent Indians'.[5] He was not far wrong. The Viceroy Don Francisco de Toledo in 1572 assigned 95,000 Indians to the Cerro Rico's mines to labour as mitimae, working for one year. Their vast numbers darkened the foot of the mountain, as in their thousands they made the daily ascent into its caverns. Only seven out of every ten Indian miners would survive this immense labyrinth of human suffering, consoled only by their addiction to coca; such hard labour left young miners with the broken and haggard features of old men, but the silver they produced dominated the largely agricultural economy of the southern Andes.

Working by candlelight day and night the Indian miners with their pickaxes and wooden ladders extracted the silver which was then taken by mule to the Casa de la Moneda. In a room with stone floors and cedar wood walls, mules turned the giant wheels that converted the stream of raw metal into bars and coins, one-fifth of which was put aside for the Crown and transported to the Pacific harbour of Arica. It was then carried by small barques to Lima's port of Callao, from where caravels took it to Panama, a journey of fifteen days. Loaded onto hundreds of mules, it was then carried overland across the isthmus to the Atlantic port of Nombre de Dios, from where great galleons sailed with it to Havana, linking up with the treasure fleets from Mexico before finally crossing the Atlantic to the Andalusian port of San Lúcar de Barrameda and Seville's Casa de la Contratación.

The wealth of Potosí's miners was legendary. In 1699 Antonio López de Quiroga died leaving a fortune in excess of one hundred million pesos of silver. Referring to the thousands of peasant immigrants and impoverished hidalgos and nobles from Spain who travelled halfway across the world to reach the Imperial City, Arzáns remarked that 'a person who would never have been able to possess in his lifetime 100 pesos of silver, would within time spend that sum on a single meal in the city'.[6]

The Augustinian chronicler Antonio de la Calancha, who for some years lived and preached in the city, and who was an adept of astrology, recorded that: 'In Potosí the signs of Libra and Venus predominate, and because of this most of its inhabitants incline to avarice and festivity, zealous in the pursuit of riches, and somewhat given to conceit.'[7] The friar's greatest admirer was the city's unofficial chronicler Arzáns, a reclusive and impoverished figure from the Creole nobility, who over the years was to write almost a million words describing the opulence and decadence of his city. Very little is known about his life. A self-taught man, he was the son of a Spanish immigrant of hidalgo lineage, and in 1701 he married a Creole woman, Juana de Reina, who was fifteen years his senior. He died at Potosí in 1736 at the age of sixty. His manuscript was to remain unpublished until the nineteenth century, and the original is now in the library of the Royal Palace in Madrid.[8]

Arzáns's observations, covering almost three centuries, recall not only the historical events of the city but also the lives of its citizens, their religious fervour, their crimes and their apparent obsession with death and the supernatural:

1575. This year while digging in one of the mountain's mines the workers discovered a statue made of various metals, the size of a man. His face was handsome and made of white silver, though his eyes were not well proportioned; his chest to his waist was of a reddish silver, and his arms of various other metals. They tried to pull it out of the rock, but its neck broke, which caused great distress to the Indian workers, who cried out that it was the ghost of the mountain, and that the Spaniards had beheaded it. The pieces were taken down to the city and admired by all who saw them.

1599. The news reached this Imperial City in the month of April of the death of the king, Don Felipe [Philip II]. And though the death of his father, the emperor, had been deeply felt, his death was felt even more so. The tolling of the bells began to sound from all the churches, and it was not necessary even for the towncriers to proclaim his mourning. Carpenters were chosen to build a mausoleum in the city's principal church. On the evening of 23 May the procession set out from the Royal Council Chamber, led by two hundred Indians wearing black wool garments and hoods of the same colour. They were followed by a further five hundred Indians, who were mine owners, tradesmen and artisans, wearing mourning capes, the brims of their hats turned down. After them came four companies of Indians in black garments, carrying bows and arrows, some of them trailing their lances and standards on the ground. Then came the caciques, not only from the city but from further afield, each dressed in Spanish court dress except for their headgear, on which they wore llautus, of the type worn formerly by the Incas. Then followed the Spanish citizens, led by the Captain Diego Grande with his company of harquebusiers dressed in black taffeta and holding their weapons in reverse, their military flags also trailing on the ground. After these came the Captain Escudero with his regiment of musketeers dressed in dark silk and wearing black armbands. Then came the entire nobility of the city dressed in mourning black, followed by some sixty royal officials, their long capes trailed behind and each held by two pages, their heads covered by hoods. On that day twelve hundred Masses were offered for the soul of the king. The cost of these obsequies was 130,000 pieces of eight.

1604. It was about six o'clock in the afternoon and it was raining so hard that it was virtually impossible to move through the streets, but despite all this the sound of gunfire could be heard, and the shouts of women and children; for in these streets men could be seen with swords or harquebuses in their hands, some dragging the wounded to safety. The bells of the city were tolling and priests could be seen rushing about nervously in their efforts to help the dying, hearing confessions and administering the Holy Sacrament. Thus Potosí experienced the most bloody day in its history, making Shrove Tuesday of that year, the day on which this tragedy occurred, its most infamous day.

On the following day, Ash Wednesday, all the inhabitants of the city were horrified to learn of the atrocities that had taken place, for there had been more than fifty deaths, of both men and women, and some eighty wounded; among them some ladies of the nobility, who had had their ears, legs and faces slashed. There was scarcely a house that had not suffered some loss or disgrace. The Governor went about the city trying in vain to calm people's fury and sensibilities but to no avail, and not a day was to pass without further killing and wounding of its citizens.

The outrage that aroused the greatest scandal took place on Maundy Thursday of this Lent, when after nightfall some Andalusians and Estremadurans, who had just taken part in the city's religious procession, and were still dressed in their hooded robes, murdered two Basques named Pedro de Alava and Sancho de Alledona, who at the time were performing the Stations of the Cross. On the night of Holy Saturday a group of Basques went to the home of Don Fernando Arzáns, an officer of the Royal Mint, where the Andalusians had taken refuge. The servants shouted out the alarm, rousing Don Fernando and his wife and his guests. All of them armed themselves with harquebuses and shot at the Basques, who had used ladders to climb on to the roof of the mansion.

Such was the behaviour of the wretched inhabitants of Potosí in their civil wars. And many were the brawls and skirmishes that were to take place throughout that year, and in which many noblemen of both Spain and the Indies perished.

1610. In this year there arrived in the Imperial City an hidalgo by the name of Fulgencio Orozco. He was fifty years old, a strong man with a hardened and terrible look about him, and very poor. He soon found employment as a foreman in one of the metal refineries, and was able not only to make a living but also to save a little from his wages. The years, however, brought him little fortune and in a state of despair he was admitted into the city's hospital, where he blasphemed and openly declared he wished to end his life. Apparently the Devil had spoken to him in secret and

171

he had seemed to listen to him, for he was heard to shout out: 'What is it you want from me? I am doing what you command, I have fulfilled my promise to you, yet you have done nothing of what you promised me.' When those present heard this they imagined him to be possessed and went to call the friar Antonio de la Calancha, who at the time was the principal preacher of the Augustinian monastery, and much respected in our city.

He came at once, accompanied by other priests, and they found him still blaspheming. Friar Antonio tried to make him submit but could do nothing to stop his ravings. The hidalgo Orozco became very angry, telling the friar not to wear himself out because he was a lost soul and that he could see from his bed the bonfire that had been prepared for him in Hell. The good father made several attempts to calm him. When a crucifix was placed before him, he turned his face away or merely uttered blasphemies. Friar Antonio exorcised him twice, but each time Orozco yelled: 'I do not have the Devil in my body but here at the head of my bed. He has deceived me with promises and with his lies!'

When the friar had almost worn himself out, trying to persuade him to repent and confess his sins, he asked him why he hated his Creator so much and why he was raving like some heretic. Orozco, raising his voice, said it was because he gave riches to worthless men, and that since he had come to Peru to earn money for his daughter's dowry, however much he had worked he had never been able to save any money, and what he had saved he had lost. The Friar Antonio answered him that wealth was not a gift from God, nor should he have been angry with God because He did not give him such worldly goods; rather, he should be grateful to Him, and when the Devil told him that there was no salvation for his soul and that he was damned, he should have regarded this as a falsehood.

Early in the evening Orozco finally began to make his confession. Before he died later that night he was told that several Spaniards who had listened to his agonies had agreed to give him enough silver for his daughter's dowry, which they would send to Spain, leaving everyone who had attended him greatly consoled that he would find his salvation. Little would his daughter know the price paid for her dowry.

1625. In this year there died in Potosí the well-known hermit and beggar, who for some twenty years was seen in our city's streets, dressed in sackcloth, his beard full grown, and holding a skull in his hand. Regarded by everyone who saw him as a saintly man and penitent, at times he would be seen contemplating the skull he held, as if contemplating his own death. He was buried with all the Holy Sacraments. After his burial a sheet of parchment was discovered hidden in the skull he had carried with him, and written in his hand were the following words:

I, Don Juan de Toledo, a native of this city of Potosí, declare to all who have known me in this city, and those who in the future may wish to know of my existence, that as I had the appearance of a hermit, everyone took me for a saintly man; but it is not so, for I am one of the most evil of men that this world has seen; for I wish you to know that the garments I wore were not for virtue, but for deceit; and so that it will be known to you all, I record that some twenty years ago, because of the injustices the Spaniard Don Martín de Salazar inflicted on me, I stabbed him to death, and that after his burial I opened his tomb and with a dagger I cut out his heart. I then cut off his head and skinned it, and having reburied the body I carried off his skull. I donned the sackcloth you have all seen me wear, and taking his skull in my hands I have walked about with it these twenty years, never letting it out of my sight either at my table or in my bed. And when I gazed upon his skull, I was not contemplating death as you all imagined, but the opposite – for like the crocodile, who they say groans and weeps over the skull of its victim, not because it has killed it, but because it wishes to kill it again, thus did I contemplate my enemy.

1643. This year the Creoles Doña Laura de la Cerda and Doña Estefania de Azaña were married to Spaniards. Doña Laura's dowry was 200,000 pieces of eight. Doña Estefania's dowry was 100,000 pieces of eight, together with an estate, horses and slaves.

1657. This year Gervasio de la Réa killed his wife, because he saw a ghost stroking her legs; and this was the Devil, for his wife was innocent of such a charge.

1657. It was during the governorship of the General Don Francisco Sarmiento, in this same year, that the city and its province was assailed by the wickedness and terror of certain assassins known as the 'Twelve Apostles and Magdalena', robbing villages and wayfarers, raping young women and committing a thousand other atrocities. These twelve men were said to have been of noble Spanish families. It was their custom to dress one of their number as a woman; thus disguised, he would enter people's homes to plead for shelter, or at other times claiming that her husband was pursuing her to kill her. The doors would be opened to her of the houses she would later rob – at times robbing as well the honour of its young women; and because of this most of the city was up in arms. The one who dressed as a woman was known among themselves as Magdalena.

Some time later that year the priest Tórtollo, a handsome and astute cleric, was making his way at night along the street of the city's parish of Our Lady of Copacabana. He was wearing a new cloak of taffeta and a cassock of rich cloth. When he saw he was surrounded by the brigands he asked them calmly who they were. When they told him their identity he then asked them what they wanted of him. 'Your cassock, your cloak, and the silver in your purse,' one of the men replied. 'And do you want nothing more?' the priest asked. 'No, that will do nicely,' another of the brigands said. 'Well, if you want nothing more,' the priest added, 'here is what you asked me for,' and he took all his garments off, folding them neatly.

The brigands waited for him with all civility. Standing naked before them, he said to them: 'So your worships are the Twelve Apostles?' They answered, 'We've already told you so.' The priest replied: 'Then let the Twelve Apostles follow Christ!' And he ran down the street as fast as his legs would carry him, keeping a tight hold of the bundle containing his clothes; and although they gave chase, he made his escape.

1661. Doña Magdalena Telléz was born in this Imperial City of Potosí of noble parents. She was both rich and a widow. One day at morning Mass in the Jesuit church she forcibly took the stool reserved for Doña Ana Roeles, the wife of Don Juan Sans de Barea, who slapped her for the affront to his wife. In time Doña Magdalena married once more. Her husband was the Basque treasurer Pedro Arechua, whom she had agreed to marry solely on condition that he would avenge her by killing the man who had publicly humiliated her, and who still lived in the city. Enjoying the wealth he had inherited by his marriage, and spending much of his time at her country estate, her husband felt secure enough to forget his promise. But to his cost Doña Magdalena reminded him of his vow and killed him. The records of her trial state that she then proceeded to eat his heart: a crime so vile that she was arrested and tried.

They hung her body in the square from three stakes, to the great sorrow of all who came to see her. Everyone had known her in the city for her wealth and grandeur, for she owned more than 200,000 pesos in gold, silver, jewels, pearls and slaves – and to see her there with one coarse red stocking and the other white, with an old broken pair of men's shoes on her feet, brought her much pity from those who gazed at her that morning.

1674. In his *Chronicle of Peru*, Pedro de Cieza de León, referring to the value of the coca plant, writes: 'In all the parts of the Indies where I have travelled I have observed that the Indians take great pleasure in holding in their mouths roots, branches or plants. And in the Andes some are accustomed to use a small coca leaf. It was the custom and is the custom still to this day, to place the coca leaf in the mouth; and they will keep it there from early morning until they go to bed without removing it. Inquiring why they do this, they reply that because of it they feel no hunger and that it gives them great strength and vigour. It is also greatly valued by the Spaniards and encomenderos of Cusco, La Paz and La Plata, whose encomiendas where the plant grows are valued at 80,000 pesos annually. This coca is carried to the mines of Potosí where it is sold. There is many a rich man in Spain whose fortune is derived from this plant.'

As for my own experience. It is true that those Indians who make use of the plant are given added strength and vigour – to the point that no Indian will go into the mines or to any other labour, be it building houses or working in the fields, without taking it in his mouth, even if his life depends on it. It is brought to this city in great abundance. A basket is worth some seven or eight pesos of silver. Among the Indians, and even some Spaniards by now, the custom of placing coca in their mouths when entering a mine is so well established that there is a superstition that the richness of the silver they mine will depend on it.

When I was ten years old I was in the Vilacota mine, and one day when I tried to enter the mineshaft the Indians stopped me, saying that I could not enter without putting the plant in my mouth. I was reluctant, but they insisted, until the Spanish mine owner informed me of their superstition, and said that I was either to take the plant and enter the mine or not enter. Eventually I took it in order to please the owner, who was sending me to keep watch over a storage chamber where there was a fine deposit of silver, so that the Indians would not steal it. As soon as I placed two leaves in my mouth my tongue seemed to grow thick, burning and prickling me, which I found unbearable. I told the owner that I could not enter the mine with the coca in my mouth. He laughed at me and gave me a small piece of stone, saying that I should take it along with the coca, and that its bad effects would disappear. I took it into my mouth and I swear I have never tasted anything so bitter in my life. I was then told that the Indians call that stone llipita, and that they make it from a mixture of ashes, bark and roots. When the plant is ground and placed in boiling water, if a person takes a few sips of the broth, it opens the pores, warms the body and shortens labour in women; and this plant has many other virtues beside.

1678. This year Ambrosio de Soto, a native of Mérida in Estremadura, arrived in the Imperial City. Undernourished and dressed almost in rags, he began his career as a beggar two days after his arrival, beseeching the love of God to provide him the dowries for his four daughters he had left in his homeland. Alms were given to him most generously, as is customary in Potosí, as there is no licence required for beggars. For this reason many idlers, drones and men incapable of work, in order to enjoy the privileges of poverty, dedicate themselves to this vocation.

One day when he went out on his usual begging route he collected only eight pesos and returned to his boarding house in despair, and exhausted by the distance he had walked. While he was taking a nap, his landlord woke him and said that since he had returned from his begging so early at ten o'clock that morning, he wished him to serve as overseer in the work of the rebuilding of a room in the boarding house, which would enable him [the landlord] to leave the city for some days on an errand. He promised to pay him a hundred pesos and to provide him with his meals.

Later that day the landlord set off on his journey, leaving the Estremaduran in charge of the labourers. Within a short while the masons digging the foundations of the room informed him that they had dug their way into a vault below. Intrigued by the discovery, he ordered the labourers to continue their digging elsewhere in the room and to leave that section untouched.

As soon as they had finished their work, assisted by an Indian boy with a pickaxe he began to break open the roof of the vault. After very little effort he discovered an underground chamber, into which he and the boy climbed. Illuminated in the light of their lanterns they saw what appeared to be a large altar stone in the centre of the chamber, on which lay the skeletons of two women dressed in rich garments, embroidered with gold and pearls. As they inspected the rest of the chamber they saw other bones, and on a nail, fastened to one of the walls, a large gold chain, twelve strings of pearls and nine necklaces of diamonds. Almost hidden under the rubble they found a large metal box, inside which were five thousand pesos-worth of gold ingots, together with some letters. These were signed by a certain Don Antonio and Don Pedro and dated 1620, and referred to the two women whose skeletons lay on the altar, Leonor and Damiana.

A few months later Ambrosio de Soto returned to Spain (with the hoard he had discovered) and wrote to his former landlord in Potosí, telling him that God had indeed rewarded him.

1716. On the visit of His Excellency the Viceroy Archbishop Don Diego Morcillo Rubio de Aunón to the Imperial City to mark the end of Lent, various celebrations were organized in his honour that would last for several days. On Wednesday, which was the fifth day after his arrival, bullfights were held. Before they began the city's corps of infantry entered the barricaded main square looking very smart in their new uniforms and wearing their jewellery. After circling the square, where His Excellency, the city's judges and nobility had taken their seats at the surrounding balconies, they arrayed themselves in their squadrons, fired a volley and marched out of the square. Then the bullfighters entered on foot, wearing hideous masks and dressed in exotic colours, accompanied by kettle-drummers and mules laden with spears and lances for the fight, and covered by rich trappings adorned with the city's coat-of-arms.

The chief constable Don Juan Alonso de Mena then rode into the square, sumptuously attired, and accompanied by pages in livery. He rode around until he reached His Excellency's balcony, who presented him with the key to the bull enclosure. Then a handsome youth, armed with a lance, rode into the square to fight the first bull of the day. In the course of the afternoon he was to take on three bulls, fighting with such skill that not once was his horse wounded. In one of the other bullfights that day another youth stood by the entrance of the bull enclosure, armed with a knife and a lance he had spiked in the ground. When the bull noticed him, it charged him, but he stood firm, and with his lance he struck the bull in the throat. After a few steps it swayed and fell dead. The youth's performance was later rewarded with gifts of money from all the gentlemen who had occupied the balconies of the square, and all those who were seated with His Excellency.

At five in the afternoon scores of servants entered the square to the sound of trumpets, all carrying plates of food and jugs of wine. These were offered to His Excellency and all the gentlemen and ladies in the balconies. There was, however, an unfortunate accident when His Excellency's halberdiers, standing guard outside the city's Council Chamber, were knocked down and gored by the bulls on their way to the square. Also, on a following day, one of the bullfighters was gored in the leg and dragged some distance, still on horseback. The horse was severely injured and the unfortunate youth died shortly afterwards.

On Saturday His Excellency departed from the city, accompanied by the judges and officials of the viceroyalty, and by those members of our nobility who were able to go with him. The cost of his visit was estimated at some 100,000 pesos of silver in costumes, liveries, triumphal arches, banquets and other expenditure. Another 50,000 pesos was spent in gifts, silver ingots and jewels, the approximate sum presented to His Excellency. Thus, the total figure was 150,000 pesos, though some believe it to have been much greater. He also took with him on his departure 100,000 pesos, and from the royal treasury 100,000 was sent to His Majesty. His visit had lasted for almost eight days.

Arzáns's words were a fitting epitaph for the inevitable demise of the city and its grandeur. By the end of the eighteenth century the great mountain would be exhausted of its silver. The city's palaces and convents, where nuns had once prayed for the souls of their governors, were left barren and deserted, their carved façades of lotus flowers, devils and mermaids, emblems of the moon and of the sun, of winged angels and sad-eyed Indian madonnas the sole reminder of its Inca heritage and former glory.

TWENTY

The Prisoner of Cusco

Numbed and bewildered, amid the stone palaces and churches of the city, the Indian populace of Cusco filled the streets as the news was passed from mouth to mouth of the capture of Túpac Amaru, and of his imminent arrival. Pablo Astete, a Creole colonel in the militia, described him as a handsome man in his late thirties, 'some 5 feet 8 inches tall, his nose aquiline and his light-coloured skin almost too white for an Indian'.[1]

The Visitor-General Areche had been quite explicit in his orders concerning the Inca's torture and interrogation. On 4 April 1781 he was brought into the city, his wrists tied by a rope to the tail of a mule; barefoot and shirtless, he was taken to the former seminary of the Jesuits, built on the site of Hernando Pizarro's mansion. He was to be hung naked by his arms for an hour at a time, and beaten whenever he refused to answer any question.

No one who saw him that day could have imagined he was the same muleteer who had so often brought his string of three hundred mules to the city, transporting coca from the Yucay valley and other merchandise to the mines at Potosí. Nor that he was the same black-cloaked figure, dressed in velvet breeches, silver-buckled shoes and a tricorn hat, who occasionally could be seen attending to his business among the city's merchants.

Few also knew that four years previously he had made the long journey to Lima for the first time. He stayed there for several weeks, living in a small rented room, and it was there, surrounded by the documents he had brought with him, that he compiled an account of his lineage as part of a petition he was to present to Lima's Chancery Court. He was determined to refute the claims of the rich Cusco merchant Betancur to be recognized as the last representative of the Inca royal house:

Most Powerful Lord: I, Don José Gabriel Túpac Amaru, Cacique and Governor of the villages of Surimana, Tungasuca and Pampamarca, in the province of Tinta, in defence of my litigation against Don Diego Felipe Betancur, concerning the right of succession to Don Diego Felipe Túpac Amaru, last Inca and lord of Peru, and who falsely claims such right, present the proofs of my descent in the enclosed documents. . . .

In the first of such documents Your Highness can see my proven lineage and descent from the Inca Don Felipe Túpac Amaru: in which Francisco de Vilela, Protector of the Natives of Cusco, in the name of the Coya Doña Juana Pilcohuaco, the legitimate wife of Don Diego Felipe Condorcanqui, presented to the then governor of the city, Don Pedro de Córdoba y Mejía, Knight of Santiago, the sworn evidence that she was the natural daughter of the Inca Túpac Amaru and granddaughter of the Emperor Huayna Cápac, kings of these realms.

And that it was His Excellency the Viceroy the Marquis of Cañete, who finally showed her alms by awarding her some 70 bushels of coca from the lands that had once belonged to the Inca Huayna Cápac, on the outskirts of Cusco, dated 19 October 1592.* And that at the time of her petition she was married to Don Diego Felipe Condorcanqui and was the mother of five children.

Further evidence was presented to the same governor in the year 1609, comprising the testimony of twelve witnesses, all of whom were persons of quality, Spaniards, Caciques and descendants of the Inca kings. . . . All of whom confirmed she was the Inca's natural daughter, and that when His Excellency the Viceroy Don Francisco de Toledo ordered that he be taken prisoner from the province of Vilcabamba, she had also been taken to Cusco, together with one of her sisters who was very young; and some of the witnesses stated that they saw them

---

* Don Diego Hurtado de Mendoza, 2nd Marquis of Cañete, 8th Viceroy (1589–96).

carried in litters by the Indians, being the daughters of the Inca, and that they witnessed the killing of the Inca in the gallows of the city that had been erected.

And that the witness Don Tristán de Silva stated that after the killing of the Inca, the Viceroy Toledo ordered that Doña Juana be placed in the household of Doña Teresa de Ordóñez, the witness's mother. And that after Doña Teresa's death, she remained in the household of her daughter . . . and she was the sole surviving child of the Inca, and that her sister, Doña Isabel, had long since died in the Aymara country.

Her petition was subsequently presented to His Excellency the Viceroy the Prince of Esquilache,* asking him to recognize her as the sole surviving heir of the Inca Túpac Amaru . . . and he ordered that seals be struck to that effect. He also decreed that she and her children be accorded the privileges of their rank, and that the governors of Cusco and of the province Canas and Canchis be informed of this, and that she be granted in that province the lands that had once belonged to the mamacuna.

Of her children only Don Blas left issue, who was Cacique of Surimana in the lands of his mother. From his marriage to Doña Francisca Torres, he was succeeded as cacique by Don Sebastián, who was married to Doña Catalina del Camino . . . their eldest son Don Miguel, who in turn became cacique, married firstly Doña Rosa Noguera, by whom he had two sons, my brother Don Clemente, who died childless, and myself.[2]

It was Friday 10 November 1780 and His Grace Don Juan Manuel de Moscoso y Peralta, Bishop of Cusco, had just finished celebrating High Mass in his cathedral church. It was a service he found both comforting and rewarding, especially in the light of the calumnies that had been spread against his person in the city. A Creole from Arequipa and a member of one of its most prominent families, he held the singular distinction among the prelates of Peru of having

---

* Don Francisco de Borja, Prince of Esquilache, 12th Viceroy (1615–21).

been a widower and mayor of his native city. A former bishop of the northern Argentine province of Tucumán, to whose cathedral he had gifted a gold monstrance of emeralds and pearls, he had only arrived at Cusco the previous year to take possession of his diocese.

As he left the cathedral it was brought to his notice that a billboard had been nailed to one of Cusco's convent doors, accusing him of a bias against Spanish-born citizens and of 'maintaining relations with the opposite sex'.[3] It was a calumny that would be repeated in a letter to the Council of the Indies. Portly and prone to melancholy, the bishop had done little to occupy his mind that morning other than to complain once more in his correspondence to the Viceroy about the behaviour of the provincial governor of Tinta, who had interfered in his appointment of religious in his province, and whom he had excommunicated.

Don Antonio de Arriaga, a Basque who had served in the colonies for most of his life, had been rewarded by the Crown with the governorship of Tinta, a province south of Cusco. He knew the bishop in the years when they had both lived in Tucumán, and though their relationship had initially been civil, as time passed their contempt for each other had developed into a public feud, in which the Basque had even questioned the purity of His Grace's Creole blood. So it was with a mixture of anger and impotence that Bishop Moscoso ended his letter to the Viceroy Don Agustín de Jáuregui. Shortly afterwards a messenger arrived in the city and made his way to the episcopal palace.

A year later various eyewitnesses recorded that six days previously Governor Arriaga had been invited to dine in one of the villages under his control by its parish priest to mark the birthday of the king; that the Indian Cacique of the province was also present. It had by all accounts been a fine meal, which had gone on until four in the afternoon, at which time the Cacique had excused himself and left the priest's house before the other guests departed. Later that afternoon, as the messenger informed the bishop, Governor Arriaga, on his way back to his provincial capital accompanied only by his secretary and two Negro slaves, was ambushed by a band of Indians led by the Cacique.

Every detail of Arriaga's murder was relayed to him by the messenger: he had been placed in irons by his own Negro slave, and a 'trial' was held in the Cacique's township of Tungasuca; afterwards he was shown a picture of Christ by the priest López, who had accompanied the rebels, and was told that he would be put to death. Stripped of his own clothes, he was made to wear the habit of a friar and was taken to the gallows that had been erected in the square of the township. There he was unceremoniously hanged by the neck.

The bishop had received the news of the governor's killing on 10 November, but it wasn't until two days later that he informed the authorities at Cusco. This delay would haunt him for years to come, and gave credence to the suspicion that he had been an accomplice in the governor's killing.

In the following weeks what had initially seemed to be a single act of murder was to develop into the greatest Indian rebellion against the Spanish rule since the Conquest. Within months Cusco was a city under siege, and panic swept through the entire province as reports reached the governor of the massing of Indian troops in the southern region, and of the Cacique's many declarations, variously freeing all Negro slaves and ending the mita service of forced Indian labour. Skirmishes were reported between the colonial militias and the army of Indians that the Cacique had raised from the surrounding region, and soon there was news of a battle at Sangarara, in which the troops of the provincial governors and their Indian auxiliaries were defeated.

On 2 January 1781 the Cacique had been seen on the hills above Cusco; mounted on a white stallion and holding a banner emblazoned with the royal Inca arms, he was at the head of an army of some sixty thousand Indians. For almost a month he hesitated to march on Cusco and instead spent much of his time subduing the southern provinces and converting them to his cause – much against the advice of his young wife, who implored him to attack the city without delay. Cusco was defended by some twelve thousand troops and hundreds of penitents walked its streets in despair, each knowing that their lives depended on the outcome of the coming battle.

The Cacique sent a letter to the city's governor demanding his surrender and declaring that he would no longer delay the advance of his troops; he repeated the demands of his earlier proclamations, boasted of his royal blood and then stated that his purpose was to end the exploitation of his people in the name of the king.[4] But suddenly, and without warning, on 10 January his forces fell back from their positions and began their march of retreat.

No one, not even the reinforcements urgently sent from Lima to help defend the city, believed what they saw; most had expected to die at the hands of the Indian army, regardless of the entreaties of their officers and the prayers of their chaplains. But what the bishop would describe as a miracle was largely the result of the Cacique's indecision: he was torn between his belief that the city would surrender willingly to his army and his reluctance to commit to battle the thousands of men that faced one another.

It was, recalled Bishop Moscoso years later, the moment when the great rebellion that could have changed the whole course of Andean history was extinguished by one simple mistake. The road the Cacique chose was one of retreat and retribution, and it led to a final betrayal.

In the darkness of his cell the Cacique dictated a letter to the bishop. 'I am', he wrote, 'considered a rebel or infidel to our monarch Charles III. Time will tell that I am a faithful and loyal vassal and that neither have I retracted in the slightest from my due esteem for the Holy Church . . . and that my purpose was only to end the abuse of my people.'[5]

For over a month Visitor-General Areche kept him in his cell, taking him out almost daily for a few hours at a time to face repeated torture of beatings and hangings, which dislocated one of his arms. In one of the more brutal sessions of interrogation the prisoner boldly addressed Areche with the following words: 'The guilty are you and I, your excellency: you for being an oppressor, and I for being a liberator, for which we both deserve to be sentenced to death.'[6]

Among the documents Areche supplied to the Judge Don Benito de la Mata Linares, who would preside at the Cacique's trial and sentencing, was a declaration he had supposedly made in which he declared himself king of Peru. This proved beyond doubt his treason against the Crown, but it was probably a forgery.[7] On two occasions he had attempted to send messages to his followers from his cell, written on scraps of paper in his blood. Both times he was betrayed by his gaolers.

On 18 May 1781 the execution was to take place. A regiment of mulattos and mestizos had been sent from Lima and now lined the streets of the city. At 10 o'clock in the morning nine manacled prisoners were brought out from the old Jesuit school. Placed in sacks, they were tied to horses and dragged into Cusco's main square, where a wooden gallows had been erected. The Cacique, wearing a metal spiked crown of thorns, his hands and feet in chains, was made to stand to one side and watch as four other prisoners were taken to the gallows and hanged.

At each killing a cheer went up from sections of the crowd, but the more deaths they witnessed the greater the silence that took hold of the square. When the Cacique's eldest son and elderly uncle mounted the gallows together he showed visible pain in his face, as he watched each of them have his tongue cut from his mouth before they too were hanged. It was then the turn of his wife, who, much to the amusement of her gaolers, had been dressed in the habit of a monk. She mounted the scaffold but refused to open her mouth. Placed on the executioner's stool, her neck was strapped and garrotted, but she survived. For several minutes the two executioners kicked and struck her, tightening the metal collar again and again until she finally expired.

The screams of the Cacique's other young son, who had been made to watch the killings, could be heard resonating across the square. And he screamed again as he watched his father roped by his feet and arms to four horses, one at each corner of the great quadrangle of buildings and churches. One eyewitness later recorded:

Sometimes certain things occur, as if the Devil comforts these Indians in their superstitions and omens. I say this, because, after a great period of dry and fine weather, that morning in particular was grey and not a sign of the sun could be seen, and it began to rain heavily, and at twelve o'clock in the afternoon, when the Indian was held by four horses, suspended in the air, a great gust of wind broke across the square, followed by a hailstorm . . . which is why it was said by the Indians that the elements of nature felt the death of their Inca, whom we Spaniards so inhumanely killed.[8]

Three years after the Cacique's brutal execution Bishop Moscoso was himself placed under arrest, accused of complicity in the Cacique's rebellion, and was taken by coach to Lima, escorted by a platoon of lancers. For two years he was to live under house arrest in one of the city's monasteries, forbidden to communicate with anyone. On the orders of the Viceroy he was then taken on board a ship bound for Spain and exile. On reaching Spain he suffered a similar censure for a further two years, during which time he wrote his defence against the charges of treason and complicity in the Cacique's rebellion, *Inocencia justificada contra los artificios de la calumnia*.

In 1789 he was cleared of all charges and was rewarded by the Crown with the Archbishopric of Granada. His gratitude was demonstrated by his gift of 80,000 pesos to his see. He died at the age of eighty-eight on 24 July 1811, the anniversary of Bolívar's birthday and of the discovery of Machu Picchu. His only legacy is the summer palace he built in the foothills of the Sierra de Alfacar, near Granada, in the hamlet of Víznar. It was here, in one of the olive groves, that the poet Federico García Lorca was assassinated during the Spanish Civil War.

TWENTY-ONE

The Last Inca

The old Indian had not slept much that day. He had only moved into his new lodgings a few days previously, accompanied by his elderly companion Durán, who was almost as old as he was. He knew that it was the patriot Azopardo who had convinced the Argentine government that he was far too ill to involve himself in any political activity, and that all he wished for was the solitude of a room with board and lodging, where he could die in peace. It was a request that President Rivadavia agreed to, on condition the old man wrote a journal of his past experience, a copy of which is now to be found in the Biblioteca Nacional at Buenos Aires.[1]

Argentina had become independent of Spanish rule in 1816, six years previously, but no longer was there any talk among the Argentine deputies in the newly established Congress of reviving the Inca monarchy. The Liberator José de San Martín had initially proposed such a plan, and at the time it might well have become a reality but for the lack of a suitable candidate of Inca royal blood.

It was damp and cold in the room, and once more the old man got up from his bed and lit the small fire. For a while he sat at the small desk Durán had bought for him, staring aimlessly at the white paper and inkwell, as if he could not find the words to begin writing. Earlier that week he had described the killing of his half-brother, the Cacique José Gabriel Túpac Amaru, and related how he himself had been imprisoned, after being publicly whipped through the streets of Cusco mounted on a mule, and how after his release he had once more been imprisoned for over a year in the city's jail. He wrote:

The day came for our departure, which was done with much public acclaim and notoriety to our persons: people crowded the

188

streets we were to pass through and were encouraged to spectate as if it were some attraction of ridicule. Some sixty of us unfortunates, among them children, some aged only three and eight years old, were paraded in front of the prison, chained and manacled. But it was as if neither our filthy rags and appearance, nor even our haggard faces, shrunken from months of hunger and thirst, brought any semblance of compassion to those who stared at us and insulted us. And thus we were made to walk to the main square, and around it to the applause and laughter of the common people, who seemed to be greatly amused by the sight of our degradation.

And so began our long and arduous march, from mountain village to hamlet, provided with only sufficient food and water to enable us to continue our journey. Ignoring our cries and our demands for water, we were met only with blows and curses from our guards; for that is how my dear mother died three days after we had begun our march, pleading and begging for water, until she died of thirst.

It took us some forty days to reach Lima, where we hoped we would be accorded more humane treatment. But it was not to be. We were taken to a large cell and held together by one single chain, and for the simplest movement of our bodies we were abused or struck. Our impotence was only equalled by the tortures we suffered, which were of such crudeness I do not wish to recall them. Many of my companions died chained next to me, among them my elderly uncle Bartolomé Túpac Amaru, whose frail lungs could no longer survive the stench of excrement and human misery.

For five months we were to remain in the dungeons of Lima, and on our departure for the port of Callao we experienced the same public humiliation as on leaving Cusco, where we became little more than curiosities and the butt of the crowd's humour. Shackled as we were, men, women and children, our inability to walk without falling only increased their laughter and the anger of our guards, who prodded us with their bayonets. A young man, moved by what he saw, as I remember, held out his hand to me as I fell.

My family and I were put on the frigate *Peruana*. My other companions were taken to the ship *San Pedro*. Córdoba, the captain of the frigate, was a man of a particularly unpleasant disposition; superstitious in the extreme and without any sense of morality, his years at sea had only hardened his inhumanity. There was little we could expect from such a man. All of us were placed in the main under-deck, shackled together by one chain, and with virtually no room to move. The food they fed us was so vile that by refusing to eat we remained constantly hungry; our only consolation was the bones they fed us from their meals, and which, like the dogs they called us, we chewed. The air was thick with our odour and only added to our illness and debility, leaving us with a sense of utter abandonment.

Neither the ship's captain, nor its doctor or chaplain, showed the least concern for our state. Half of my companions died of scurvy before we reached the port of Rio de Janeiro, two of them dying on top of me, where I was shackled, and their bodies remained there until the following day.* Each one of us suffered just to be alive, and even our physical proximity to one another did not alleviate our terror or our lack of ability to care for one another; and in this state my wife died, without me even being able to speak to her, or comfort her.

It was a suffering which only made me desire my own death; and it was how one of my young nephews died. One of my companions begged the captain to show us leniency in his treatment of us, but was only told that any such request would be met with the flogging of our entire company. However, later, when a Frenchman, who was also one of the prisoners, again pleaded our cause, we were allowed for a time to have our shackles taken off and to go up on deck. Also a priest, who had served as one of our confessors since the time we left Cusco, once we had reached Rio de Janeiro was given permission to hose us down with sea water, to clean the vile state of our bodies.

---

* The frigate *Peruana* had sailed round Cape Horn into the Atlantic.

For four months we remained in the port of Rio de Janeiro until finally we again set sail for Spain, which we had been told was at war with England; this only added to the irritation and nervousness of our captain, who feared we would be captured by an English man-of-war. It was a fear that became for us our only hope of salvation. Their unease only increased their ill-treatment of us, our hunger, the heat we endured and the biting cold of the night. It also added to our desperation and the risks we took to find food. A few scraps of biscuit I had managed to obtain in the few times we were allowed up on deck were discovered by one of our guards, who hit me so violently with the butt of his rifle that he broke my ribs; denied any assistance by the ship's doctor I recovered only through the affection of my fellow prisoners, who did what they could for me, and in time I was healed of my wounds, even though to this day I carry the pain.

One small incident I will add, which in itself demonstrates the cruelty of our gaolers. It became our custom to recite the Rosary aloud together to alleviate our suffering, in the hope that God would free us, but even this was forbidden us.

It was ten months after we left Lima that we finally reached Cádiz. We hoped that the king would have been informed of our situation, and would have allowed us to defend ourselves of the crimes of which we had been accused.

On 1 March 1785 we disembarked in the port. I was taken in chains to the city's castle of San Sebastián, arriving there at midnight, my arms supported by two soldiers, without whose assistance I would not have been able to walk. Each of us was placed in a special cell underground, made of stone, and possessing a small metal shaft to let in air and light. The floor was also of stone, and damp. My cell had a small bunk, where I was able to make a bed from an old and dirty woollen garment I had been given; it was my only worldly belonging, other than the rags I wore. I cannot describe the sense of pain and loneliness I felt that night: alone in an unknown land, separated from my companions who had survived the voyage; it all seemed so far from the killing of my brother and all that I had suffered in the aftermath of his death.

In the three years and three months I remained a prisoner in the castle of San Sebastián I cannot recall one single occasion when I was treated with a semblance of charity or compassion. It was decided that all the prisoners from Peru were to be separated. Some were taken to Orán, others to Alhucema, Mellilla, El Peñon and Málaga. At Málaga a number of them died from ill-treatment.

One morning I was woken by one of the prison commanders, who was escorted by several soldiers; they tied my arms and hands with their usual harshness and took me to a large cell where I was surrounded by common criminals, some of them thieves and murderers, and some of whom, believing I had some fortune at my disposition, appeared only too willing to kill me to gain favour from my guards. Only by the help of a Mexican prisoner, who protected me from the abuse and blows of our fellow inmates, did I survive the four or five days I spent there, until finally I was taken away and placed on board a small barque and brought to the island of León, and then across the Straits of Gibraltar to Ceuta, which we reached after four days' sailing on 16 June 1788.

On the ship, which was a transporter of salt, I was met by the curiosity of my fellow prisoners, few of whom had ever seen an Indian before, and they examined me as if I were some object. They looked upon me as some dangerous brigand purely because of the length of my sentence, and two of their leaders made it known to me that my fate and life were in their hands; one of them commanded me to follow him with his group of prisoners when we disembarked. But the captain of the ship told him that he had no rights over me, and he escorted me to the house of the colony's governor, the Count of Las Lomas, to whom he expressed his opinion that I was not like the rest of the other prisoners he had brought, and that I should not be put in their company, but allowed a measure of freedom to serve out my sentence; and to this the governor agreed, and ordered one of his officers to see to it that I was lodged for the time being in someone's house. A tradesman, who happened to overhear our conversation, and who had been present, offered to provide a room for me. This was agreed upon as a temporary measure, though I soon discovered that his motive had little to do with human kindness, nor hospitality, but was more a means of ingratiating himself with the governor. After much maltreatment at his hands within a few days I made my way to the prison commander.

It was there that I asked to serve my sentence alone, devoid of any human contact. I was given a small kitchen garden to cultivate, beside the hut where I was to live. And like the living dead, in this occupation I preserved my life.

It was on 1 June 1813 that I first met the Augustinian friar Don Marcos Durán Martel, the one human being who made amends for my injuries and suffering, and who I know had been destined to save me in these last years of my life with the simple joy of friendship and kindness. When I got to know him he told me, being as he was a Creole and fellow American, that he had himself been persecuted for his beliefs, because of which he had also been imprisoned and exiled. I offered to share my lodging with him, which he accepted. As by then I was an old man, I was no longer able to dig and work my garden with the same vigour as before, and it was a task he took up in my stead; and in truth it was his help and goodness that brought me the care and comfort I had never imagined possible. And it was at that time that I once more felt the dream and desire to see my homeland again, after almost forty years of imprisonment, in a world that had changed so radically.

Until the year 1820 we continued as we had before, dreaming a little more of one day being set free and of our homeland, which neither of us old men really believed we would ever see again. But in that year the Cortes of Spain announced the release of all American political prisoners, each of whom would be given 10 reales per day until they were embarked on ships to take them to their homeland, the cost of which would also be paid. My companion helped me finally leave to find a ship that would take us to Algeciras, and then to Gibraltar. . . .

The old Indian could write no more that night. His mind was full of memories – how he had spent months evading the various impositions that were placed on his right to freedom, and how eventually his companion the friar Durán had managed to find them a berth on a ship from Cádiz bound for Buenos Aires, which they reached on 3 August 1822.

That same year he presented his memoir to the Argentine Congress, and a reproduction of it was published in Buenos Aires in 1825 as a pamphlet entitled *The Long Imprisonment in Spain of Juan-Bautista Túpac Amaru – fifth lineal grandson of the last Emperor of Peru.*[2] In May of that year, having heard the news of the independence of Peru, he wrote in gratitude to its liberator Simón Bolívar, informing him that his forty years of imprisonment and exile had been rewarded by the freeing of his people, and expressing his desire to meet with him before he died. It was something he was never able to fulfil. He died in Buenos Aires on 2 September 1827 at the age of eighty. The site of his burial remains unknown.

Chronology

1513	Vasco Núñez de Balboa, accompanied by the isthmian slaver Francisco Pizarro, discovers the Pacific Ocean.
1514	Diego de Almagro and Hernando de Soto arrive in the isthmus in the armada of its new governor, Don Pedro Arias Dávila, known as Pedrarias.
1515	St Teresa of Ávila born.
1519	Hernán Cortés conquers Mexico.
1522	The Basque Pascual de Andagoya reconnoitres the Pacific coastlands of Colombia and Ecuador, the northern empire of the Incas.
1524–7	Exploratory voyages of Pizarro and Almagro to the Ecuadorian coast.
1526	The Venetian ambassador Andrea Navagero attends the wedding at Seville of the Emperor Charles V and the Portuguese Infanta.
1527	Death of the Inca Emperor Huayna Cápac.
1529	Civil war breaks out between the Inca Emperor Huáscar and his half-brother Atahualpa.
1529	At Toledo the Empress Doña Isabel awards Pizarro the right to conquer Peru.
1530	The conquistador Cristóbal de Mena sails from Panama in Pizarro's expeditionary force for the conquest of Peru.
1532	The capture of the Emperor Huáscar by Atahualpa's generals and the imprisonment of his sisters, the Princesses Marca Chimbo and Quispiquipi.
1532	Pizarro's conquistadores seize Atahualpa at Cajamarca.
1533	Distribution of treasure at Cajamarca.

1533	Cristóbal de Mena is the first of Pizarro's veterans to return to Seville.
1533	Execution of Atahualpa at Cajamarca.
1533	Capture of Cusco.
1535	Hernando de Soto leaves Peru for Spain.
1535	Almagro leaves Cusco for the conquest of Chile.
1535	Pizarro founds the City of the Kings at Lima as the capital of the colony.
1536–7	Cusco besieged by the Inca Manco.
1537	Almagro relieves Cusco and captures the city for himself.
1538	Almagro's forces defeated at the Battle of Salinas by Hernando Pizarro's loyalist army. Almagro executed.
1539	Birth of the future historian Garcilaso de la Vega at Cusco.
1539	Hernando de Soto leads an expedition of conquest to Florida.
1539	Gonzalo Pizarro leads the first invasion of Vilcabamba.
1541	Francisco Pizarro killed by supporters of Almagro's isthmian mestizo son.
1541	Hernando de Soto dies on the banks of the Mississippi River.
1542	The Governor Vaca de Castro defeats Almagro's son at the Battle of Chupas.
1544	Gonzalo Pizarro leads an armed rebellion in Cusco and governs the colony for four years until his defeat at the Battle of Jaquijahuana.
1545	Discovery of the silver mine at Potosí.
1553	Year-long rebellion of the encomendero Francisco Hernández Girón.
1555	The Princess Doña Inés gives testimony in Lima on behalf of the orphaned children of Atahualpa.
1556	Abdication of the Emperor Charles V.
1557	The Inca Sayri Túpac induced to leave Vilcabamba.
1560	Death of Sayri Túpac in the Yucay.
1560	The young Garcilaso de la Vega leaves Peru for Spain, never to return.
1561	Hernando Pizarro released from the castle of La Mota.

1562   Hernando de Soto's abandoned daughter testifies on behalf of her mother, the Princess Doña Leonor.

1571   Death of the Princess Doña Beatriz at Cusco.

1572   The Viceroy Don Francisco de Toledo's enquiry into the history of the Incas.

1572   Toledo orders the second invasion of Vilcabamba; capture and execution of the Inca Túpac Amaru.

1590   Death of the last of the conquistadores at Cusco.

1598   Death of King Philip II.

1616   Death of Garcilaso de la Vega at Córdoba.

1676   Birth of Bartolomé Arzáns de Orsúa y Vela, future chronicler of Potosí, in the Imperial City.

1781   Execution at Cusco of the Cacique José Gabriel Túpac Amaru.

1827   Death at Buenos Aires of the Cacique's half-brother Juan Bautista Túpac Amaru.

Genealogy

Children of the Emperor Huayna Cápac

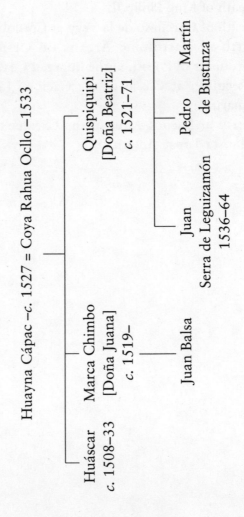

Huayna Cápac –*c.* 1527 = Coya Rahua Ocllo –1533

Huáscar
c. 1508–33

Marca Chimbo
[Doña Juana]
c. 1519–

Juan Balsa

Quispiquipi
[Doña Beatriz]
c. 1521–71

Juan
Serra de Leguizamón
1536–64

Pedro

Martín
de Bustinza

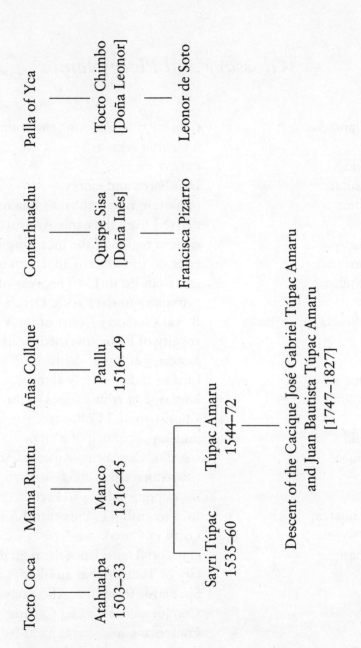

Concubines

Tocto Coca   Mama Runtu   Añas Collque   Contarhuachu   Palla of Yca

Atahualpa
1503–33

Manco
1516–45

Paullu
1516–49

Quispe Sisa
[Doña Inés]

Tocto Chimbo
[Doña Leonor]

Sayri Túpac
1535–60

Túpac Amaru
1544–72

Francisca Pizarro

Leonor de Soto

Descent of the Cacique José Gabriel Túpac Amaru
and Juan Bautista Túpac Amaru
[1747–1827]

Glossary and Place Names

adelantado: military title, denoting the command of a frontier region.

alcalde: mayor.

amauta: Inca bards and elders.

Andes: mountain range; the quéchua name derived from the name Antisuyo.

Antisuyo: eastern region of the Inca Empire.

Apurímac: river on the western approach to Cusco.

Arequipa: city founded in 1540 because of its proximity to the Pacific Ocean.

Audiencia de Lima: Royal Chancery Court of the Viceroyalty of Peru; governed by its judiciary and president.

ayllu: Inca or Indian family clan.

Aymára: language of ethnic tribes of the Cuntisuyo and Collasuyo.

cabildo: municipal council of a city.

cacique: word of Caribbean–Amerindian origin denoting a tribal chief, introduced by the conquistadores to Peru.

Cajamarca: Inca township in the central Andes, north of Cusco.

Cañari: equatorial tribe from the region and city of Tumibamba; auxiliaries of the Spaniards from the earliest days of the Conquest. The Cañari Cacique Don Francisco Chilche was awarded by the Crown an encomienda in Cusco's Yucay valley and the rank of a hidalgo.

Cápac:	Inca title meaning a powerful sovereign.
captain:	commander of a squadron of horse or infantry.
Chachapoya:	tribe of the north Andean region.
chicha:	maize wine.
Chile:	the most southern region of the Inca Empire; the settlement at Santiago was founded in 1541 by Pedro de Valdivia.
Chinchasuyo:	the northern region of the Inca Empire.
Chuquinga:	Battle of, in Cuntisuyo, 30 March 1554; defeat of the royalist army of the Mariscal Alonso de Alvarado by Francisco Hernández Girón.
Coca:	narcotic plant sacred to the Inca nobility. Cocaine is derived from it and it was grown in abundance by encomenderos in sub-tropical valleys for the mining markets of Potosí.
Collasuyo:	the southern region of the Inca Empire.
converso:	convert to Christianity, of Jewish ancestry.
Copacabana:	religious colonial shrine on a promontory of Lake Titicaca; the Aymara name signifies 'stone from where all can be seen', and refers to the view from its former Inca temple; an early chapel was replaced by a sanctuary dedicated to the Virgin, built between 1610 and 1619. A wooden sculpture of the Madonna was donated to the sanctuary by the Indian sculptor Tito Yupanqui in 1592. The Augustinian chronicler Antonio de la Calancha y Benavides in the mid-seventeenth century published a history of the sanctuary entitled *Historia del*

	Santuario de Copacabana y del Prado.
cordillera:	mountain range.
corregidor:	governor of a city or province.
Council of the Indies:	governing body of the Indies.
Coya:	title of the sister-queen of the Inca emperor and of their daughters; used indiscriminately after the Conquest by various illegitimate daughters of the Emperor Huayna Cápac.
Creole:	children of Spaniards born in the Indies.
Cristiano viejo:	Old Christian lineage.
Curaca:	quéchua name for a tribal leader.
Cusco:	capital of the Inca Empire of Tahuantinsuyo, established as a Spanish municipality in 1534.
Don/Doña:	courtesy title among royalty, nobles and principal governors and military commanders, among them Pizarro and Almagro, some of whom were hidalgos. Though in later years its use would become more common, in sixteenth-century Peru only the wives and daughters of hidalgos and conquistadores were addressed as Doña. The conquistador Mansio Serra de Leguizamón's courtly relatives were accorded the title of Don, but neither he nor his father, though hidalgos, were ever addressed as such. A few of the Inca princes who had converted to Christianity were, however, awarded the title, among them the conquistador's son Don Juan Serra de Leguizamón, as recorded in his father's will.
encomienda/encomendero:	land grant of Indian vassals awarded by the Crown in lieu of feudal service and

conditional upon the evangelization of their domains. The award could only be inherited once, either by the encomendero's son or grandchild as heir, or by his childless widow and any future husband of hers. No mestizos or illegitimate children were allowed to inherit, unless authorized by the Crown.

Guayaquil: equatorial coastal city, founded as Santiago de Guayaquil in 1535.

hidalgo: term of ancient Spanish nobility; *hijo de algo* = son of a man of rank.

Hispaniola: Caribbean island, partitioned into Dominican Republic and Haiti.

huaca: Inca nature shrine.

Huanacauri: huaca mountain shrine, south-west of Cusco.

Huarina: Battle of, on south-eastern shore of Lake Titicaca, 20 October 1547; defeat of Diego de Centeno's loyalist army by Gonzalo Pizarro.

Iñaquito: Battle of, near Quito, 18 January 1546; defeat of the Viceroy Blasco Núñez Vela's army by Gonzalo Pizarro.

Inca: name of ruling ayllu of Quéchua tribe; title of emperor.

Indian/Indies: name given by the Spaniards to the natives of the Americas and Caribbean islands because of their belief that the continent formed part of India.

Inti: Inca sun deity.

isthmus of Panama: known formerly as Castilla del Oro because of its purported abundance of gold, and later as Tierra Firme; the port city of Panama on its western coast was founded as a result of the discovery of the Pacific Ocean by Vasco Núñez de Balboa in 1533.

Jaquijajuana: Battle of, in the valley and plain of that name, north of Cusco, 9 April 1548; defeat of Gonzalo Pizarro's army of encomenderos by the President La Gasca.

Jauja: Inca township in central Andes; founded by Francisco Pizarro as the first Spanish municipality in 1533.

La Paz: city in the Collasuyo: Nuestra Señora de la Paz, Our Lady of the Peace, founded in 1548 to commemorate the defeat of Gonzalo Pizarro's rebellion; administrative capital of Bolivia.

La Plata: city in the southern Collasuyo, founded in 1538 and deriving its name from its abundance of silver mines; known also by its indigenous name of Chuquisaca and Las Charcas, the name of its region; renamed Sucre in 1825 in honour of Mariscal Antonio de Sucre; capital of Bolivia.

league: 3½ miles.

León: capital of the early settlement of Nicaragua.

Licentiate: lawyer.

Lima: city, capital of the Viceroyalty of Peru; name for the lands of the Curaca Taulichusco, where Pizarro in 1535 founded the capital of his governorship which he named Los Reyes, the City of the Kings, in honour of the Feast of the Epiphany.

Lupaca: Aymara tribe of the Cuntisuyo and Collasuyo, though principally of the

	north and western regions of Lake Titicaca.
mamacuna:	virgins of the sun.
Manco Cápac:	The mythical founder of the Inca dynasty, son of the sun and of the moon, founder of Cusco.
mariscal/marshal:	commander of cavalry or army; empowered to act as a legal authority during a campaign.
mestizo:	person of mixed Indian and Spanish parentage.
mitimae:	labourers of the subject tribes; transported to various regions of the empire for a period of time – mita – by Incas and then Spaniards.
Morisco:	of Moorish parentage.
morrión:	curved steel helmet used by conquistadores.
Mudéjar:	Moors allowed to live in Christian lands; also a term to describe Moorish influence in architecture.
mulatto:	person of mixed Negro and Spanish parentage.
Nazca:	western region of the Cuntisuyo; pre-Colombian civilization; site of the giant Nazca lines.
New Castile:	Francisco Pizarro's governorship of Peru.
New Spain:	Mexico.
New Toledo:	governorship awarded to Almagro of the region of the Collasuyo.
ñusta:	niece or daughter of the emperor by a concubine.
oreja:	ear: name given by the Spaniards to Inca lords because of the gold and silver ear ornaments they wore.

Pachacamac: quéchua name for the creator.
Pachamama: earth deity.
palla: daughter of a cacique.
panaca: name for the Inca lineages and their
                       custodians; the spiritual and secular
                       heirs of the emperors, numbering at the
                       time of the Conquest eleven in all.
Parinacochas: north-western region of the Cuntisuyo.
Pastu: northern Ecuador; the most northern
                       region of the Inca Empire.
Peru/Birú: name of equatorial cacique mistakenly
                       given to the Inca Empire of
                       Tahuantinsuyo by the early Spanish
                       explorer of the Pacific coast Pascual de
                       Andagoya.
peso: name of coinage, originally meaning
                       weight. Estimated present-day value of
                       gold and silver: Peso de Oro: £25. Peso
                       or mark of silver: £17. Peso of stamped
                       silver (*plata ensayada*): £25. Unmarked
                       silver: £20. The value in Spain during
                       the early colonial period would have
                       been possibly threefold.
piece of eight: coin, approximately equivalent to
                       ½ peso of gold.
Písac: encomienda situated in the valley of
                       that name in the Yucay.
Piura: equatorial township.
Potosí: city in Bolivia, founded in 1545 because
                       of the great wealth of the nearby silver
                       mine, the Cerro Rico.
procurator: title of a governorship.
Pucará: Battle of, north of Lake Titicaca,
                       8 October 1554; defeat of Francisco
                       Hernández Girón by the royalist army
                       of the Judges of Lima.

Puerto Viejo:	the old port, north of Guayaquil.
Quéchua:	language and ruling tribe of the Inca Empire.
Quipucamayoc:	guardians of the quipu, coloured strings used for numeration, historical and astrological records.
Quito:	northern capital of the Inca Empire; founded in 1534 as San Francisco de Quito; capital of Ecuador.
regidor:	alderman.
Sacred Valley of the Incas:	the valley of the Yucay, just north of Cusco.
San Mateo:	equatorial bay.
Sapa Inca:	emperor.
Sucre:	*see* La Plata.
Surampalli:	country retreat of the Emperor Huayna Cápac, capital of the Cañari tribe, site of the present-day Ecuadorian city of Cuenca, which he later named Tumibamba, the name of his panaca.
Tahuantinsuyo:	name of the Inca Empire of the four suyos or regions: Antisuyo, Chinchasuyo, Collasuyo and Cuntisuyo.
tambo:	Inca fortress or storehouse.
Titicaca:	lake in the Collasuyo, sacred to the Incas; 12,500 feet above sea level and 3,500 square miles; bordering Peru and Bolivia.
Tucumán:	southern province of the Collasuyo in northern Argentina.
Túmbez:	early Spanish settlement on the equatorial coast.
Tumibamba:	Surampalli, equatorial Andean capital of the Cañari tribe; birthplace of the Emperor Huayna Cápac, who gave it

	the name of his panaca; site of the present-day city of Cuenca, the Spanish municipality of which was founded in 1557.
Veragua:	north-western province of Nicaragua.
Vilcabamba:	Inca fortress settlement north-west of Cusco; built by the Inca Manco; known as the Lost City of the Incas; probable site is Espíritu Pampa.
Villaoma:	title of the Inca High Priest of the Sun.
Viracocha:	cosmic Andean deity.
Vitcos:	Inca township near Vilcabamba, north-west of Cusco.
Yanacona:	nomadic servant caste.
Yucay:	valley north of Cusco; personal fiefdom of the Emperor Huayna Cápac and of his panaca; renowned for its climate and beauty.
yupanqui:	quéchua title denoting royalty.

Notes

The transcription of Spanish manuscripts is by Josefa García Tovar, and their translation is by the author, as are all other translations.

Preface

1. Alfredo Varela (ed.), *Memorias del Hermano de Túpac Amaru, escritas en Buenos Aires*.

1. The Gateway to the Indies

1. Antonio María Fabie (ed.), *Viajes por España de Jorge de Einghen, del Barón León de Rosmithal de Baina, de Francisco Guicciardini y de Andrés Navajero*.
2. Ibid.
3. Ibid.
4. Diego de Trujillo, 'Relación del Descubrimiento del Reino del Perú', p. 196.
5. Pedro Pizarro, *Relación del Descubrimiento y Conquista de los Reinos del Perú*, p. 15.
6. Garcilaso de la Vega, *La Florida del Ynca, Historia del Adelantado Hernando de Soto, Gobernador y capitán general del reyno de la Florida, y de otros cavalleros Españoles e Indios*, Libro 5, Primera Parte, Capítulo VII.
7. Diego de Trujillo, 'Relación', p. 197.
8. James Lockhart, *The Men of Cajamarca*, pp. 380–4.
9. Diego de Trujillo, 'Relación', p. 199.
10. Ms. Información de méritos y servicios del Adelantado Hernando de Soto, Archivo General de Indias, Seville, Patronato 109, N1.R4.
11. Cristóbal de Mena, *La Conquista del Perú, llamada la Nueva Castilla*, p. 81.
12. Ibid., pp. 45–6. Diego de Trujillo, 'Relación', pp. 200–3.
13. Ms. Información hecha por el fiscal en el pleito de Doña Francisca Pizarro y Don Hernando Pizarro, Archivo General de Indias, Seville, Legajo 496.
14. Ms. Pedimiento de Don Diego y Don Francisco, hijos naturales que se dicen de Don Francisco Atahualpa, Archivo General de Indias, Seville, Patronato 188.
15. Francisco de Xerez, *Verdadera Relación de la Conquista del Perú*, p. 123.

16. Miguel de Estete, *Noticia del Perú*, vol. 1, p. 378.
17. Pedro Pizarro, *Relación*, pp. 65–9.
18. Ibid., p. 240.
19. Rafael Loredo, *Los Repartos*, pp. 72–4. Stuart Stirling, *The Last Conquistador: Mansio Serra de Leguizamón and the Conquest of the Incas*, pp. 42–4. The original spelling of the family name – Serra de Leguizamón – has been retained, though the phonetic spelling – Sierra de Leguízamo – was adopted in error by various notaries and historians.
20. Stirling, p. 43.
21. Ms. Información . . . Doña Francisca Pizarro.

2. The Kingdom of the Snow Mountains

1. Sir William Stirling-Maxwell, *The Cloister Life of the Emperor Charles V*, p. 246.
2. Garcilaso de la Vega, *Comentarios Reales de los Incas, Historia General del Perú*, Libro 3, Capítulo XX.
3. Martín de Murúa, *Historia General del Perú*, vol. 1, p. 99.
4. 'Información Acerca el Señorío del los Incas hechas por mandado de Don Francisco de Toledo, Virey del Perú, 1570–2', in Fernando Montesinos, *Memorias Antiguas Historiales y Políticas del Perú*, p. 254.
5. Ms. Información de los conquistadores, Cuzco, 1572. Archivo General de Indias, Seville, Lima 28 B.
6. Waldemar Espinoza Soriano, *Los Orejones del Cuzco*, p. 95.
7. Pedro Pizarro, *Relación*, p. 46.
8. Pedro de Cieza de León, *La Crónica del Perú*, p. 367.
9. Roberto Levillier (ed.), 'Gobernantes del Perú, Cartas y Papeles del Siglo XVI', vol. VII, p. 124.
10. Ibid., p. 18.
11. 'Discurso de la Sucesión y Gobierno de los Incas', reproduced in Julío Luna, *El Cuzco y el Gobierno de los Incas*, pp. 31–5, 40–1.
12. Gonzalo Fernández de Oviedo, *Historia General y Natural de las Indias*, Tomo IV.
13. Ms. Declaración de los Indios que residen en Potosí, Año 1550, Archivo General de Indias, Seville, Justicia 667, N2.
14. Ms. Información de los conquistadores.
15. *Pedro Sancho de la Hoz, Relación de la Conquista del Perú*, Italian translation by Joaquin García Icazbalceta, pp. 88–92.
16. Pedro de Cieza de León, *El Señorío de los Incas*, pp. 97–8.
17. Juan de Betanzos, *Suma y Narración de los Incas*, p. 260. Marca Chimbo would later be known as Doña Juana and her younger sister Quispiquipi as Doña Beatriz Manco Cápac. Both were full sisters of Huáscar and daughters

of Huayna Cápac and the Coya Rahua Ocllo. Ms. Información de méritos de Juan Serra de Leguizamón, Archivo General de Indias, Lima, Patronato 126.
18. Ms. Antonio de Ribera. Archivo General de Indias, Seville, Patronato 188.

3. The Marquis of Las Charcas

1. Ms. Información de Francisco Pizarro, Archivo General de Indias, Seville, Patronato 145, N2, R2.
2. It is quite valid to describe Pizarro as a slaver – the slave trade was one of the principal sources of wealth in the isthmus, along with mining gold – for both he and his partner Diego de Almagro had for years made a living by catching slaves. Of Almagro, it was recorded 'he could follow an Indian through the thickest forests merely by tracing his tracks, and in the event the Indian might have a league's advantage on him, yet would he catch up with him'. Pedro Pizarro, *Relación*, p. 168.
3. Raúl Porras Barrenechea, *Pizarro*, p. 667.

4. The Nephews of Doña Inés

1. Ms. La Querella de Francisco Sánchez Curujano, Archivo General de Indias, Seville, Justicia.
2. Ms. Pedimiento de Don Diego y Don Francisco.
3. Garcilaso de la Vega, *Comentarios*, Libro 9, Capítulo XXXVIII.

5. The Child Empress

1. Cristóbal de Molina, *Conquista y Población del Perú*, Tomo III, pp. 342–3.
2. William Prescott, *The History of the Conquest of Peru*, Appendix, pp. 496, 497.
3. Garcilaso de la Vega, *Comentarios*, Libro 9, Capítulo XXXVIII.

6. The River of the Holy Ghost

1. Hidalgo de Elvas, *Expedición de Hernando de Soto a Florida*, Capítulo XXX.
2. Garcilaso de la Vega, *La Florida*, Libro V, 1, Capítulo VII.
3. Hidalgo de Elvas, *Expedición*.
4. Ibid.
5. *The De Soto Chronicles, The Expedition of Hernando de Soto to North America in 1539–1543*, vol. 1, p. 369.
6. Ms. Información de Hernando de Soto.

7. The Old Soldier

1. Ms. Información de méritos del Capitán Mansio Serra de Leguizamón, Archivo General de Indias, Seville, Patronato 126.

2. José Antonio del Busto Duthurburu, *Diccionario de los conquistadores del Perú*.
3. Ibid.

8. The Haunting

1. Ricardo Palma, *Tradiciones Peruanas*, pp. 180–2.
2. Garcilaso de la Vega, *Comentarios*, Libro 5, Capítulo XXXVI.
3. Ibid., Libro 5, Capítulo XLIII.
4. Ibid., Libro 4, Capítulo XL.
5. Ibid., Libro 5, Capítulo XXXVIII.
6. Ibid., Libro 5, Capítulo XLI.
7. Diego Fernández, *Historia del Perú*, Primera Parte, Libro 2, Capítulo 90.
8. *Colección de Documentos Inéditos para la Historia de España*, Madrid, 1842–1895, vol. XLIX, pp. 277, 278.
9. Pedro Pizarro, *Relación*, p. 238.

9. The Requiem

1. Ms. Carta de Fray Vicente de Valverde, Obispo del Cuzco, escrita al Emperador Carlos V desde la ciudad del Cuzco a 2 de Avril de 1539. Número 3216, Biblioteca Nacional, Madrid.
2. Emilio Lisson Chavez (ed.), *La Iglesia de España en el Perú*, p. 77.

10. The Blind Man of La Mota

1. Gonzalo Fernández de Oviedo, *Historia General*, Tomo CXXI, p. 61.
2. Ms. Orden de Santiago, Número 6525, Biblioteca Nacional, Madrid.
3. Ms. Archivo Arzobispal, Lima.
4. Ruth Pike, 'Sevillian Society in the Sixteenth Century: Slaves and Freedmen', *Hispanic American Historical Review* 47, 1967.
5. María Rostworowski de Díez Canseco, *Doña Francisca Pizarro*.
6. Ms. Orden de Santiago, Número 6525, Biblioteca Nacional, Madrid.
7. Roberto Levillier (ed.), *Gobernantes del Perú*, vol. II, pp. 139–40.
8. Ms. Doña Francisca Pizarro y Don Hernando Pizarro, Archivo General de Indias, Seville, Lima, Legajo 496A.

11. The Emperor's Daughter

1. Ms. Autos seguidos por Martín García de Licona, Archivo General de la Nación, Lima, Perú, Legajo 15, Cuaderno 80.
2. Ms. Información de Juan Serra de Leguizamón. She was also referred to by her territorial title Huaylla (Guaylla) in the Yucay, which she had inherited from

her father. Ms. Autos seguidos por Martín García de Licona. José de la Puente Brunke, *Encomiendas y Encomenderos en el Perú*, pp. 359, 378.

3. Ms. Información de Juan Serra de Leguizamón.
4. Juan Díez de Betanzos, *Suma y Narración*, p. 260.
5. Carlos Sempat Assadourian, *Transiciones Hacia el Sistema Colonial Andino*, p. 144.
6. Ms. Información de Juan Serra de Leguizamón.
7. Ms. Información de méritos de Diego Maldonado, Archivo General de Indias, Seville, Patronato 99.
8. Edmundo Guillén Guillén, *Versión Inca de la Conquista*, p. 120.
9. Ibid., pp. 35, 121.
10. Ibid., p. 122.
11. Ms. Información de Juan Serra de Leguizamón.
12. Ibid.
13. Joaquín Pacheco et al. (eds), *Colección de Documentos inéditos relativos al descubrimiento, conquista y colonización de las posesiones Españolas en América*, vol. 3.
14. Emilio Lisson Chavez (ed.), *La Iglesia de España en el Perú*, vol. 3, pp. 79–80.
15. Ibid.
16. Ms. Información de Diego Maldonado.
17. Ibid.
18. Ms. Información de Juan Serra de Leguizamón.
19. Garcilaso de la Vega, *Comentarios, Historia del Perú*, Libro 6, Capítulo III.
20. Ms. Autos seguidos por Martín García de Licona.
21. Ms. Información de Juan Serra de Leguizamón.
22. Stuart Stirling, *The Last Conquistador*, p. 111.
23. Diego Fernández, *Historia del Perú*, p. 76.
24. Henry Kamen, *The Spanish Inquisition*, p. 254.
25. Ms. Información de los conquistadores.
26. Ms. Información de Juan Serra de Leguizamón.
27. Ibid.
28. 'Información Acerca el Señorío de los Incas', p. 256.
29. José de la Puente Brunke, *Encomienda y Encomenderos*, p. 359.
30. Sir Clements Markham, *The Incas of Peru*, p. 57.
31. Ms. Autos seguidos por Martín García de Licona.
32. Ibid.

12. The Mestizo Prince

1. Ms. Informaciónes de María Ramírez, 1569, Archivo General de Indias, Lima, 206, N.2.

13. *The Bride of Santa Clara*

1. 'El Monasterio de Santa Clara de la ciudad del Cuzco', *Revista del Archivo Nacional del Perú*, 1938.
2. Ms. Baltasar de Ocampo, 'Descripción de la Provincia de San Francisco de la Victoria de Vilcabamba', Hispanic Manuscripts, British Library.
3. Ibid.
4. Ella Temple Dunbar, 'El Testamento inédito de Doña Beatriz Clara Coya de Loyola, hija del Inca Sayri Túpac', *Revista Fenix* 3, nos 7–8, 1951–2, p. 113.
5. Ibid., p. 121.
6. Ibid., p. 114.
7. Ibid.

14. *The Lost Treasure*

1. Alfred Bingham, *Portrait of an Explorer: Hiram Bingham, Discoverer of Machu Picchu*.
2. John H. Rowe, 'Machu Picchu a la luz de los documentos del Siglo XVI', *Histórica* 14, 1990, pp. 139–54.
3. Stephen Clissold, *Conquistador: The Life of Don Pedro Sarmiento de Gamboa*.
4. Ms. Fray Antonio Martínez de la Orden de San Agustín, Archivo General de Indias, Seville, Lima 327.
5. Ibid.

15. *The Sacristan of Córdoba*

1. Garcilaso de la Vega, *Comentarios*, Libro 9, Capítulo XXXI.
2. John Varner, *El Inca: The Life and Times of Garcilaso de la Vega*, p. 176.
3. Ms. Información de méritos del Capitán Pedro del Barco y de Pedro del Barco, hijo, Archivo General de Indias, Seville, Justicia 429, Lima 204, Patronato 283.
4. Garcilaso de la Vega, *Comentarios*, Libro 9, Capítulo XL.
5. Garcilaso de la Vega, *Historia General del Perú*, Libro 8, Capítulo XXI.
6. John Varner, *El Inca*, p. 281.
7. Ibid., pp. 368, 369.

16. *The Last of the Conquistadores*

1. Ms. Información de méritos de Francisco Serra de Leguizamón, Archivo General de Indias, Seville, Patronato 126.
2. Ms. Expediente de Don Tristán de Leguizamón y Esquivel, Caballero de Santiago, Bilbao, Año 1530, Archivo Histórico Nacional, Madrid.

3. Richard Ford, *Handbook for Spain*, London, Centaur Press, 1966, vol. III, p. 1374.

4. Lope García de Salazar, *Las Bienandanças e Fortunas*. Capítulo: 'Del Linaje de Leguiçamon e de su fundamento, e donde sucedieron'.

5. Raúl Rivera Serna, 'El Primer testamento de Mancio Sierra de Leguízamo', Mar del Sur, Lima, p. 27.

6. Diego de Mendoza, *Crónica de la Provincia de San Antonio de las Charcas*, Libro 3, Capítulo VII, pp. 399–405.

7. Juan Perez de Tudela (ed.), *Documentos Relativos a Don Pedro de la Gasca*, vol. 2, p. 354.

8. Ms. Información de méritos de Gómez de Mazuelas, Archivo General de Indias, Seville, Lima 177.

9. 'Carta de los licenciados Cepeda y Vera a Felipe II, La Plata, 14 Febrero 1585', in *Monumenta Misionem, Monumenta Peruana*, ed. Antonio Egaña, Lima, 1961. Prior of Huamanga. Emilio Lisson Chavez (ed.), *La Iglesia de España*, vol. IV, p. 142.

10. Ms. Protocolo 11, 1586, Luis de Quesada, fol. 25, Archivo Regional del Cusco.

11. Ms. Doña Elena Girón Heredia y Francisco Serra de Leguizamón. Contratación 5239, N1, R10, Archivo General de Indias, Seville.

12. Ms. Información del Capitán Mansio Serra de Leguizamón.

17. *The Torture of Doña Catalina*

1. Información de Doña Catalina de Urbina, viuda del Licenciado Gregorio de Gamarra, Archivo General de Indias, Sevilla, Patronato 139, N1, R3.

18. *The Bishop's Legacy*

1. Carlos Alonso, 'Pedro Perea, Obispo de Arequipa', Archivo Augustiniano, vol. LXI, Madrid, 1977. M.A. Cateriano, *Memorias de los SS. Obispos de Arequipa*.

2. Emilio Lisson Chavez (ed.), *La Iglesia de España en el Perú*, vol. 5, no. 23, p. 27.

3. Ms. Expediente de Hidalguía de Martín Díez de Medina, Legajo 106, Año 1568, Sala de Hijosdalgo, Real Chancillería de Valladolid.

4. Ms. Private Collection.

5. Ms. Información de Mansio Serra de Leguizamón.

6. The Palacio Díez de Medina in La Paz was completed in 1775 by the Judge Don Francisco Tadeo Díez de Medina, although its construction had been initiated by his father Don Andrés Díez de Medina, on the foundations of an earlier family mansion. It is now the Museo Nacional de Arte of Bolivia.

19. The Imperial City

1. Miguel de Cervantes, *El Celoso Extremeño*, in *Novelas Ejemplares*, Madrid, 1917.
2. Ms. 'Historia de la Villa Imperial de Potosí', Palacio Real, Madrid.
3. The Master of Calamarca may perhaps be identified as the late seventeenth-century painter of the La Paz region, José López de los Ríos.
4. Ms. 'Historia de la Villa Imperial de Potosí'.
5. Rubén Vargas Ugarte, *Historia del Perú*, Lima, 1949, pp. 36, 37.
6. Ms. 'Historia de la Villa Imperial de Potosí'.
7. Antonio de la Calancha, *Córonica Moralizada del Orden de San Agustín en el Perú*.
8. Ms. 'Historia de la Villa Imperial de Potosí'.

20. The Prisoner of Cusco

1. Boleslao Lewin, *La Rebellión de Túpac Amaru*, p. 391.
2. Ms. José Túpac Amaro, Archivo General de Indias, Audiencia de Lima, Legajo 1619.
3. Lillian Estelle Fisher, *The Last Inca Revolt 1780–1783*, p. 43.
4. Letter of Túpac Amaru to the Cabildo of Cusco in Boleslao Lewin, *La Rebellión de Túpac Amaru*, pp. 456, 457.
5. Lillian Estelle Fisher, *The Last Inca Revolt*, p. 220.
6. Daniel Valcárcel, *La Rebellión de Túpac Amaru*, p. 162.
7. Lillian Estelle Fisher, *The Last Inca Revolt*, p. 135.
8. Daniel Valcárcel, *La Rebellión de Túpac Amaru*, p. 166.

21. The Last Inca

1. 'El dilatado cautiverio bajo del gobierno español de Juan Bautista Tupamaro', folleto. Biblioteca Nacional de Buenos Aires.
2. Ibid.

Bibliography

Acosta, José de, *Historia Natural y Moral de las Indias*, ed. José Alcina Franch, Historia 16, Madrid, 1987.

Alonso, Carlos, *Pedro de Perea, Obispo de Arequipa*, Archivo Agustiniano, vol. LXI, Madrid, 1977.

Álvarez Rubiana, Pablo, *Pedrarias Dávila*, Madrid, 1944.

Arzans de Orsúa y Vela, Bartolomé, *Historia de la Villa Imperial de Potosí*, eds Lewis Hanke and Gunnar Mendoza, Brown University, 1965.

Betanzos, Juan Díez de, *Suma y Narración de los Incas*, ed. María del Carmen Martín Rubio, Ediciones Atlas, Madrid, 1987.

Bingham, Alfred, *Portrait of an Explorer: Hiram Bingham, Discoverer of Machu Picchu*, New York, 1989.

Browser, Frederick, *The African Slave in Colonial Perú*, Stanford University Press, 1974.

Busto Duthurburu, José Antonio del, *Diccionario Histórico Bibliográfico de los conquistadores del Perú*, Lima, 1986–7, Vols 1 and 2.

Calancha y Benavides, Antonio de la, *Corónica Moralizada del Orden de San Agustín en el Perú*, ed. Ignacio Prado Pastor, Universidad Nacional de San Marcos, Lima, 1974.

Cateriano, M.A., *Memorias de los SS. Obispos de Arequipa*, Arequipa, 1908.

Chavez, Emilio Lisson (ed.), *La Iglesia de España en el Perú*, Seville, 1943.

Cieza de León, Pedro de, *La Crónica del Perú*, ed. Manuel Ballesteros, Historia 16, Madrid, 1984.

——, *Descubrimiento y Conquista*, ed. Carmelo Sáenz de Santa María, Historia 16, Madrid, 1986.

——, *Las Guerras Civiles*, vols 1–2, ed. Sáenz de Santa María, Consejo Superior de Investigaciones Científicas, Madrid.

——, *El Señorío de los Incas*, ed. Manuel Ballesteros, Historia 16, Madrid, 1988.

Clissold, Stephen, *Conquistador: The Life of Don Pedro Sarmiento de Gamboa*, Derek Verschoyle, London, 1954.

Colección de Documentos Inéditos Relativos al Descubrimiento, Conquista y Colonización de las Posesiones Españolas en América, ed. Joaquín Pacheco, Francisco de Cárdenas y Luis Torres de Mendoza, Madrid, 1864–84.

Colección de Documentos Inéditos para la Historia de España, Madrid, 1842–1895.

Cook, Noble David, *Tasa de la Visita General de Don Francisco de Toledo*, Universidad Mayor de San Marcos, Lima, 1975.

——, *Born to Die*, Cambridge University Press, 1998.

Del Valle Siles, María Eugenia (ed.), *Diario de Francisco Tadeo Díez de Medina*, Banco Boliviano Americano, La Paz, 1994.

Delamarre, Catherine, *Las Mujeres en tiempos de los conquistadores*, Planeta, Barcelona, 1994.

De Soto Chronicles, The. The Expedition of Hernando de Soto to North America in 1539–1543, eds Lawrence Clayton, Vernon James Knight and Edward Moore, University of Alabama Press, Alabama, 1995.

Díez de Medina, Fernando, *Thunupa*, Juventud, La Paz, 1990.

Díez de San Miguel, García, *Visita hecha a la provincia de Chuquito . . . 1567*, Casa de Cultura, Lima, 1964/72.

Dunbar Temple, Ella, 'La Descendencia de Huayna Cápac', in *Revista Histórica*, Lima, vols 11 (1937), 12 (1939), 13 (1940), 17 (1948).

Estete, Miguel de, *Noticia del Perú*, Biblioteca Peruana, vol. 1, Lima, 1968.

Fabie, Antonio Marie (ed.), *Viajes por España de Jorge de Einghen, del Barón León Rosmithal de Baina, de Francisco Guicciardini y de Andrés Navajero*, Madrid, 1879.

Fernández, Diego, 'Historia del Perú', in *Crónicas del Perú*, Biblioteca de Autores Españoles, Madrid, 1963.

Fernández de Oviedo, Gonzalo, *Historia General y Natural de las Indias, Islas y Tierra Firme del Mar Océano*, Madrid, 1851. (Repr. ed. Juan Pérez de Tudela, Biblioteca de Autores Españoles, Madrid, 1959.)

Fisher, Lillian Estelle, *The Last Inca Revolt 1780–1783*, University of Oklahoma Press, Norman, 1966.

García de Salazar, Lope, *Las Bienandanças e Fortunas*, ed. Maximiliano Camaron, Madrid, 1884.

Garcilaso de la Vega, *Comentarios Reales de los Incas, Historia General del Perú*, ed. Angel Rosenblat, Emecé Editores, Buenos Aires, 1945.

——, *La Florida del Inca, Historia del Adelantado Hernando de Soto, Gobernador y capitán general del reyno de la Florida, y de otros cavalleros Españoles e Indios*, ed. Gabriel Daza de Cárdenas, Madrid, 1723.

Guillén Guillén, Edmundo, *Versión Inca de la Conquista*, RA Ediciones, Lima, 1974.

Hemming, John, *The Conquest of the Incas*, Papermac, London, 1970.

Hidalgo de Elvas, *Expedición de Hernando de Soto a Florida*, ed. Miguel Muñoz de San Pedro, Colección Austral, Espasa Calpe, Buenos Aires, 1949.

Hyslop, John, *Inca Road System*, Orlando, Florida, 1984.

Bibliography

Instrucción del Inca Tito Cussi Yupanqui, ed. María del Carmen Martín Rubio, Atlas, Madrid, 1988.

Kamen, Henry, *The Spanish Inquisition*, Weidenfeld & Nicolson, London, 1997.

Levillier, Roberto (ed.), 'Gobernantes del Perú, Cartas y Papeles del Siglo XVI', Documentos del Archivo General de Indias, Madrid, 1924.

Lewin, Boleslao, *La Rebellión de Túpac Amaru*, Sociedad Editora Latino Americana, Buenos Aires, 1967.

Lockhart, James, *The Men of Cajamarca*, University of Texas Press, Austin, 1972.

——, *Spanish Peru, 1532–1560*, Wisconsin, 1994.

López Martínez, Hectór, *Diego Centeno y la Rebelión de los Encomenderos*, Villanueva, Lima, 1970.

Loredo, Rafael, *Los Repartos*, Miranda, Lima, 1958.

Luna, Julío, *El Cuzco y el gobierno de los Incas*, Miranda, Lima, 1962.

McNeill, William, *Plagues and Peoples*, Oxford, Blackwell, 1977.

Markham, Sir Clements, *The Incas of Peru*, Librerias ABC, Lima, 1965.

Means, P.A., *Biblioteca Andina*, Yale University Press, Blaine Ethridge, Detroit, 1973.

Mena, Cristóbal de, 'La Conquista del Perú, llamada la Nueva Castilla', in Raúl Porras Barrenechea, *Las Relaciones Primitivas de la Conquista del Perú*, Instituto Raúl Porras, Lima, 1967.

Mendiburu, Miguel de, *Diccionario Histórico-Biográfico del Perú*, Lima, 1874–90.

Mendoza, Diego de, *Crónica de la Provincia de San Antonio de las Charcas*, Editorial Casa Municipal de la Cultura, Franz Tamayo, La Paz, 1976.

Molina, Cristóbal de, *Conquista y Población del Perú*, ed. Francisco Loayza, Biblioteca Peruana, Lima, 1943.

Montesinos, Fernando, 'Memorias Antiguas Historiales y Politícas del Perú', *Colección de Libros Españoles Raros*, ed. Jiménez de la Espada, Madrid, 1882.

Montoto, Santiago, *Nobiliario Hispano-Americano del Siglo XVI*, vols 1–2, Madrid, 1927.

——, *Sevilla en el Imperio*, Nueva Libreria, Sevilla, 1937.

Morales Padrón, Francisco, *Los Conquistadores de América*, Colección Austral, Espasa-Calpe, Madrid, 1974.

Murúa, Martín de, *Historia General del Perú*, Wellington MS, vols 1–2, ed. Manuel Ballesteros, Madrid, 1964.

Palma, Ricardo, *Tradiciones Peruanas, Obras Completas*, Aguilar, Lima, 1968.

Pérez de Tudela, Juan (ed.), *Documentos Relativos a Don Pedro de la Gasca*, Real Academia de Historia, Madrid, 1964.

Pizarro, Pedro, *Relación del Descubrimiento y Conquista de los Reinos del Perú*, eds Guillermo Villena, Pierre Duviols, Fondo Editorial, Pontificia Universidad Católica del Perú, Lima, 1986.

Polo de Ondegardo, Juan, *El Mundo de los Incas*, eds Laura González and Alicia Alonso, Historia 16, Madrid, 1990.

Bibliography

Poma de Ayala, Felipe Guaman, *Nueva Crónica y Buen Gobierno*, ed. Franklin Pease, Biblioteca Ayacucho, Caracas, 1980.

Porras Barrenechea, Raúl, *Las Relaciones Primitivas de la Conquista del Perú*, Instituto Raúl Porras, Lima, 1967.

——, *Pizarro*, Lima, 1978.

——, *Los Cronistas del Perú*, ed. Franklin Pease, Biblioteca Ayacucho, Caracas, 1980.

Prescott, William, *The History of the Conquest of Peru*, George Allen & Unwin, London, 1913.

Puente Brunke, José de la, *Encomienda y Encomenderos en el Perú*, Diputación Provincial, Seville, 1992.

Quipucamayos, *Relación de la Descendencia, Gobierno y Conquista de los Incas*, ed. Juan José Vega, Colección Clásicos Peruanos, Lima, 1974.

Rostworowski de Díez Canseco, María, *Doña Francisca Pizarro*, Instituto de Estudios Peruanos, Lima, 1994.

Salles-Reese, Verónica, *From Viracocha to the Virgin of Copacabana*, University of Texas Press, Austin, 1997.

Sancho de la Hoz, Pedro, *Relación de la Conquista del Perú*, trans. Joaquin García Icazbalceta, Biblioteca Tenantíla, Ediciones José Porrua Turanzas, Madrid, MCMLXII.

Sarmiento de Gamboa, Pedro, *Historia de los Incas*, Miraguano Ediciones, Madrid, 2001.

Sempat Assadourian, Carlos, *Transiciones Hacia el Sistema Colonial Andino*, México, Instituto de Estudios Peruanos, 1994.

Soriano, Waldemar Espinoza, *Los Orejones del Cuzco*, Proceso, Huancayo, 1977.

Stirling, Stuart, *The Last Conquistador: Mansio Serra de Leguizamón and the Conquest of the Incas*, Sutton Publishing, Stroud, 1999.

Stirling-Maxwell, Sir William, *The Cloister Life of the Emperor Charles V*, John Parker, London, 1891.

Trelles Arestegui, Efrain, *Lucas Martínez Vegazo: Funcionamiento de una encomienda Peruana inicial*, Pontificia Universidad Católica del Perú, 1982.

Trujillo, Diego de, 'Relación del Descubrimiento del Reino del Perú', in Francisco de Xerez, *Verdadera Relación de la conquista del Perú*, ed. Concepción Bravo Guerreira, Historia 16, Madrid, 1988.

Uhle, Max, *Las Ruinas de Tomebamba*, Academia Nacional de Historia, Quito, 1923.

Urbano, Henrique y Sánchez, Ana, *Antigüedades del Perú*, Historia 16, Madrid, 1990.

Valcárcel, Daniel, *La Rebellión de Túpac Amaru*, Lima, 1970.

Valera, Blas, *Relación de las Costumbres Antiguas de los Naturales del Perú*, in *Antigüedades del Perú*, ed. Henrique Urbano y Ana Sánchez, Historia 16, Madrid, 1990.

Bibliography

Vargas Ugarte, Rubén, *Historia de la Iglesia en el Perú*, Lima, Santa María, 1953.

——, *Historia del Perú*, Lima, 1949.

Varner, John, *El Inca: The Life and Times of Garcilaso de la Vega*, University of Texas Press, Austin, 1968.

Varón Gabai, Rafael, *Francisco Pizarro and his Brothers*, Oklahoma Press, 1997.

Varela, Alfredo (ed.), *Memorias del Hermano de Túpac Amaru, escritas en Buenos Aires*, Editorial Boedo, Buenos Aires, 1976.

Xerez, Francisco de, *Verdadera Relación de la Conquista del Perú*, ed. Concepción Bravo Guerreira, Historia 16, Madrid, 1988.

Zimmerman, Arthur, *Francisco de Toledo*, Greenwood Press, New York, 1968.

Index

Index

Index